FINGAL COUNTY

I0411502

ME

Swords
Library
Ph: 8905894

Comhairle Contae Fhine Gall
Fingal County Council

Items should be returned on or before the last date shown below. Items may be renewed by personal application, writing, telephone or by accessing the online Catalogue Service on Fingal Libraries' website. To renew give date due, borrower ticket number and PIN number if using online catalogue. Fines are charged on overdue items and will include postage incurred in recovery. Damage to, or loss of items will be charged to the borrower.

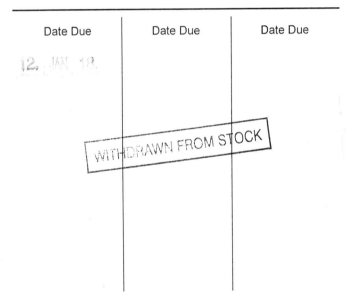

Date Due	Date Due	Date Due
12. JAN. 18.		

BRITAIN'S BAND OF BROTHERS

For Edward Stanley D. Sewell, my grandson, with my love. Who, although he doesn't know it yet, enjoys a life of freedom purchased with the courage of men such as these.

BRITAIN'S BAND OF BROTHERS

Tom Keene

The Germans have a phrase for heroes: 'Always the tallest poppies [*Mohnblumen*] are taken'. These were proper people and I hope that some day a book will be written about them.

Lord Lovat, *March Past*

First published 2014

The History Press
The Mill, Brimscombe Port
Stroud, Gloucestershire, GL5 2QG
www.thehistorypress.co.uk

© Tom Keene, 2014

The right of Tom Keene to be identified as the Author
of this work has been asserted in accordance with the
Copyright, Designs and Patents Act 1988.

British Library Cataloguing in Publication Data.
A catalogue record for this book is available from the British
Library.

ISBN 978 0 7524 8990 2

Typesetting and origination by The History Press
Printed in Great Britain

Contents

Acknowledgements

My thanks go, first and foremost, to the relatives of the men whose wartime exploits are described below. Without them, Britain's 'band of brothers' would have stayed in the shadows of history: To 'J.E.A.', Ernest Appleyard, whose labour of love and sorrow – the publication of *Geoffrey*, a slim volume of letters sent home by his son – has provided the framework for all that follows and has been quoted from frequently; to John Appleyard, Geoffrey's half-brother, for his help and support, and for escorting me around Linton, the one-time family home; to the distant relatives of Gus March-Phillipps, Christina Bennett and Harriet Greer, for the loan of family photographs and whose retrieval of a tape and a long-forgotten transcript brought the story of Gus to life; to Jennifer and Tom Auld; to Malcolm Hayes, Graham Hayes' nephew, for the loan of other photographs and for filling in some of the gaps; to Annabel Grace Hayes, Graham's niece, who shared a suitcase of forgotten letters and papers; to Chris Rooney, son of Oswald 'Mickey' Rooney, for photographs and useful background; to Peter Stokes, MBE, son of Horace 'Stokey' Stokes, whose almost-forgotten, unpublished, well-written memoirs brought those days so vividly to life; and to James Edgar in Australia, doughty survivor of Operations *Branford* and *Basalt*, and a veteran who still, at 93, enjoys total recall of those turbulent days. I am grateful also to Phil Ventham, local Dorset historian, and to the current owners of Anderson Manor, who allowed me into their beautiful home, patiently answered my questions and showed me where the ghosts once walked.

My thanks also go to historian Major General Julian Thompson, CB, OBE, commander of 3 Commando Brigade during the Falklands conflict and Visiting Professor at the Department of War Studies, King's College, London; to Lt Col David Owen, MBE, curator of the Royal Corps of Transport (formally RASC) Medal Collection, held at the headquarters of the Royal Logistic Corps at Deepcut, Surrey; to Colour Sergeant Gary

Chapman at 3 Commando Brigade Headquarters, Stonehouse; and to David Harrison, respected amateur SOE historian. I am most grateful also to the helpful staff at the Imperial War Museum and at The National Archives, Kew; to Dr Steven Kippax, whose efforts on my behalf have greatly assisted in the retrieval of important wartime documents. Geoff Slee and his Combined Operations website were also able to open several doors. I am most grateful also to staff of the highly efficient National Meteorological Archive, Exeter, who were able to retrieve – instantly, it seemed – wartime weather conditions on what was to become Omaha beach and I am grateful also for the help of the United Kingdom Hydrographic Office, Taunton.

I have drawn heavily upon the works of other authors to compile this history: *Dunkirk* by Hugh Sebag-Montefiore, one of the very best accounts of the fighting withdrawal to the French coast in 1940; *The Commandos 1940–1946* by Charles Messenger; *The Green Beret* by Hilary St George Saunders; and *Anders Lassen VC, MC of the SAS* by Mike Langley. I am also grateful to French authors Gérard Fournier and André Heintz for '*If I Must Die …*', their account of the *Aquatint* raid and to the late Peter Kemp's now out-of-print *No Colours or Crest*. I am grateful also to Steven Forge of Oundle School in Sussex for his help in sourcing photographs of ex-Oundle pupil Patrick Dudgeon, MC.

Lastly, I am more grateful than words can express to my wife, Marguerite, whose support and patience remained unwavering as I pieced together the untold story of *Maid Honor* and the men of the Small Scale Raiding Force. Because it mattered to them, it mattered to me and to her, that was enough.

List of Abbreviations

AA	Anti-Aircraft	MEW	Ministry of Economic Warfare
ACNS(H)	Assistant Chief of the Naval Staff (Home)	MBE	Member of the British Empire
ADC	Aide-de-Camp		
AuxUnits	Auxiliary Units	MC	Military Cross
BEF	British Expeditionary Force	MI(R)	Military Intelligence (Research)
BREN	Section light automatic weapon, .303 cal.	MGB	Motor Gun Boat
'C'	Head of SIS	MTB	Motor Torpedo Boat
CCO	Chief of Combined Operations	NID(C)	Naval Intelligence Division (Clandestine)
COHQ	Combined Operations Headquarters	POW	Prisoner of War
		RA	Royal Artillery
CD	Executive Director, SOE	RAF	Royal Air Force
C-in-C	Commander-in-Chief	RAFVR	Royal Air Force Volunteer Reserve
CIGS	Chief of the Imperial General Staff	RASC	Royal Army Service Corps
CND	*Confrérie de Notre Dame*	RTU	Returned to Unit
CSDIC	Combined Services Detailed Interrogation Centre	SAS	Special Air Service
		SO	Chairman, SOE
DDOD (I)	Deputy Director Operations Division (Irregular)	SO2	Fusion of Section D and MI (R) that became SOE
DFC	Distinguished Flying Cross	SOE	Special Operations Executive
DMO	Director of Military Operations	SIS	Secret Intelligence Service
		SS	*Schutzstaffel*
DSO	Distinguished Service Order	SSRF	Small Scale Raiding Force
DZ	Drop Zone	STEN	Personal automatic weapon, 9mm cal.
OC	Officer Commanding		
GOC	General Officer Commanding	VC	Victoria Cross
		W/T	Wireless Telegraphy
GRT	Gross Register Tonnage	ZNO	*Zone Non-occupée*
GS(R)	General Staff (Research)	ZO	*Zone Occupée*
'M'	Brigadier Colin Gubbins, Director of Operations & Training, SOE	ZP	Foreign Office

Foreword

Major General Julian Thompson, CB, OBE

This is a story about a group of men, of whom Brigadier Lord Lovat wrote 'These were proper people and I hope that some day a book will be written about them.' Well, here it is at last.

The Second World War saw the birth of a host of special units, many in response to Winston Churchill's wish to strike back at the foe after the ejection of the British Army from France in June 1940. Those who joined them did so for a variety of motives: adventure, revenge for the shame of defeat in France and Flanders, to have a 'crack at the enemy'.

Many of these men were what might be described as 'self-starters'. They did not hang about waiting for someone to give them a job to do, but often initiated the task themselves. The people in this book were no exception. In this case soldiers in the Special Operations Executive (SOE), but actually part of the Combined Operations Small Scale Raiding Force (SSRF) founded by Vice Admiral Lord Louis Mountbatten in February 1942. In the early days of Special Forces, units often found themselves serving two or more masters. Occasionally members of such a unit were able to play on the 'left hand not quite knowing what the right hand was up to' to their advantage. This could be counter-productive. For example, the leaders of the SSRF exerted pressure on their masters to authorise nightly raids along the whole coastline of occupied Europe, unaware whether or not this fitted in with the overall plan which might call for a more selective approach. For example, one might wish to avoid drawing attention to a particular stretch of coastline because it figured in future invasion plans, in which case a more clandestine operation might be appropriate. The problem: there was a lack of overall co-ordination of raiding policy at the time.

But the story starts well before the founding of the SSRF and among other escapades includes an operation involving a trawler called *Maid*

Honor, two tugs and an expedition to West Africa. The operation, code-name *Postmaster*, breached Spanish neutrality and resulted in a cover up including some creative lying by Sir Anthony Eden, Secretary of State for Foreign Affairs; Sir Francis Drake would have heartily approved.

On return to England, the leader of the *Postmaster* force, Major Gus March-Phillipps, suggested that a small scale raiding force of around 100 men be formed to raid the German-held coastline of France – hence the SSRF. The small matter of ownership of the force was sorted out: it would belong to SOE, but Mountbatten's Combined Operations Headquarters (COHQ) would task it. To add to the tangled lines of command and control, the Secret Intelligence Service (SIS) also had a 'vote' when it came to deciding whether or not an SSRF raid would go ahead or not.

At first the SSRF was given two motor launches for passage across the Channel, but these were replaced by a Motor Torpedo Boat – MTB 344 – known as '*The Little Pisser*' because of its speed. *The Little Pisser* carried a dory or a collapsible canvas-sided Goatley assault boat in which the raiders made their final approach to the beach from the MTB anchored or loitering offshore.

Starting on 14 August 1942, the SSRF carried out three successful raids over a period of twenty-four days. The fourth, set for 11–12 September 1942, but delayed until the night 12–13 September because of fog, was a different story. By now the enemy, who were not stupid, were on high alert after the abortive Dieppe Raid a month before. The beach selected for the SSRF landing was an ideal invasion beach; it became Omaha Beach eighteen months later. It was well defended. The raid was a disaster. But this should not be allowed to detract from the reputation of the 'proper people', the men of the SSRF, including March-Phillipps, killed in the raid, described by SOE agent Peter Kemp as 'the gallant idealist, and strange quixotic genius who had been our commander and inspiration'. The force remained in being, led by Appleyard, mounting its last raid in April 1943. By then the reconnaissance plan for the forthcoming invasion of France was tightly controlled and mainly done by the Combined Operations Pilotage Parties, the COPPs, the forerunners of today's SBS. The SSRF was disbanded, but many of its members joined other organisations and continued to engage the enemy to the end, some dying in the process, including Appleyard and Anders Lassen, VC.

Tom Keene is to be congratulated on his book and for telling us about these gallant men.

Prelude

0531: the first pale flush of sunrise.

Soon, this beach will become famous as 'Bloody Omaha', a gently shelving killing ground to the east of the Cotentin peninsula in Normandy, France. Here, on another dawn, green American troops from the unblooded 29th and veterans of the US 1st Divisions of V Corps will slog ashore in the face of withering enemy fire from the bluffs behind the beach. Here they will endure the worst losses of D-Day as they attempt to claw a fingertip's hold on Hitler's *festung Europa*. An estimated 1,900 Americans will die on this beach on that single day.[1] But not yet, for this is 13 September 1942 and D-Day is almost two years away.

The beach is long, flat and billiard-table smooth: like Rommel himself, his anti-invasion obstacles have yet to be put in place. As dawn breaks along this 5-mile strand of empty, golden sand that stretches from Vierville-sur-Mer in the west to Sainte-Honorine-des-Pertes in the east, a slight haze lifts slowly from the flat, gun-grey sea and the low, crumbling waves that roll in on the last of the ebbing spring tide. Now, this morning, this dawn, this same tide brings with it to the gleaming shore the broken, sea-tumbled detritus of war: three bodies that now lie still, humped and sodden, rolled in on the falling tide. They wear British khaki battledress but have lost their boots and pistol belts. Two were wounded before drowning; a third has died from a gunshot wound to the head. Faces waxy pale and drained in death, they lie in crumpled abandon on this, the enemy shore.

††††

The dawn light gathers strength; visibility lengthens. Very soon the three bodies are spotted by the binoculars of the German sentries of 726th Infantry Regiment who man the six concrete strong points – *Stützpunkt* – that overlook this sector of beach within the prohibited coastal zone.

Later this same morning German troops will recover a bullet-ridden assault boat containing 2 gallons of drinking water. They will also recover twelve wooden paddles, five sub-machine-guns, several primed Mills No 36 hand grenades – some in a small bag – three British army webbing belts, each with pistol and dagger attached in webbing holster and leather sheath, and a British naval anchor tied to 40 feet of hemp rope whose standing end has been severed by the sharp blow of an axe. Later that same day two British prisoners, their battledress still damp and caked in salt, will be ordered to drag the bodies of their three comrades above the high tide mark. They will be filmed doing so by a German film unit and this sequence will form part of the Nazi propaganda film entitled *Midnight at Cherbourg*. A further sequence, filmed on the morning of 15 September, will show sheaves of flowers and three coffins being lowered into the ground whilst the synchronised rifle shots of a Wehrmacht firing detail provide full military honours in the civilian cemetery of Saint Laurent-sur-Mer. *Dulce et decorum est pro patria mori.*

All three men who died were members of Britain's Special Operations Executive and were on loan to Combined Operations' Small Scale Raiding Force. Their mission, as so often before, had been straightforward, if hardly simple: to gather information, destroy enemy installations and capture prisoners to bring back to England for interrogation. That mission failed. Of the eleven raiders who had embarked on MTB 344 at Portsmouth at 2012 the previous evening, not one would return to Britain before the end of the war. And some would lie in the soil of France for eternity.

Today, in England, there is little trace of their passing: a wind-swept secret mooring among the shelduck, heron and curlews of the Arne peninsula; a tiny hilltop church where brave men once hunched in prayer; a lawn of moles who garnish their burrowings with the tarnished .45 cartridge cases of Colt automatics and Thompson submachine-guns once ejected onto a home-made firing range in the kitchen garden above their heads; a haunted seventeenth-century manor house whose ancient oak staircase still echoes to the shouts of hurrying men, the clatter of cleared weapons and the skitter of hob-nailed boots; names remembered in a Yorkshire village hall and, in Dorset, a simple brass plaque, golden in lamplight, that pays tribute to men once needed but who have now stepped back into the shadows of history.

This, then, is their story, written in detail for the first time before those shadows fade into darkness. There is no fiction. It is the story of the men of *Maid Honor* and the Small Scale Raiding Force. It is the untold story of Britain's own Band of Brothers.

1

Das Sichelschnitt – the 'sickle cut'

Dunkirk. It was not a miracle, it was a disaster.

Committed across the Channel to honour a promise, block an enemy and support an ally, British troops moved to northern France in autumn 1939, with advanced units crossing into France the day after war was declared. By the end of September 1939 more than 152,000 troops of the British Expeditionary Force were on French soil. By early October the first two BEF divisions had moved up to the front line on the Franco-Belgian border. The BEF: the very title of the formation of under-equipped, under-armoured units hints at a glance back to the reassuring certainties of Empire that were to have no place in the fast-moving battlefield of this new war that now awaited them, hull-down over the horizon.

To begin with, of course, very little happened. War may have been declared, but it was hardly being waged. In one of the wettest and coldest winters on record, British troops simply dug in and waited out a miserable, muddy *Sitzkrieg*, their line of further advance hindered by Belgian neutrality: only if German troops invaded Belgium would French and British troops move forward in the execution of 'Plan D'. To the British left and right were the French Seventh and First armies, units of what was commonly recognised to be the best army in the world. But, as cursing British troops hunched down into their greatcoat collars, stamped frozen feet on wooden duckboards and rubbed wet, gloved hands together for warmth, they were aware of a niggling and growing unease about the calibre of the much-vaunted *poilus* on their flanks: the French soldiers *they* saw manning concrete defences and on muddy route marches did not look to them like the best soldiers in the world, not at all. Slovenly, ill-disciplined, permitted to smoke on duty, poorly dressed, the word that came down the line was that some sentries even stood guard *in bedroom slippers*. And no one seemed to mind. Senior officers noticed too. General Alan Brooke of 2 Corps and subsequently 2 BEF wrote after watching a parade of French troops:

Seldom have I seen anything more slovenly and badly turned out. Men unshaven, horses ungroomed, clothes and saddles that did not fit, vehicles dirty and complete lack of pride in themselves and their unit. What shook me most however was the look in the men's faces, [their] disgruntled and insubordinate looks, and, although ordered to give 'Eyes Left', hardly a man bothered to do so.[1]

It was not just the French rank and file who preferred not to look their allies in the eye. The malaise of martial disinterest, of a basic reluctance to *fight*, it transpired, was a contagion that infected the entire French chain of command; a chain of command, moreover, that Britain had agreed could control the tactical deployment of all British troops in France. It was an agreement that was based upon the premise, the unquestioned British assumption, that France would fight and that France would hold. Yet it was a premise that would prove to be fatally flawed. That process of realisation began on 10 May 1940 when *Sitzkrieg* exploded into *blitzkrieg*. The waiting war was over.

As the German High Command had both hoped and predicted, France's generals fell for the sucker punch, the feint. As *Generalfeldmarschall* Von Manstein's *Fall Gelb* (Plan Yellow) kicked into action, the twenty-nine divisions of General von Bock's Army Group B stormed across Holland and the northern Belgian frontier supported by massed formations of Ju 87 Stuka dive-bombers, the Luftwaffe's aerial artillery. As they did so the BEF carried out their pre-planned Operation *David*: they left their carefully prepared defensive positions and lumbered forward obligingly towards the River Dyle in Belgium to block the threat to their front. Even as they abandoned those carefully prepared positions, far to their right, the *forty-five* divisions and massed armoured units of von Rundstedt's Army Group A poured through Luxembourg and the supposedly impenetrable forests of the Ardennes to hook right into the British rear and crash north-westwards towards Calais and the coast. It was what *Generalfeldmarschall* Erich Von Manstein, the author of *Fall Gelb*, called *Sichelschnitt* – the 'sickle cut' – and sickles have sharp edges. In the days of terror, rout and onslaught that followed, French units collapsed and British forces found themselves in chaotic, headlong retreat westwards towards the coast, their corridor of access through to the channel port of Dunkirk held open by an ever-shrinking British and French rearguard who sacrificed their own chances of escape so that comrades could move back to the coast. These harassed units retreated down a pinched and shrinking corridor that initially was 60 miles deep and between 15 and 25 miles wide. They struggled north-westwards under constant attack from three sides as German artillery, infantry and armoured units hacked into the retreating columns where a rag-tag of jumbled, exhausted and often leaderless units wrecked and then abandoned their weapons, stores and vehicles as they edged closer to the sea.

The leading German Panzer units of General Heintz Guderian's XIX Panzer Korps reached the Channel coast at Abbeville, west of Dunkirk, on 20 May after just ten days of brutal, exhilarating advance. To those dust-caked, red-eyed, sleep-starved, deafened tankers gazing out across the Channel in sudden, bruising silence as engines were switched off after advancing 180 miles since crossing their start lines on 10 May, it must have seemed that the end of the war was in sight.

Yet, if there *was* a miracle of Dunkirk, then perhaps it was the controversial German 'halt order' of 25 May that stopped German armoured units at Gravelines south-west of Dunkirk for three days to regroup and permit their rear echelon of supplies, ammunition and replacements to catch up. That, and the gift of good Channel weather that ensured mostly light winds and flat seas, permitted that armada of 'little ships' and Royal Navy warships to pluck a weary BEF from those sandy, smoke-shrouded beaches and shuttle them back to England. Most returned with their personal weapons, yet many came home with little more than helmet and damp, salt-stained battledress to be greeted with buns and sandwiches, hot tea, survivor postcards and a cheering crowd at every railway halt who hailed them as the returning victors they manifestly were not.

At the outset it had been hoped that perhaps 30,000 men might be evacuated in two days by the Royal Navy's well-organised Operation *Dynamo* before German intervention made further evacuation impossible. In the event – and after nine days and nights of heroic endeavour, shared by the French whose First Army, surrounded at Lille, fought on alone for four vital days thus delaying the advance of seven extra German Divisions to Dunkirk – 338,226 French and British troops were lifted off the French beaches and moles of Dunkirk and spirited away to England. Yet 68,111 members of the British Expeditionary Force did *not* return home. Excluding combat casualties, 41,030 British soldiers were left behind to be either wounded or marched into a long captivity. Also left behind were most of the British army's weapons, cased food, ammunition and vehicles. The statistics of loss make sober reading, for every round of ammunition, every Bren gun and rifle, every hand grenade, mortar round and field gun would be needed in the fight to repel the invasion of Britain which must now surely follow. Yet left behind in France were 2,500 artillery pieces, 377,000 tons of stores, 162,000 tons of petrol and 68,000 tons of ammunition. Britain's military cupboard was now bare. Little wonder then that the early Local Defence Volunteers drilled with broom handles while troops on the south coast practised rapid deployment from corporation omnibuses. And 65,000 vehicles and 20,000 motorcycles had also been left behind for the Germans.

It was the loss and self-destruction of the cars and lorries under his own command that one particular subaltern, 24-year-old Second Lt Geoffrey Appleyard, RASC, found particularly shaming. Vehicles, after all, were to that particular corps what field guns were to the Royal Artillery and field dressings were to the Royal Army Medical Corps. A Cambridge University Engineering graduate with First Class Honours, Appleyard had heeded the climate of an increasingly war-nervous Europe and volunteered to join the Supplementary Reserve of officers in the Royal Army Service Corps in 1938. On 1 September the following year he and his fellow Reservists were mobilised. He soon found himself at Bulford Camp, Wiltshire, commanding the skilled mechanics, fitters, turners, blacksmiths, coppersmiths, carpenters, drivers and mobile workshop personnel who made up his forty-five-strong unit in the Workshops of 'E' Section, No 6 Sub Park, 11 Ammunition, RASC. A week earlier, on 23 August 1939, Molotov and von Ribbentrop had stunned the world by signing their two nations' non-aggression pact, thereby virtually guaranteeing both the German invasion of Poland and the world war that would follow. Appleyard was one of those who permitted himself to peer into a bleak future, writing home to his family in Yorkshire:

So Russia is in. How awful. And what a swinish thing to do. It means a long war, but I'm sure we must win. I'm certain we've got right on our side and I even feel we've got God on our side – if God could conceivably be on any side in anything so bloody as a war. We *must* win. Funny how relative everything is – you don't really appreciate a holiday till it's over. The same way you don't really appreciate your liberty until it's threatened. But I'll *never* be *made* to say 'Heil Hitler'. I'd sooner die.

The Germans invaded Poland, Britain's ultimatum ran its course, the war began and a weary, self-pitying, lacklustre Neville Chamberlain addressed the nation on the wireless. On 29 September 1939, crammed with 1,500 other mobilised troops into the SS *Lady of Mann*, one of the early vessels to be pressed into service to carry the BEF to France, Appleyard and his unit endured a rough crossing to France. There they joined the rear echelon in support, for they did not form one of the front-line fighting units: they were tail, not teeth. They spent that long, cold and muddy winter moving from billet to billet behind the static front line repairing vehicles and supplying various artillery units with ammunition from the railhead and waiting for something, anything, to happen. Transferred by his colonel without the option from Workshops to Ammunition Section and then to Headquarters, Appleyard was an inveterate letter-writer to a loving family back home in Linton-on-Wharfe, near Wetherby, Yorkshire. Prohibited by the censor from disclosing his exact location, he left them in no doubt about conditions, writing in October:

> With the arrival at this village quite a lot of the fun has gone out of this war. Quite suddenly winter has come with a bang, and there is mud everywhere. Mud, mud, mud wherever you go. It rains off and on all through the day and the sky is heavy, misty and overcast. Cheerful prospect! The village here is much smaller than Linton and consists solely of farms ... The first night here the men were billeted in a cowshed – absolutely filthy.

He added a little later: 'I'm not learning to love this mud-soaked corner of Europe any more – it must be the most utterly God-forsaken piece of land in the world. Did someone say something about "*La Belle* France"? I prefer La Bl... France.'

As the months dragged by, Appleyard's thoughts turned increasingly to home and an overdue leave. In April 1940 he was writing: 'My leave prospects are very bright! There is every chance that I should get home on my original date; that is, leaving here the 8th May, home 9th, which is sensational.' On 25 April he felt confident enough to write:

> Hurrah! My leave date is now definitely confirmed. I am leaving here May 7th, arriving home May 8th – possibly very late as it is a late boat that day, I think. That's terrific, isn't it! I'm thrilled to have so early a prospect of seeing you all again ... Just think – only twelve days hence! And the date is quite definite unless leave is suspended again, or something else very unto-ward happens!

Unfortunately for Appleyard and his eagerly anticipated home leave, something very untoward *did* happen. The British anglicised it to *blitz-krieg* but it meant the same thing: lightning war – the German thunderclap advance into Belgium, Holland, Luxembourg and France by a co-ordi-nated force of tanks, motorised infantry, artillery and on-call air support. As German mechanised units smashed across the Belgian border and headed deep into France to start their swing towards the Channel coast, Appleyard and his unit were caught up in the initial advance to contact. He wrote about those dangerous days – perhaps with an eye to an anxious family waiting at home – in terms that suggested he might almost be on some sort of private Grand Tour:

I am very well, fairly comfortable (at times) and having a terrific experience. There will be masses to tell you when I am home again, but I am afraid it must all wait until then. Sufficient to say that my days are very full and very interesting. I am very brown with continually being out in the open air in the open car ... You know, in spite of everything, this is an amazing and invaluable experience for me and in certain ways will be of immense value in later life. I had better stop – things are beginning to happen again.

No mention, then, of wailing, gull-winged Stukas or of thundering German armour hacking into soft-skinned British columns; no mention of collapsing French armies amidst rout; of valiant last-ditch, last bullet stands by both French and British troops; no mention of British units in chaos or nervous officers relieved of their command and sent home, or British rifles being turned on fleeing British officers and soldiers with orders to shoot to kill.

Appleyard's RASC unit had reached Armentières just before the evacuation of Dunkirk began. By then the chatty letters home had ceased. Armentières was at the western edge of the Gort line of five interlinked British divisions that hooked in a sickle of their own to the north and east protecting Lille. Armentières was bombed into ruin and Appleyard and his men did what they could to help, then headed north-west down the corridor towards Dunkirk taking with them all their vehicles and ammunition stores. It says much for his early skills as both leader and young subaltern that not a man of his unit was lost in what is arguably that most difficult of all military manoeuvres, the fighting withdrawal. His letters do not describe that fighting retreat to the coast, nor the eventual link-up with the crescent-shaped, shrinking perimeter that guarded Dunkirk itself. When he got there, every lorry and car lovingly intact, his CO told him to take his vehicles to a nearby canal, destroy them with fire and pick-axe to make them useless to the enemy and then tip them into the canal. Appleyard's father was to write later:

> The Commanding Officer later, with some amusement, recounted to Geoff that he seemed dazed by the order, that his jaw dropped, his eyes opened wide with horror and, forgetting military discipline, he ejaculated 'What? Me destroy *my* cars, *my* lorries!' On these vehicles Geoff had laboured through days and nights of the long rigours of winter and the rains of spring, to keep them in the pink of perfection on the road. The shock of the order was to him as to a father told to ill-treat his children.[2]

Second Lt Appleyard followed his orders. Then, on foot, he led his men into the Dunkirk perimeter. On 30 May, that perimeter stretched from

Mardyck, 5 miles west of Dunkirk's west mole, to Nieuport Bains 23 miles to the east and inland to a depth of 6 miles. Three days later those 23 miles of British-held shoreline had shrunk to a perimeter just 10 miles long and, at its maximum, 4 miles wide. Amidst the chaos of the evacuation from Dunkirk we do not know exactly where or when Appleyard and his men entered the perimeter down roads lined with wrecked vehicles, spilled stores and guns of every description as they straggled down to the beach in the hope of possible evacuation. But we do know from contemporary accounts that, by then, the once-pleasant summer resort that held fond memories for thousands of European holiday-makers had descended into a vision of Hell itself. More than a thousand of its civilians were dead, many lying bloated in the heat, disfigured and stinking in their own streets. Under incessant German shelling, hundreds of homes and municipal buildings had been shredded and blasted into ruin. One French officer wrote about entering Dunkirk:

> Entire columns of soldiers have been annihilated by the bombardment. Not far from Bastion 32 lay a line of corpses who had fallen on top of each other. It was as if a gust of wind had blown over a row of wooden soldiers. The dark road was so full of obstructions that it was impossible to avoid some of the corpses, which were run over by my car.[3]

Now, shattered glass crunched under hob-nailed boots; bricks, piles of rubble and tangled telephone wire lay everywhere, impeding progress. There was no electric street light or running water, the town was lit at night by the lurid flickering glow of many fires, the streets were thick with the cloying, throat-greasing, back-of-the-mouth taste of death and burning oil that drifted in on the wind from the storage tanks to the west of the town. Another French officer observed approaching the west mole:

> We walk along the beach which is obstructed by isolated soldiers, cars, English cannons, dead men and horses … This suburb is sinister. It is completely ruined, and burned, with more dead horses and unimaginable disorder. None of the cars have tyres anymore; they have been taken and used as lifebelts.[4]

No 3 Brigade's headquarters was moved to the beach at Bray Dunes just inside the eastern perimeter on 31 May. The unit's war diarist recorded:

> The scenery provided a … picture of the abomination of desolation. Ruined and burnt out houses … salt water spreading everywhere, vehicles

abandoned, many of them charred relics of twisted metal on the roadside and overturned in the ditches. Light tanks and guns poking up out of the floods. Horses dead or dying from want of water. Here and there civilian or French army corpses lying in the open. An unforgettable spectacle.[5]

A few days later a German Officer would concur as he reviewed the abandoned beaches after the last grey British warship had slid back over the horizon:

> It's a complete mess. There are guns everywhere as well as countless vehicles, corpses, wounded men and dead horses. The heat makes the whole place stink. Dunkirk itself has been completely destroyed. There are lots of fires burning … We moved to Coxyde Bains by the beach [4 miles west of Nieuport] but we cannot swim since the water is full of oil from the sunk ships, and is also full of corpses … There are tens of thousands of cars, tanks, ammunition cases, guns and items of clothing.[6]

Above all, Dunkirk was, as it had always been, a place of beaches and sand dunes but with this difference: now it was also a place of patient and sometimes not-so-patient evacuation where long black lines of soldiers, three or four abreast, waited their turn for salvation. Weary, thirsty men were standing up to their chests in water or queuing for hours on life-saving piers of lorries: these had been driven out into the sea, lashed together with their tyres shot out, filled with sand and then topped off with planks to provide a shallow-water jetty for the heroic 'little ships' that had put out from a dozen English ports to ferry what remained of the BEF to deeper-draught vessels waiting offshore. Others, crammed with troops, sailed straight for England. German aircraft and artillery had bombed the beaches incessantly, lobbing bomb and shell into the packed clusters of waiting troops. They could hardly miss. Many men had died there on the beaches within sight of rescue. But if there was a third miracle, it was that the beaches at Dunkirk were soft. Many bombs and shells had simply buried themselves deep in the sand before exploding.

One of those who had taken shelter in the sand dunes from the incessant bombing whilst awaiting his turn to get away was Geoffrey Appleyard. Crouching in one of those deep sand holes as the bombs rained down, Appleyard was suddenly sent sprawling into the sand by something hitting him hard in the middle of the back. 'As he lay, his mouth full of sand, thinking: "Well, this is it – they've got me" a voice sounded in his ear: "I say, I f-feel a bl-bloody coward, how about you?"'[7] It was a startling and unorthodox introduction to Capt. Gustavus March-Phillipps, Royal

Artillery, a man who would shortly become his commanding officer. Crouching there in the sand dunes of Dunkirk during the long hours of fear and boredom that followed as they dodged the shells and waited for evacuation, the two officers formed a bond of friendship that was to last a lifetime.

At its inception, Operation *Dynamo* had hoped to lift perhaps 30,000 British soldiers off the beaches at Dunkirk. In the event, 338,226 British and French servicemen had been saved. Amongst them were Appleyard and March-Phillipps. Had the German High Command realised just how much trouble the stuttering gunner and the Yorkshire engineer who liked writing letters home were about to cause the German war effort, they would have been justified in diverting an entire Stuka *Geschwader* to ensure their particular and personal destruction. But they did not.

And so Gus March-Phillipps and his new friend Geoffrey Appleyard came home to the country they loved: England.

2

Backs to the Wall

Geoffrey Appleyard and his men were amongst the very last to leave the Dunkirk beaches. They returned home in a destroyer doomed to be sunk the next day and which was bombed repeatedly on their way back to England as brave surgeons worked below decks to save the lives of the wounded. Landing at Dover, Appleyard telephoned home to Yorkshire to report his safe arrival. The family immediately drove south to meet him at Tenby, South Wales: 'There followed the happiest renion this family has ever known', wrote his father simply of a time of closeness made precious by the uncertainty of repetition. After brief home leave in Linton, Appleyard reported back to Aldershot where he helped in the rebuilding of his decimated unit.

March-Phillipps also returned to his parent unit, although there remains today no trace in the records or his personal file as to his actual deployment. In France with the BEF he had served on General Brooke's Headquarters staff at 2 Corps and subsequently 2 BEF where he 'served with some distinction'.[1] It was a distinction recognised by the award of the MBE (Military Division) although, again, no trace of the actual citation appears to exist beyond the bald facts of its promulgation in the *London Gazette* of 11 July 1940. (This is recorded erroneously in his own military file as 29 July 1942.)

At 32, March-Phillipps was an Ampleforth-educated former regular soldier, commissioned into the Royal Artillery at the age of 20, but who had left the army after active service with 23 Field Battery RA on India's North-West frontier in the 1930s. Tiring of inaction and a hill bungalow social life that looked endlessly in on itself, March-Phillipps handed in his papers in 1932, sold his kit and used the proceeds to fund his way back to England. Here he settled in the family home in Eastway House, Blandford Forum, and began pecking out a living as a novelist. Gordon Winter knew him then:

He was very much a young man just out of the army in his manner, much more than anything else, and he had all the mannerisms which I don't think he ever lost ... impatience with anybody who was slow or dithery, the importance of getting on with something quickly, importance of doing whatever you did well, and a kind of built in dislike of any sort of slackness – these are the things which he carried on. And a great scorn of anybody who was carrying an ounce of too much weight (laughs). I can well remember that.[2]

March-Phillipps was then 24. *Sporting Print* (1937), *Storm In A Teacup* (1937) and *Ace High* (1939) were all well received but, by the time war came, he was neither famous nor wealthy. Of light frame and medium height, he was single, aesthetic, romantic, whipcord lean and sometimes impetuous. He had protruding ears, receding light brown hair brushed back flat from a high forehead and a small moustache grown to disguise a hardly noticeable upper-lip disfigurement, the legacy of being bitten by a horse as a child. An expert horseman, he was also afflicted by a startling stammer that became worse when he was angry or frustrated. Cursed – or perhaps blessed – with a short fuse, he had a fierce temper and forthright views. To his family, he had huge charisma. His niece, Jennifer Auld, now aged 83, remembers with great fondness the Gus March-Phillipps she knew before the war:

My mother was his elder sister ... He was a great chap and a lovely uncle. He used to take us for walks and that lovely car he had, the Vauxhall. He called it Gert and he used to tell us stories about it. 'When I'm tired', he used to say, 'I'd just say: Gert, take me home' and we always wondered – we were only young – and we used to think 'Did it really happen? It can't *really* happen like that, can it?' He told it very convincingly. I can hear him now. He was a lovely chap; he was great. He used to take us for walks – but it was never just a walk, it was always – I don't remember birds but it was flowers and trees and the other thing was: take you for a walk and now find your way back to Gert ... there was a puzzle there; there always something a bit more to it than just a walk. He was fun; he was adventurous. He was tall and thin; athletic; a bit of a dare-devil. I remember my grandmother telling me he had broken his collarbone but he still rode in the point-to-point. He was a great sportsman. He was a sports journalist and he wrote books. When he came to our house in Goring – we weren't very old I don't think – and he was up in the second floor and we were told to play one side but of course we went round and he was writing one of the books and put his head out of the window and yelled at us; he was quite cross.[3]

Tim Alleyn shared a cottage with him in the Thames Valley. Recalling those sunlit pre-war days: 'My recollection is that we just had a whale of a time. Dashing around in large cars to various places with various friends, in and around the Thames Valley, Maidenhead and other places. You know, life was just one enormous party.' But a party, it appears, with edge:

> We quarrelled. He had a violent temper. Oh, terrific, yes. He used to go off into sulks for weeks – well, that's an exaggeration, but certainly he would sulk and he'd turn absolutely white with rage if you disagreed with him sometimes, or he stammered very badly. But of course when he was very cross it got very much worse.[4]

He was also fiercely patriotic and deeply religious, a practising Roman Catholic with a devout belief in God. Appleyard recalled:

> He is the first Army officer I have met so far who kneels down by the side of his bed for ten minutes before he goes to sleep. M-P is a great worshipper and disciple of the Knights of Old, believes that the spirit of Drake and Raleigh, of Robert The Bruce and of Oliver Cromwell is the spirit that will save England today and give her a name that the world will once again look up to. And I'm sure he is right.

Deeply religious he may have been, but March-Phillipps was no saint. Another who formed a shrewd opinion of the former officer and novelist now returned to the colours was Sir Brooks Richards, a future member of SOE who was later to become a distinguished British diplomat: 'Gus was a really rather extraordinary man. Before the war he had had expensive tastes and slender means. He'd loved foxhunting and driving very fast cars and indulged these two tastes by becoming someone's kennel huntsman and by being a racing driver.'[5]

Nine years older than Appleyard, March-Phillipps was also a born and an inspirational leader, a man others would follow without hesitation. The late SOE historian Professor Michael Foot once described him memorably as possessing 'a fiery, disdainful manner that left an unforgettable impression of force'.[6] Wars need men like that.

The Britain both these officers returned to had changed, and not simply because the lisping new prime minister many still distrusted now had a growl in his voice: there was everywhere a new, hard-edged realism that seemed to shrug off the mists and obfuscations of the Chamberlain years and the phoney war. Britain was rolling up her sleeves. Despite the euphoria with which she had greeted her heroes returning from Dunkirk, a

Britain now braced for invasion did not need the prime minister to tell them that wars were not won by evacuations. As the news from across the Channel deteriorated still further, there was a brief scare that Appleyard and his unit might be amongst formations earmarked for a swift return to France – at one point three-quarters of his unit's replacement vehicles had actually been loaded onto ships in Southampton before wiser counsels prevailed and the Movement Order was cancelled.

Even as Appleyard and his men had struggled towards Dunkirk, the Chiefs of Staff had considered a Top Secret paper entitled 'British Strategy in a Certain Eventuality'.[7] That 'certain eventuality' was the collapse of France. Its essential conclusion was that, if France went to the wall, Britain would indeed still have the will, the morale, to fight on – if necessary, alone: 'The real test is whether the morale of our fighting personnel and civil population will counter-balance the numerical and material advantages which Germany enjoys. We believe it will', concluded the Chiefs of Staff with unequivocal, prescient courage. Now, on 4 June, with the last troops snatched back from France and the door to Europe closed, bolted and barred, Prime Minister Winston Churchill lost no time setting out his stall in what was to become one of the defining speeches of the Second World War:

> I have, myself, full confidence that if all do their duty, if nothing is neglected, and if the best arrangements are made, as they are being made, we shall prove ourselves once more able to defend our island home, to ride out the storm of war, and to outlive the menace of tyranny, if necessary for years, if necessary alone. At any rate, that is what we are going to try to do. That is the resolve of His Majesty's Government – every man of them. That is the will of Parliament and the nation ... Even though large tracts of Europe and many old and famous States have fallen or may fall into the grip of the Gestapo and all the odious apparatus of Nazi rule, we shall not flag or fail. We shall go on to the end. We shall fight in France, we shall fight on the seas and oceans, we shall fight with growing confidence and growing strength in the air, we shall defend our island, whatever the cost may be. We shall fight on the beaches, we shall fight on the landing grounds, we shall fight in the fields and in the streets, we shall fight in the hills; we shall never surrender.[8]

Churchill could have made it no plainer: the next significant battleground was likely to be the southern shores and rolling green fields of England. 'I'd rather be fighting overseas', Appleyard admitted:

> There you do at least feel you are doing something to keep the 'wolf from the door' so to speak, but to form up in England and wait for him to come

means that this country of ours will be turned into a battlefield. Still, I suppose it will at least have the advantage of making certain people in England know that we are at war, and realise what invasion really does mean. And we really shall feel that we are fighting to protect English soil.

Despite the strength of Churchill's soaring rhetoric on that date and his 'finest hour' speech to the Commons a fortnight later which together managed, for those remaining months of 1940, to excite the British population to a never-to-be-recaptured selfless nationalism and resolve, not everyone shared Appleyard's pragmatic acceptance of the inevitably of fighting on British soil. Kingsley Amis wrote in the *New Statesman* that same month: 'To talk to common people in and out of uniform is to discover that determination to defend this island is coupled with a deep and universal bitterness that we have been reduced to such a pass.'[9]

†††

As German armoured units swung south towards the French capital, the roads south of Paris filled with fleeing, panic-stricken civilians. Officials too abandoned their posts and the people they had once pledged to serve. They called it *L'Exode*: the Exodus. The German army entered Paris unopposed on 14 June. On that same day, in Chartres, an hour south of the capital by train, that beautiful cathedral town was abandoned by its mayor, its director of public works and its chief water engineer. Although Chartres was bombed and burning, the fire chief announced that now was the time to head south and take the town's four fire engines to safety away from the flames.[10] With him rode the town clerk. Chartres was also abandoned by its doctors, its entire force of gendarmes and by its bishop. It was a scene of shame, of fear and civic betrayal that was repeated in a hundred towns across northern France. Two days later, on 16 June, after finding himself unsupported by his own Cabinet when he suggested continuing the fight from Algeria, right-wing Republican Premier Paul Reynaud resigned. He was succeeded by the still-revered 84-year-old Marshal Philippe Pétain, the hero of Verdun in 1916, who told his nation, on the radio, that it was his intention to seek an armistice with Germany. On 22 June in the same railway carriage in Compiègne forest and on the same spot where Germany had signed the armistice in 1918, Pétain signed the instrument of surrender that would take France out of the war and divide his own country in two: a German-occupied zone in the north and west and a *Zone Non-occupée* in the south to be known as Vichy France. Out went the discredited Third Republic with its heart-stirring *Liberté*,

Égalité, *Fraternité*, in came the French State of Vichy with Pétain Chef de l'État Français. It would soon prove to be a state, a government and a betrayal of shameful collaboration. The French armistice and ceasefire came into effect on 25 June 1940. France's particular 4-year Calvary had begun. Now, at last, Britain stood alone. To many, the realisation came as a relief. For good or ill, Britain's destiny, her very survival as a sovereign state, now lay in no one's hands but her own.

†††

Already, within that beleaguered island, Britain's combative new prime minister and soon-to-be self-appointed minister of defence, the portly, cigar-smoking, scotch-drinking former soldier of 65 who would in short measure prove himself to be *exactly* the man who would chart Britain's survival and eventual victory, had begun to lean forward and think of ways in which Britain could take the fight back to the enemy. As Appleyard and his men awaited evacuation on the crowded beaches of Dunkirk, Winston Churchill had minuted his Chiefs of Staff on 3 June 1940:

> The completely defensive habit of mind, which has ruined the French, must not be allowed to ruin all our initiative. It is of the highest consequence to keep the largest numbers of German forces all along the coasts of the countries that have been conquered, and we should immediately set to work to organise raiding forces on these coasts where the populations are friendly.[11]

Others, too, were already thinking along the same lines. The following evening, 4 June, Lt Col Dudley Clarke, Royal Artillery, was walking back from the War Office to his flat in Stratton Street, Mayfair. Clarke was a General Staff Officer, First Grade, and serving at that time as Military Assistant to Sir John Dill, the newly appointed Chief of the Imperial General Staff. Aged 59, Dill had just taken over from General Sir Edmund Ironside and was now Britain's most senior soldier. Dill was also on the Chiefs of Staff Committee and thus one of the recipients of Winston Churchill's 'highest consequence' minute of the day before. As Clarke made his way home through the early evening summer twilight of sandbagged, barb-wired and barrage-balloon protected London, his thoughts were grim for, he remembered, 'in the War Office on that night it was not easy to view the future with optimism.' He cast his mind back to other times and other armies: what had *they* done when their backs were to the wall? Clarke had served in Palestine in 1936. He had seen with his own eyes what 'a handful of ill-armed fanatics' had been able to achieve against the regular, cumbrous

British army. He remembered also South Africa, where he had been born, where mounted units of Boers, sharp-shooting farmer 'commandos', had successfully harried more than a quarter of a million British troops conventionally deployed almost half a century before. Could they – could not Britain – now create something similar? A lightly armed, lightly equipped amphibious strike force that could take the fight to the enemy anywhere and everywhere along the coastline of his vastly extended occupied territories? It was an exciting thought. Clarke hurried home and there 'before I went to bed I tried to marshal my ideas into the outline of a plan jotted down in note form on a single sheet of … writing paper.'

The next morning Clarke took his paper to Sir John Dill, who took it straight to Churchill. Both Clarke and Dill found themselves knocking at an open door. That very next day, 6 June 1940, perhaps as a direct result of Clarke's ideas, Churchill was urging General Ismay:

> Enterprises must be prepared with specially trained troops of the hunter class who can develop a reign of terror first of all on the 'butcher and bolt' policy … I look to the Chiefs of Staff to propose me measures for a vigorous, enterprising and ceaseless offensive against the whole German occupied coastline. Action This Day.[12]

Thus, within two days, Clarke had the Premier's authorisation to create exactly the sort of 'commando' strike force he was proposing. Colonel Clarke was appointed to head a new section of the War Office secretariat of Military Operations – MO9 – and to organise 'uniformed raids'.[13] Churchill imposed only two conditions: first, that no unit should be diverted from its primary task of defending the shores of Britain against invasion and, second, that this new strike force should make do with a minimum of weapons. Which, given the quantity of arms of every description left behind at Dunkirk, was probably just as well:

> So urgent was the need of every sort of arm and equipment to refit the BEF that raiding had to be carried out on a Woolworth basis. For this reason the Commandos were armed, equipped, organised and administered for one task and one task only – tip-and-run raids of not more than 48 hours from bases in England against the continent of Europe.[14]

So short, in fact, was the supply of weapons in England that tommy guns and other weapons used on the early commando raids had to be issued and later returned to a single communal store.

But … commando! The name stuck:

I suggested the name 'commando' from the very start. At least, it was arrived at without much effort and I don't remember any rival titles having been seriously considered – although it was a long time before War Office circles would unbend sufficiently to use the word in official papers without visible pain ... but it did seem at once to suggest exactly what was wanted ... A little further thought seemed to show one conditions far more favourable than most guerrillas had had to contend with. First, we had in England a safe and well-stocked base from which to operate within close range of many tempting targets; second, we had plenty of intelligent and trained soldiers who could individually be just as well armed as their opponents and, third, we had in the sea lines of approach and retreat where we could expect to be more mobile and more secure than our opponents.[15]

The troops Clarke needed were, indeed, close at hand. He had only to look to Norway.

Like Dunkirk, the British Norwegian campaign of April 1940 had been a disaster, its comprehensive mishandling shovelled under the carpet, eclipsed by Chamberlain's mauling in the Commons Norway debate, his subsequent departure from office and the German launch of European *blitzkrieg* on 10 May. The land campaign overall in Norway may have been a failure but the deployment and handling of what had become known as the 'Independent Companies' had shone a pale gleam of light onto an otherwise bleak landscape of confusion and gross senior officer incompetence. Britain had been wrong-footed by the speed, precision and brutal professionalism of the long anticipated but, in the event, unexpected German seizure of key ports and strategically important, widely scattered towns in the Germans' unprovoked simultaneous invasion of both Denmark and Norway on 9 April 1940. It was an assault aimed at securing German naval bases from which, in their sea war with Britain, Germany could break out of the confines of the North Sea.

Britain's makeshift response, according to one leading historian, 'defied parody'.[16] But someone, somewhere, *had* been thinking ahead. Military Intelligence had been ordered to make plans for amphibious raids on Norway's western coast. Accordingly, MI(R) – one of the early forerunners of the soon-to-be-created Special Operations Executive – had set about the creation of a number of irregular units whose task would be to prevent German troops from setting up those air and submarine bases and to harry the extended lines of German supply and communications. Proposed by the head of MI(R), Lt Col Jo Holland, DFC, RE, on 15 April 1940, he envisaged a number of special units, each lightly equipped and capable of operating alone for up to a month at a time. His proposal was immediately approved.

Called initially 'Guerilla Companies', then 'Special Infantry Companies' and finally 'Independent Companies', ten of these new units were formed in haste from those Territorial Army formations that had not been sent to France with the BEF. Each consisted of 21 officers and 368 other ranks drawn from units across the British Isles. Each company was to be self-sufficient and allocated a mother ship which would be both its floating base and its means of transport to and from its area of operations. Soon, five of those companies – Nos 1,2, 3, 4 and 5 – were on their way to Norway.

All five seaborne Independent Companies – the other five remained in Scotland and were intended to follow later – were commanded by Lt Col Colin Gubbins. His formation was given the name 'ScissorsForce'. If Admiralty signals reflected the uncertainty of times dominated by little more than confusion and a lurching, impulsive reaction to German military initiatives, then the Norway briefing on 4 May in Whitehall of the Officer Commanding No 4 Independent Company was of a piece: Major Patterson returned to his unit clutching 'maps' which consisted of little more than an illustrated pre-war guide to Norway as a holiday destination.

For Gubbins' men, the Norwegian campaign that ensued was chaotic and largely reactive. ScissorsForce sprang a successful ambush on German bicycle troops on the main road near Mosjøen and staged hit-and-run raids along the deeply indented coastline using commandeered Norwegian vessels. These limited, small scale successes did nothing, however, to halt the German advance and were followed by a series of withdrawing actions north to Bodø. Picked up and evacuated by the Royal Navy, by 10 June 1940 all five Independent Companies, unsure of what they had actually accomplished, were back in Scotland where they were reunited with the other five Independent Companies, most of whom had moved little further than garrison duties in Gourock and Glasgow. For those units that *had* bloodied themselves in Norway, their homecoming represented a lucky escape from which few senior officers had emerged with credit. One of those who had, however, was Colin Gubbins. Already the holder of the Military Cross from the First World War, Gubbins was awarded a DSO for his deft command and control of the ScissorsForce Independent Companies and for his part in an otherwise disastrous land campaign that had seen him relieve of his command a Scots Guards colonel who had shown a marked and persistent reluctance to hold his ground and engage the enemy. Gubbins cut a deceptively mild, well-mannered figure in peacetime and in his immaculately tailored colonel's service dress uniform with its highly burnished brasses appeared a 'slight, dapper full Colonel with a small moustache'. But beneath the surface stirred darker waters. For Gubbins was also – and most proudly – half Scots and the chieftain's love of mayhem, of smoke and battle and bloody murder was never far beneath that placid surface:

> A naval officer who met him during the 1940 Norway campaign described a brute in a khaki shirt with the sleeves cut off, snoring prodigiously in a twenty-minute squirt of sleep, then waking up alert and talking coherently 'an extraordinary man, very short and thick, with vast hairy arms that looked as if they could crush rocks and hung down almost to his knees'.[17]

Peter Kemp, a later SOE agent who, according to commando leader Lord Lovat, was 'hell bent on adventure'[18] – he had fought on Franco's side in the Spanish Civil War – was one of those destined to become closely involved with both March-Phillipps and Appleyard. He observed later:

> The invasion of Norway showed clearly the possibilities of partisan warfare. Paramilitary formations known as 'Independent Companies' had been employed in the last stages of the Norwegian fiasco. In spite of angry controversy, they were considered to have proved their usefulness. There was, however, no organised instruction in this kind of warfare, no school or centre where troops could be trained in its principles.[19]

One of those aware of just that failing was Colonel Gubbins. At the end of the First World War Gubbins had served as ADC to General Ironside, who in 1940 was Commander-in-Chief of UK Home Forces and then GOC of the Archangel Expeditionary Force to North Russia. That was in 1919 and Gubbins had seen the work of the Bolsheviks at first hand. A few years later he had served in Ireland fighting Michael Collins and those who championed the cause of Sinn Féin and Irish independence from Britain; he had fought, survived and learned much about unconventional warfare, of fighting round corners. In 1931 he began working with the British Military Intelligence Directorate specialising in Soviet intelligence. Now, returned home from Norway, Gubbins had written a far-sighted paper that urged the War Office to embrace the idea of guerrilla warfare and, moreover, provide a training ground and instructors. These men would give those freshly blooded soldiers of the Independent Companies the training they had shown they needed in Norway and would now need most certainly in the new world of clandestine, irregular warfare that was just developing. There was, he knew, an untapped reservoir of outdoor experts – explorers, soldiers, skiers, adventurers, frontiersmen –

just waiting to be approached. As a Scot brought up in part on the island of Mull, opposite Oban, he knew just the place, too: western Scotland. There was water for amphibious training, there was rugged, demanding countryside, a broken, jagged coastline where they could practise small boat insertion techniques and derelict houses that could be requisitioned for accommodation. Best of all there was space – lots and lots of space and isolation far away from prying eyes.

A similar idea had occurred to former Scots Guards officer and MI(R) 'Sleeper' Bill Stirling whose brother, David, would later go on to form the Special Air Service Regiment. It was Bill Stirling's idea to take six friends – Peter Kemp among them – with a particular outdoor interest and expertise, reinforced by a few carefully chosen officers and NCOs, and set up a new Special Training Centre at Inverailort for those engaged in irregular warfare. In time his idea would evolve into the legendary Commando Depot, later renamed the Commando Basic Training Centre at Achnacarry. In May and June 1940, however, that was still a little way in the future. 'As the Battle of Britain opened', wrote Peter Kemp:

> provisional agreement had been obtained from the War Office for our establishment, the selection of training areas and setting requisitioning machinery in motion. [Lord] Lovat, an officer who owned property in the West Highlands, was sent ahead to requisition all available premises astride the Fort William–Mallaig Road and railway line which, in fact, meant six deer forests and their lodges covering a land mass for training purposes of not less than 200,000 acres of wild country.

Better yet, this vast potential training area for Gubbins' Independent Companies – and anyone else who might be sent north to sharpen their killing skills, learn small boat work, close-quarter combat, stalking, cross-country navigation, explosive demolitions, weapon handling and endurance – lay within the Protected Area established that same year. It stretched in a diagonal line from Mull to Inverness and took in everything to the north, excluding the Isle of Skye, as far as John O'Groats. Anyone wanting access to that remote area of bleak, desolate, rain-swept beauty needed a permit: reasons to the Military Permit Office in London, in writing. Kemp and Lovat and others – with Stirling as Chief Instructor – moved up to Scotland at the end of May: 'With the help of the War Office, Stirling had been able to recruit some outstanding officers and NCOs to bring our staff of instructors to full strength. Three stalkers – great rifle shots and expert telescope men – were provided from the Lovat estate wearing their civilian plus fours.'[20]

Perhaps with an ear and an eye to the security concerns of the time in which he was writing – *No Colours or Crest* was published by Cassell in London in 1958 when the Cold War was chilling down by degrees – Kemp is being a little economical with the truth. 'The War Office' he refers to was, in fact, rather more than that. It was Jo Holland, Colin Gubbins and MI(R) in that most secret part of the War Office far from public gaze that stood behind Bill Stirling's Special Training Centre in its various guises. It would become the clandestine military *alma mater* from which so many future members of *Maid Honor*, the commandos and the Small Scale Raiding Force were to graduate.

Many of their instructors and experts had been members of the 5th (Supplementary Reserve) Battalion Scots Guards, the British Army's first unit of ski troops. Initially created to support the Anglo-French expedition to Finland during the Finns' Winter War with Russia, that war had ended before 5th Scots Guards could deploy in anger and the unit, to their dismay, had been disbanded. A further mission during the Norwegian campaign had been Operation *Knife*, an ambitious plan to land six ex-5th Scots Guards volunteers, now rebadged as MI(R) agents, from the submarine HMS *Truant* with orders to help Norwegian resistance fighters destroy the road and rail bridges that linked Oslo with the north. Attacked by an enemy U-boat and damaged, HMS *Truant* promptly turned about, limped home and never reached Norwegian waters. Disembarked at Rosyth, the unused but still optimistic MI(R) *Knife* team responded with enthusiasm to Bill Stirling's idea that they wait out the mission's new start date, not in London, but at his ancestral home estate at Keir some 30 miles west. They did so, taking with them the weapons, explosives and equipment they had planned to use in Norway. It was while they were honing their sharpshooting and explosive skills in Keir, not in London, that MI(R)'s ski-experts and recent passengers aboard HMS *Truant* leant that their days of undersea adventure were over: with the collapse of the British campaign in Norway their mission too had been overtaken by German success. There would no longer be a mission to blow up railway tracks near Oslo. Operation *Knife* was cancelled.

Thus it was in Keir, not in London, after they learnt that MI(R)'s Operation *Knife* was cancelled, that Bill Stirling had the idea of setting up a training school for Special Forces personnel. It was from Keir that Stirling and others took their idea of a special training school to Jo Holland in Whitehall only to find that he and Gubbins had embraced the same idea. Holland, Gubbins and MI(R) gave them their blessing. In return, Stirling and his friends offered skilled instructors – mostly from 5th Scots Guards – and an ideal location with no landlord problems: the hills for miles around were owned by the School's chief fieldcraft instructor, Lord Shimi Lovat.

They settled in, but there was little time to admire the stunning Highland scenery: the first course for twenty-five recruits was scheduled to start in early June. Two of those who would pass that course were David Stirling and Fitzroy Maclean, both destined to survive the war and become legends, one in Egypt, the other in Yugoslavia. Meanwhile, in Scotland, the midges were bad, they were short of rations, transport and cooks and there were never enough tents. They just got on with it.

Gubbins was not there to see the first Special Training Centre or School of Special Warfare take shape. German troops and armour were on the Channel coast and daily aerial reconnaissance missions showed that barges were being collected in ports and harbours facing England. Invasion appeared imminent. Any measure that would help Britain defend herself either before or after German troops landed in Britain – that was the overwhelming national priority. Gubbins, with his experience in Russia, Ireland, India, Poland and Paris, and with a recent DSO earned in Norway, was a man whose military currency had suddenly increased in value. Something else kept him in Whitehall, too.

In 1936 General Adam, the then Deputy Chief of the Imperial General Staff, had set up a department known as GS(R) within the War Office. The letters stood for General Staff (Research) and the purpose of the unit was nowhere near as anodyne as it sounded. The idea behind Adam's creation was to free up a single officer within GS(R) to spend a year studying a specific subject of current interest to the Army Council, to think 'out of the box' as they would not have described it at the time. In October 1938 the officer appointed to GS(R) was Lt Col Jo Holland and, by then, advanced thinking within the supposedly hide-bound War Office – despite what might be said elsewhere in Westminster and in the leader columns of *The Times* newspaper – was that Hitler was likely to invade Eastern Europe before turning his attentions to the west. If he were to do so, they reasoned, then revolt inside the occupied countries was likely. And resistance from *within* that expanded German empire was something that might be turned to the advantage of Hitler's enemies. Ostensibly, Holland's formal brief within GS(R) was to study recent guerrilla warfare in both China and Spain. But there was a deeper, top secret layer to Holland's briefing that very few knew about: he was to report on the possibility of providing clandestine support to any Eastern European country that might be overrun by Hitler.

Holland's first report was ready in January 1939 and, whatever it contained, it must have been persuasive for, as a result, he was permitted to recruit two more officers to GS(R), one to be an expert in explosives and demolitions and the other to be in charge of organisation, recruitment and training. For the first he chose an eccentric Sapper Major, Ellis Jefferis. For the second he chose Colin Gubbins. Jo Holland already knew Gubbins well and knew of his experience and language skills in Russia and Ireland. Remembered Colin Gubbins:

> A cold hand took me literally by the back of the neck and a voice I knew said: 'What are you doing for lunch today?' I whipped round – it was Jo Holland – and I replied that I was going to my regimental race at Sandown; there, beside me, were my field-glasses. 'No, you are not', he replied. 'You are to lunch with me; the CIGS says so.' We knew each other very well and I naturally agreed. In a private room at St Ermin's Hotel I found that the real host, who was waiting for us there, was another sapper officer whom I also knew well [Laurence Grand]. Over lunch he told us that he was the head of Section D and explained his charter ... He [Holland] started me off on the preparation of secret pamphlets on guerrilla warfare which were entitled *The Art of Guerilla Warfare*, *The Partisan Leader's Handbook* and *How To Use High Explosives*, and which were intended for the actual fighting partisan, tactical and not strategic.[21]

In the late spring of 1938, Holland and Gubbins worked together producing papers on the theory and practice of guerrilla warfare. By April 1939, Gubbins had been formally established as Holland's assistant. The next month Holland was authorised to further expand his department and recruit and train suitable potential saboteurs, whilst GS(R) now came under the Director of Military Intelligence and assumed a new acronym as anodyne as the last: MI(R), Military Intelligence (Research). In June 1939 Holland's newly named unit produced a report entitled *GS(R) Report No 8: Investigation of the Possibilities of Guerilla Activities*, which enclosed Gubbins' training manuals. The next month he was told that, if he were mobilised, he would be sent to Poland as part of Britain's military mission. Gubbins had been in Poland when the Germans invaded. He made contact with Polish Intelligence but, so swift was the German advance, he and his mission were unable to achieve anything. They pulled out via Bucharest and were lucky to get home. After a further fruitless MI(R) mission in Paris chasing underground contacts, Gubbins returned to London at the start of 1940. And then there had been Norway.Now, back in Britain, Jo Holland, Gubbins' friend and mentor within MI(R), offered Gubbins a further clandestine post: to set up Britain's top secret quasi-military guerrilla 'stay behind' forces that would go to ground after the Germans had invaded Britain. After being overrun by invading forces these small, four- to eight-man operational patrols would then rise up from their secret camouflaged operational bases buried deep in the woods and farmland of rural Britain and attack the Germans in the rear. Their task would be to destroy stores, blow up aircraft, bridges and fuel dumps, cut rail lines, disrupt convoys, kill senior German officers and even assassinate British collaborators. They were to be called Auxiliary Units – Auxunits – and their chances of long-term survival were slim indeed. Would Gubbins care to organise and lead them? Gubbins accepted. It was a desperate plan conceived in desperate times, times when speed, decision and, above all, action were of the critical essence. For what was at stake was Britain's very survival.

Meanwhile, as Stirling and his instructors began whipping each of MI(R)'s ten Independent Companies into shape on Stirling's home-devised, two-week course of intensive training at Lochailort, their future client-base was taking shape to the south.

On 9 June 1940 the War Office ordered Northern and Southern Commands to issue a call for 'volunteers for Special Service' from their sub units. It was a call that did not meet with universal approval: many conventional units feared the attraction of 'special service' would strip them of their best men. The orders of compliance they themselves received did little to ally such fears: 'Commanding Officers were to ensure that only the best were sent; they must be young, absolutely fit, able to drive motor vehicles and unable to be seasick. It was a leap in the dark for absolutely nothing was said as to what they were to do.'[22] Predictably, there was a huge response from regular, territorial and reservist alike, from every corps, support unit and front-line regiment. Here, perhaps, was a way of striking back; something that offered challenge, danger, excitement and a change from the boredom inherent in barrack-room duties: 'The great majority had never been under fire. They were just fed up with being told that the Germans were supermen and that they themselves were "wet". And so they revolted against their age and went to war in a new spirit of dedicated ferocity.'[23] Most may have done, but not everyone: in addition to those who volunteered out of patriotism, boredom, a yearning for excitement or a combination of all three, some turned up at the Special Training Centre for selection and found themselves under commando scrutiny whilst entirely ignorant of what sort of unit they might be joining.

The day after General Sir Alan Bourne was appointed Director of Combined Operations, the Director of Military Operations and Plans, Major General R.H. Dewing, put out a secret memorandum spelling out precisely how these newly named 'commando' units were to be created, formed and deployed. It was a timely, clearly reasoned attempt to shed a little light into an area already generating much heat, undirected excitement and not a little resentment and suspicion:

Irregular operations will be initiated by the War Office. Each one must necessarily require different arms, equipment and methods, and the purpose of the commandos will be to produce whatever number of irregulars are required to carry out the operations. An officer will be appointed by the War Office to command each separate operation and the troops detailed to carry it out will be armed and equipped for that operation only from central sources controlled by the War Office.

The procedure proposed for raising and maintaining commandos is as follows: One or two officers in each Command will be selected as Commando Leaders. They will each be instructed to select from their own Commands a number of Troop Leaders to serve under them. The Troop Leaders will in turn select the officers and men to form their own Troop. While no strengths have yet been decided upon, I have in mind commandos of a strength of something like ten Troops of roughly fifty men each. Each Troop will have a commander and one or possibly two other officers.

Once the men have been selected the commando leader will be given an area (usually a seaside town) where his commando will live and train while not engaged on operations. The officers and men will receive no Government quarters or rations but will be given a consolidated money allowance to cover their cost of living. They will live in lodgings, etc., of their own selection in the area allotted to them and parade for training as ordered by their leaders. They will usually be allowed to make use of a barracks, camp or other suitable place as a training ground. They will also have an opportunity of practising with boats on beaches nearby.

When a commando is detailed by the War Office for some specific operation, arms and equipment will be issued on the scale required and the commando will be moved to the jumping off place for the operation. As a rule the operation will not take more than a few days, after which the commando would be returned to its original 'Home Town' where it will train and wait, probably for several weeks, before taking part in another operation.

To many officers rusticating in some administrative backwater counting water-bottles, supervising the whitewashing of curb-stones or training reluctant recruits with two left feet, that appeal for volunteers for 'special service of a hazardous nature' came not a moment too soon. One of those who heeded the call was Capt. Gus March-Phillipps, MBE. After the shame of Dunkirk, he had a score to settle.

3

Commando Training

Each Command was responsible for raising commandos from troops within their own area and for selecting and appointing their own commando leaders. These leaders would appoint their own troop commanders who, in turn, would select their own volunteers:

- No 1 Commando, it was envisaged, would be formed from disbanded Independent Companies. In fact, this commando never actually formed because the Independent Companies remained in being for some months to come.
- No 2 Commando was to be raised as a parachute unit with volunteers stepping forward from both Northern and Southern Commands.
- Nos 3 and 4 Commandos would be formed from troops with Southern Command.
- Nos 5 and 6 Commandos would be formed from Western Command.
- No 7 Commando would be made up of volunteers from Eastern Command.
- No 8 Commando was also supposed to take its volunteers from Eastern Command but in fact recruited from London District and the Household Division.
- Nos 9 and 11 Commandos would come directly from Scottish Command.
- No 10 Commando was intended to be raised from Northern Command, although – perhaps curiously given the mood of bellicose enthusiasm elsewhere in the country for 'special service of a hazardous nature' – this unit did not attract enough initial volunteers to take its place in the new Order of Battle. It would be summer 1942 before it did so.
- No 12 Commando was also formed in Northern Ireland in early 1941 but, with only 250 men, it was roughly half the strength of the other commandos. Selected men from this commando, however, were to make a significant contribution to the units at the centre of this history.[1]

Capt. Gus March-Phillipps, meanwhile, was languishing, under-used and bored, within Eastern Command. Here the very inertia he wished to escape nearly thwarted his own attempts to respond to that appeal for 'hazardous service' volunteers that appeared on his unit notice board. Fearful that he might have left his application too late, he enlisted the help of a well-placed contact within Southern Command. This was Tim Alleyn, with whom he had once shared that cottage in the Thames Valley when he returned from India:

Dear Mate –
I've been recommended for the post of a commando leader, but owing to a fatuous Major in A [Administration] Branch I was unable to get the forms directly to Eastern Command. It has to go round the Corps tip and they take a week. So HO won't get it until too late unless you can tell them what has happened. The thing arrived here late in the first place, and they sat on it in the office. My God, they are awful. Anyway, I've been recommended a second time, and could you tell them that? If I come up for an interview, we'll have a terrific dinner. I'm feeling much too well, terribly fit and nothing to do ...[2]

Whilst others dragged their heels, officers elsewhere worked in haste to carry out Churchill's orders to strike back, to mount that all-important first raid across the Channel. To this end, a further special Independent Company, No 11, was formed on 14 June and began training around Hamble and Southampton Water. Less than three weeks after Colonel Dudley Clarke had his 'commando' idea whilst walking home from the War Office, Churchill's order became reality. Operation *Collar* was mounted on the night of 23/24 June 1940. It achieved little, claimed just two German lives and became dangerously close to making the concept of cross-channel raiding a risible joke. Its only British casualty was Colonel Dudley Clarke himself.

The objective of Operation *Collar* was to cross over at night to the Hardelot, Stella Plage and Berck areas of Boulogne by fast motor boat and make several landings to obtain information on German defences, destroy enemy outposts and kill or capture enemy soldiers. The raiders, under Major Ronnie Tod with Colonel Clarke along as Observer, would land at midnight, spend no more than eighty minutes ashore and then return by sea. Initially 180 men of No 11 Independent Company were detailed to take part in the raid but a shortage of weapons – there were just forty tommy guns in the whole of Britain at the end of June 1940 – and suitable raiding craft reduced that number to 120 after the failure of two of the engines of half-a-dozen air–sea rescue craft borrowed for the night from the

Air Ministry. The sea was calm, the sky cloudy with a light north-easterly breeze. Mid-Channel a rum ration was issued to the black-faced raiders. Soon after that the naval commander became unsure of his position until a sudden German searchlight obligingly revealed that he was about to motor straight into Boulogne harbour. They swung away into the safety of the darkness and landed a little further down the coast among sand dunes.

Tod and his men disappeared purposefully into the darkness. Nothing was heard for a while. Then Tod returned, armed with a tommy gun with which he was less than familiar. As Clarke disembarked to warn him that a darkened vessel had been seen nearby, a German bicycle patrol was reported moving along the beach towards them. As they prepared to open fire, Tod managed to knock the magazine off his unfamiliar weapon. It fell to the ground with a clatter. The Germans heard the noise and opened fire. Colonel Clarke was knocked back into the boat by the impact of a bullet that caught him behind the ear. He was not seriously wounded.

Major Tod's men returned without loss, and waded out into a rising tide to clamber back into their boat. They then headed back out to sea. Elsewhere, two boats had landed among the sand dunes. One had bumped into a German patrol and been fired on without loss and had not returned fire. The second had seen nothing; a third boat of armed raiders had not actually landed but attempted to stalk a seaplane which had then suddenly taken off over their heads like a startled goose. A fourth had landed at Merlimont Plage, 4 miles south of Le Touquet. Here they stumbled upon a large hotel surrounded by barbed wire which, they thought, might have been some sort of local headquarters. An enemy patrol of two soldiers was encountered. Both were killed with sten-gun fire from a range of 15 yards. Despite post-war claims that a German corpse was carried back to the beach[3] and then towed towards England behind a crowded boat only to be lost mid-Channel, the two bodies were left where they lay and nothing was removed.[4] A fifth landing party achieved nothing at all. Dawn found Colonel Clarke's crowded rescue boat approaching Dover: 'Grimy, dishevelled and triumphant and accompanied, appropriately enough, by a bandaged officer with bloodstains, they were cheered by every ship in harbour.'[5]

Men returning elsewhere suffered mixed fortunes. Outside Folkestone – unexpected, unannounced and evidently bearing the smoke-grim of distant battle – one boat of raiders was refused permission to enter harbour and ordered to lie off under the muzzles of Folkestone's defences whilst checks were made. All of which took time. Again, the rum ration was opened and two stone jars of SRD – Service Rum Dilute – were passed round the boat-load of weary heroes. Eventually permitted to proceed, upon arrival on *terra* by now not so very *ferma* they were arrested by the military police who believed them to be deserters.

The raid was reported in the newspapers the next day with only the vaguest of details. It proved a timely tonic for the battered British public – and caused near apoplexy amongst members of the British Cabinet who had no idea Operation *Collar* had been authorised to take place. It hadn't. Fearful of security leaks from high places, Director of Combined Operations General Bourne had told no one. He was only saved from court-martial by the timely intervention of the Minister of War, Anthony Eden.

German troops occupied the Channel Islands on 30 June 1940. Two days later General Hastings Ismay, Churchill's Chief Military Assistant and critical point of liaison between the Prime Minister and his Chiefs of Staff, received a memorandum from the Prime Minister. This stated: 'If it be true that a few hundred German troops have landed on Jersey or Guernsey by troop-carriers, plans should be studied to land secretly by night on the Islands and kill or capture the invaders. This is exactly one of the exploits for which the Commandos would be suited.'[6]

Thus began Operation *Ambassador*, Britain's formal second raid upon a shore occupied by the enemy. It took place twelve days later on the night of 14–15 July 1940. The target this time was Guernsey. Its objective? To inflict casualties on the German garrison, capture prisoners and destroy any German aircraft and equipment found on the island. To carry out this operation No 11 Independent Company was joined by members of the newly formed No 3 Commando commanded by Major John Durnford-Slater. He and 140 of his men were to land at three separate points on the southern side of the island: the Major at Moulin Huet Bay supported by the destroyer HMS *Scimitar*, No 11 Independent Company at both Le Jaonnet Bay and Pointe de la Moye. The landing parties were to be transported by the destroyer, then transferred to an RAF launch whilst still some distance off to make their own silent and unobserved approach to the enemy shore.

Durnford Slater and his men moved to Dartmouth, using the gymnasium at the Royal Naval College above the town as a makeshift gun room where naval cadets helped them load magazines for the precious Brens and tommy guns that had been sent down on loan from London. The attacking force left Dartmouth at 1845 on 14 July and arrived off the coast of Guernsey a few hours later in poor visibility, mist, drizzle and with a slight swell running. So far so good. But that, really, was as good as it got.

The two parties from No 11 Independent Company never made landfall. The coast was too rocky and the compasses of both boats, apparently, had been knocked out of true during degaussing. One vessel headed off smartly, in error, towards Sark. The other developed engine trouble and barely managed to struggle back to the mother ship, HMS *Scimitar*. An earlier postponement of forty-eight hours now meant that the anticipated half-tide landing onto smooth sand was now a high tide landing onto rocks and boulders from wooden, V-hulled boats that were anything but flat-bottomed: 'I jumped in, armpit-deep. A wave hit me on the back of the neck and caused me to trip over a rock. All around me officers and men were scrambling for balance, falling, coming up and coughing salt water. I doubt there was a dry weapon amongst us', recorded Major Durnford-Slater. He led the way towards the enemy, battle-dress heavy with seawater:

> I set off running up the long flight of concrete steps which led to the cliff top, 250 feet up. In my eagerness I went too fast. By the time I got to the top I was absolutely done … and my sodden battledress seemed to weight a ton. My legs were leaden, my lungs bursting, I could hear the squeak and squelch of wet boots as the rest of the troop followed us up from the beach.[7]

Once on the clifftop high above the beach they sent out patrols, established road blocks and searched for enemy to kill. Not a German was found. Although Second Lt Hubert Nicolle, an officer whose pre-war home had been on Guernsey, had landed a few nights before the raid to carry out a stealthy reconnaissance, the Germans appeared to have altered their dispositions in his absence. Reluctantly, and with time for the RV with HMS *Scimitar* running out, Durnford-Slater ordered his men back to the boats. Down the steep steps they hurried:

> I was last down from the cliff top with Peter Young clattering just ahead of me. Near the bottom I accelerated and suddenly realised that my feet had lost the rhythm of the steps. I tripped and tumbled the rest of the way, head over heels. I had been carrying my cocked revolver at the ready. During the fall it went off, seemingly tremendously loud and echoing against the cliffs. This, at last, brought the Germans to life. Almost at once there was a line of tracer machine-gun fire from the top of the cliff on the other side of our cove.[8]

They reached the beach. Heavy swell and a change of tide meant the men had to swim out to their rescue boats waiting 100 yards out in deep water beyond the growl of surf and pounding waves. Which was when three of his party admitted that, unfortunately, they were non-swimmers. They were left behind to give themselves up. Some of the men stripped off naked for the swim out to the boats. One man – Gunner John McGoldrick of the Royal Artillery – was later reported missing, believed drowned. Durnford-Slater left his battledress blouse on the beach for the Germans. It had his name sewn into the collar.

†††

And so, eventually, they came home.

Operation *Ambassador*, evidently, provided a learning curve for these new raiders that was almost vertical. Although much was learned – about boat suitability, personnel selection, the need for good small boat navigation and, above all, proper beach reconnaissance – nothing could disguise the fact that *Ambassador* was another disappointment, another fiasco. Churchill himself recognised it as such: 'Let there be no more silly fiascos like those perpetrated at Boulogne and Guernsey', he said. 'The idea of working all these coasts up against us by pinprick raids is one strictly to be avoided.'[9] Churchill had a point. Lord Lovat, one of the war's outstanding commando leaders, wrote:

> The sailors got a reprimand and Churchill ordered an immediate reorganisation. There would be no more slackly planned, uncoordinated efforts mounted by a collection of amateurs – naval or army – against targets of insignificant importance. With a hostile War Office, limited resources, our poor track record and the disapproval of every Army Command, it required courage to reinforce the concept of a corps *elite*.[10]

So far, despite all his frustration and impatience, March-Phillipps appeared to have missed very little. Yet already, thanks to the fiascos of Operations *Collar* and *Ambassador*, the very commando concept was already under fire and in question. It was Churchill, once again, who waded to the rescue. On 25 August he wrote to Anthony Eden, Secretary of State for War:

> I hear that the whole position of our commandos is being questioned. They have been told 'no more recruiting' and that their future is in the melting pot. I thought therefore I might write to let you know how strongly I feel that the Germans have been right, both in the last war and in this, in the use they have made of storm troops ... The defeat of France was accomplished by an incredibly small number of highly equipped *elite*, while the dull mass of the German army came on behind ... There will certainly be many opportunities for minor operations, all of which will depend on surprise landings of lightly equipped, nimble forces accustomed to work like packs of hounds

instead of being moved about in the ponderous manner which is appropriate to the regular formations … For every reason therefore we must develop the storm troop or commando idea. I have asked for five thousand parachutists, and we must also have at least ten thousand of these small 'bands of brothers' who will be capable of lightning action.[11]

March-Phillipps got his commando interview. He appeared before the Commanding Officer of newly formed No 7 Commando, Lt Col D.S. Lister, M.C., formerly of The Buffs, at the Cricket Pavilion, Hounslow Barracks, and on 16 July 1940 was duly selected as 'B' Troop Commander. He was then told he could select his own section leaders from the thirty other officers who had volunteered from within Southern Command. His first choice was a subaltern from the Royal Tank Corps, John Colbeck, who had served with him in France at Advance Headquarters. Appleyard had served there too, albeit in the rear, and knew and liked Colbeck; and, though now serving with Headquarters II Corps at Aldershot, he had kept in close touch with the gunner captain who had jumped into his foxhole in Dunkirk. Now he too wanted to join the same unit:

> Until then I had not heard anything about this at all, and then I heard March-Phillipps discussing it and knew it was the thing for me. I know him very well and after he knew I wanted to volunteer he accepted me as the other subaltern immediately. The proposal went up to Colonel Lister together with my 'on paper' qualifications and March-Phillipps' strong recommendation. Col. Lister accepted it and approached the War Office, they communicated with Brig. Gale of this HQ who apparently 'did his stuff by me' and yesterday the War Office wired that I was appointed! This all happened in about twenty-four hours and now I am only waiting for the official written confirmation to come through – perhaps in a day or two – a relief to come to take over my job here, and then we can start interviewing the volunteers and pick our men.[12]

Appleyard's appointment was confirmed on 21 July 1940. He was in.

The truth was that, in Second Lt Geoffrey Appleyard, RASC, Colonel Lister had something of a catch. Not only had Appleyard acquitted himself with calm, dependable courage during the chaos of the Dunkirk evacuation, but those 'on paper' qualifications he mentioned hid other formidable talents. He had been Head of Boats at Caius College Cambridge, where he had taken a First in Engineering. He was a skiing Blue at Cambridge, had won the Slalom Race for Cambridge against Oxford on his twenty-first birthday in 1937 and was an international downhill competitor at the highest level. He had won outright – and in a blinding snowstorm – the 'Roberts of Kandahar', the oldest and best known British downhill ski race. Also, as British team captain in 1938 he tied with the Norwegian champion – on his own ground at Myrdal on the west coast of Norway – for first place in the downhill, during which he descended 2,000 feet in 1 minute 33.1 seconds at speeds often in excess of 60mph to lead Britain to overall victory and himself to become the Anglo-Norwegian Champion, 1938. Unsurprisingly, he also held the Ski Club of Great Britain's gold badge for downhill ski-racing.

Born into a wealthy family that owned a prosperous engineering company in Leeds, Appleyard had, from a carefree childhood, enjoyed a life of unconscious privilege. It had not spoilt him. Fair-skinned, dark-haired and good looking with a strong physique toned by days of skiing and competitive rowing, from an early age he had loved the outdoors and, amidst boisterous high spirits, had been a keen and serious ornithologist with an interest in 'ringing' migrant birds. He even had a special British Museum reporting name – Whippletree – which he shared with three friends. He also appears to have had that happy knack of making friends wherever he went, a trait detected with insight by early teachers: 'A boy of very attractive character who causes a great deal of trouble by thoughtless high spirits', observed Donald Gray, Headmaster of Bootham school, York, in March 1932. 'He takes punishment in the right spirit but generally contrives to do it again, very soon. Good manners, healthy and friendly.' Added Housemaster Leslie Gilbert that same year: 'I admire his absolute straightforwardness; it seems to be the pattern on which he builds his life. It is difficult to praise enough his sincere, friendly attitude in all things, even in his occasional outbreaks of harmless disorder.' One day, everyone knew, Appleyard minor would inherit his father's business and responsibilities. Engineering was where his future lay. He spent the summer of 1938 in overalls on the shop floor, working in his father's motor repair depot, learning the job from the bottom up, skinning knuckles, getting grease and engine oil under his fingernails. Reading a copy of the speech he made at that first Appleyard Christmas annual staff dinner, it is difficult to find fault with his teachers' early judgement:

Facing all of you tonight, some of whom have been with us for ten or fifteen years, I feel that it is rather out of place for me to be getting upon my feet at all – even for only two minutes. You see, I have always been told that children should be seen and not heard and, as I've only been working since September, I'm really only an infant three months old … First of all I want to say how tremendously proud I am to have at last joined this organisation, and to feel that I am taking some part – even though it's still a very small part indeed – in the running of it. Of course, I'm far from being a mechanic yet. In fact, I'm still the chap that passes the tools to the man that passes the tools to the man that's actually doing the job. However, there is some talk of me getting a rise soon, and then I'll be the chap that actually passes the tools to the man that's doing the job.

You can almost hear the ripple of laughter, of quiet approval of Mister Appleyard's eldest son from that warm room of seasoned, Yorkshire mechanics sitting there with their beer, their wives in their Christmas frocks surrounded by the glitter of Christmas lights and decorations, the growing fears of a war in Europe momentarily thrust aside:

I also want to tell you how proud I am to be getting to know all of you. I want to know each one of you in this business individually, and whether I am working under you or with you, or whether you are working for me, I want to know each one of you as a friend.

To a different, more cynical age, his words may appear touchingly naive, even callow. They were not so, then, to him. A few months later, in uniform, he would receive a dressing down from a senior officer who found him, stripped to the waist, down in the earth with his men, helping them dig trenches on Salisbury Plain. He received a severe reprimand for being improperly dressed and for Conduct Unbecoming An Officer. Second Lt Appleyard would have shrugged. He was simply doing what he always did, mucking in. A war and a single gold pip on each shoulder shouldn't change that.

With his formal appointment as one of March-Phillipps' two section commanders in 'B' Troop, No 7 Commando, came a second gold pip on those shoulders and promotion to Lieutenant. To Geoffrey, or 'Apple' as he had come to be called, the new job offered a blast of fresh air. His enthusiasm was infectious:

Of course, it's absolutely terrific – it's the grandest job in the army that one could possibly get, and is a job that, if properly carried out, can be of enormous value. Just think of operating under direct orders from the C-in-C! No red tabs, no paperwork, none of all the things that are so cramping and infuriating and disheartening that there are in the army. Just pure operations, the success of which depends principally on oneself and the men one has oneself picked to do the job with you. It's terrific! It's revolutionary, and one can hardly imagine it ever happening in this Old Army of ours, but

I am convinced that the Commandos can be of very real value in ensuring ultimate victory in this war.

He was right: it *did* all depend, ultimately, upon the men they chose. He, Colbeck and March-Phillipps, their new Officer Commanding, toured the battalions and units of 18 Division choosing the very best from the 200 men who had volunteered. '[It] was hard work but great fun. After asking endless questions of candidates all day long at one point I caught M-P asking a fellow "Can you marry? Are you swim?!!"' Each section had twenty-three men:

The whole strength of the Troop is 50 men. Thus I shall be in command of 23 *picked* men – all volunteers ... Everything depends on the men we choose ... it is rather frightening, this selection of the men. This thing can either be a flop or a colossal success, and so much depends on the men. They must be utterly reliable, steady and intelligent. But with the right men what a wonderful fellowship we can have in the unit – just picture it – a command of 23 of my own picked men. I can know every man personally, the sort of job he can do, his good points and his weak ones. On parade and on a job there must be rigid discipline. Off parade there will be a great fellowship. At all times there must be absolute trust and confidence ... Well, don't you agree with me now that it's a real job? I can't imagine a better.[13]

By early August No 7 Commando, with its Headquarters now based at Felixstowe, boasted 17 officers and 249 other ranks. Not everyone, however, went through the standard medical and interview selection procedure. One of the SSRF's future stalwarts, Jan Nasmyth, was recruited that summer whilst March-Phillipps was on horseback:

Gus was out riding with a girl on a beautiful summer evening in peaceful English countryside. It's very hard to describe, but Gus seemed to live an almost inspired life at times when he reached some sort of balance within himself. I always remember him on that horse. He seemed part of the evening, part of everything and perfect in a way that you often don't see perfection in a lifetime. I said that I had only one eye and asked if that mattered. He said: 'Do you ride a horse – and can you judge a distance from a fence when you are going to jump it?' I said that I thought so and he said: 'That's all right, then. You'll do.' Much to Jan's surprise, he was in. Noting that, his new commanding officer learned down from the horse and, twinkling with glee, whispered: 'I have absolute powers.'[14]

'In' he might be, but March-Phillipps had a rude awakening in store for his latest recruit with a romantic idea of coastal raiding:

> Well, I thought we were going to sort of rush up the beach in France and stay there long enough to grab a bottle of Pernod and come back again and then have sort of three days holiday in London … [But instead] we went marching. Marching, I think is an immensely boring occupation. It's not like walking, and you march in formation and the number of strides to take per minute is fixed and the people you're next door to are fixed and it goes on and on and on and on and on and on.[15]

Their men selected, 'B' Troop under Capt. March-Phillipps moved to a large, requisitioned house in Newmarket, east of Cambridge, where the men slept eight to a room. Apple shared with John Colville; March-Phillipps had a room to himself. The place was entirely unfurnished except for tables and benches. There was a bathroom with running water. None of it was hot. The officers ate the same good food as the men, prepared for them by two cooks loaned from the Provost Company. But they were not there to stay indoors. They were there to work outside in all weathers, to get fit and prepare themselves for an as yet undisclosed strategic purpose:

> One of our first objects is to get really fit! Think of it – training again! I've been longing to do that for months! Cross-country runs, P.T., up early, riding in the mornings (by the way, I've been out 6 to 8 a.m. for the last seven mornings now), getting really fit is to be one of the first objects for all. Then map-reading, night patrol and compass work in unknown country by night will all come into the training which is going to be very strenuous. Think of it – a job that is operational instead of purely paper work!

Unit transport consisted of March-Phillipps' own private motor car – a 30–98 Velox – two motorcycles and a single 30-hundredweight lorry. But they did not use them much. Whenever the unit went anywhere they marched: 'Our primary object is to get as tough as possible. When we finally move from here to a new location on the coast we shall walk – 60 or 70 miles – in two or three days, bivouacking at night in barns and haylofts and living on our ration allowance.' Apple took to the life immediately, writing home in early August:

> This life is absolutely terrific. There is something about the fellowship and hardship and toughness of it that appeals to me enormously … there is such a tremendous spirit of keenness, smartness and discipline in the Troop, that

I know these Commando units are going to mean something … We have got a grand crowd of chaps, keen as mustard, exceptionally fit physically and very alert mentally.

A typical day's schedule for 'B' Troop whilst they were at Newmarket began with reveille at 0630 followed by a 1-mile training run and PT. Breakfast at 0800 was followed by a parade and inspection at 0900 before a two-hour, fast-paced route march interspersed with cross-country work, map reading and compass work, moving through cover and crossing obstacles. Lunch at 1300 was followed by an hour and a half's break before ninety minutes of swimming, running or exercising. Tea was at 1630 followed by a unit lecture given by March-Phillipps that lasted from 1700 to 1745. Commented Apple:

A fairly full day and hard work, but makes one feel grand, even though a little stiff! Later, of course, there will be weapon training, range practice, cross-country runs, hare and hounds, treasure hunts, mock operations, night operations, etc. The training programme can and will be made more fascinating.

It would not all be hare and hounds, or treasure hunts, and Apple knew it. Increasingly, he was thinking of what must surely lie ahead, of leading the men he had picked, and whom he regarded now so highly, into action, into danger. A little later that same year he wrote home to his family: 'Don't pray for my safety or for my speedy return, but pray that I am alive to my responsibilities, courageous in danger and that I have the strength to do my bit of the job to the utmost. Remember – I am responsible for 25 men – I mustn't let them down.'[16]

That particular letter was written at the tail end of the year and by then 'B' Troop, No 7 Commando, had moved north to Scotland for boat training. By then Appleyard's regard, respect and affection for his commanding officer had deepened: 'M-P is a very stout fellow – we have a great deal in common. He is a keen naturalist, a great lover of the open air, of country places and, above all, of this England of ours and all its unique beauty and life.'

Late summer fitness-training near Newmarket in Suffolk for No 7 Commando was disrupted in the autumn by that move north to Scotland and the outlying islands. Apple's security-conscious letters home did not disclose its destination, but, with the unit's headquarters now at Girvan on the west coast of Scotland, it was probably close to Arran, off the Firth of Clyde. Some 19 miles long and 10 miles wide, the steep, rugged hills of the island's interior would now replace the flat countryside of Suffolk. The move north, in winter, represented a ramping up of their training, its close proximity to water a reminder that commandos were primarily raiders, and that raiders would come from the sea. Their living conditions too reflected that hardening of condition. 'This is certainly going to be a "memorable" Christmas,' wrote Appleyard two days before Christmas:

> but memorable because of its apparent lack of merriment and what-not. Actually, we shall manage to have quite a lot of fun. We are on an island, a tiny little place, with hardly any form of life whatsoever, but very picturesque and very lovely. There is no sort of amusement whatever for the troops, though, and there is not a pub within eight miles. We are living in a hotel which is only open in summer and is utterly unfurnished and empty except for tables and chairs.[17]

The officers were offered better accommodation in private houses nearby. Typically, March-Phillipps, Appleyard and some of the others chose to stay with their men. There was no heating beyond wood-burning open fires and no lighting except for the candles and the small oil lamps they brought with them. Running water was invariably cold, and cooking, sleeping and living were all done in the same room. For a bed – at least until his officer's valise and camp bed arrived – Appleyard had a pile of blankets on the wooden floor. It was all, he admitted cheerfully, 'a bit of a shambles'.

Nearby March-Phillipps spotted a disused, laid-up, 5½ ton sailing boat owned by an ex-fisherman called up by the Royal Navy. He decided to buy it; or, rather, he decided his unit should buy it. The agreed cost of the *I'm Alone*, a yawl-rigged 32-foot vessel with a 9-foot beam and a 15hp auxiliary paraffin engine, was £35. Each man was required to stump up between 10s and £1. It is doubtful if they were given the option:

> Her general condition is excellent, but she needs a certain amount doing before we can use her. We hope to teach the men how to sail, navigate, use a compass and run an engine and generally be 'handy' with a boat. But apart from that, it is an excellent thing to have her, as it gives the men a new interest – partly due to delay and postponement, and partly due to our training, the men were going very stale. This ship has really made them enthusiastic and given them a real interest. Also, it is a job of work to keep all really busy over Christmas when there will be nothing whatever to do … As you know, Gus is an experienced yachtsman and so is the 'skipper' whilst I have been appointed 'first mate'! …

We are getting quite a Christmassy spirit in our room as we have Christmas cards spread across the mantelpiece and tomorrow will be getting some holly to decorate the walls. I am thinking of you all continually and wishing you the very happiest of Christmasses. And now it is past midnight and all is silent in the room except for the snores of my companions and the crackle of a few dying embers in the grate. Good night, all!

Very much Love,

Geoff.

They took *I'm Alone* out to sea in a gale of wind with a running sea and driving rain, not on Christmas Day but on 28 December:

We were soaked through all day and took many a wave right over the bows and decks, but she never showed a sign of misbehaviour and shook herself straight out of everything ... She is a marvellous craft. That seems to be about all. Only 1½ hours left of 1940 so I'll wish you the best of days for 1941. May it see a reunited family again before the year is over and the war a thing of the past.

Good night and God bless!

Geoffrey

4

Cloaks and Rudders

While March-Phillipps and his men were learning to sail and navigate *I'm Alone* through winter gales in the Sound of Bute, toiling up and down the rugged hills of Arran beneath heavy packs and sleeping out in ditches and against hillside walls in all weathers, events elsewhere were taking place which were to have a lasting effect upon them all.

In July 1940, while No 7 Commando were still forming up in Newmarket, Suffolk, Dr Hugh Dalton, the newly appointed Minister of Economic Warfare, had been placed in charge of a new and highly secret organisation, the Special Operations Executive (SOE). SOE's business was sabotage and subversion; clandestine warfare. It was unavowable, secretly funded and answered only to the War Cabinet and Churchill himself. It sprang from – and immediately replaced – both Jo Holland's MI(R) in the War Office and Lawrence Grand's Section D in the Secret Intelligence Service (SIS). Yet SOE was, essentially, new: it embraced a new concept, ruffled old feathers. As a consequence it was disliked and distrusted, feared also for the power it might wield and the change it might bring to a Whitehall that resented and resisted newcomers.

Dalton was the political head of SOE. Supported by the able Gladywn Jebb, a career Foreign Office civil servant, 'Doctor Dynamo', as Dr Dalton was called – though not to his face – was its chairman ('SO') and abrasive, braying champion in the corridors of power and the tea rooms of Westminster. He needed two immediate subordinates, an executive director ('CD') and a director ('M') to organise and co-ordinate training and operations. For 'CD' he chose Sir Frank Nelson, a former businessman in India, European SIS officer and one-time Tory Member of Parliament for Stroud. For the latter he needed someone quite different: a man who understood the new form of 'ungentlemanly' warfare and a man who, preferably, had a wealth of military experience with which to back it up. By chance he had met Colin Gubbins at a dinner at the Polish Embassy in

November 1939 and liked what he saw. When Gubbins' name was suggested for a senior role at SOE, Dalton grabbed him: 'I had to fight for his body against C-in-C Home Forces but, with the backing of the DMO [Director of Military Operations], I got him.'[1] Until his transfer to SOE, Gubbins had been responsible to Jo Holland and MI(R) for the AuxUnits. Now that had to be left behind. Colin Gubbins came across to SOE – then still known as SO2 – as Director of Training and Operations on 18 November 1940 with immediate promotion to acting brigadier 'specially employed'.

The same month Gubbins moved across to SOE, the Special Training Centre at Lochailort opened its draughty doors just a little wider to permit selected army personnel to attend its courses: the days of 5th Battalion Scots Guards ascendancy, of Bill Stirling, Peter Kemp and Lord Lovat, were already on the wane. Lord Lovat reflected:

> Inverailort had served a useful purpose: the significance of its toughening-up process, virtually under active service conditions, had not escaped the notice of the War Office. The *coup de main*; ambush and sabotage, forced marches, opposed landings and long swims, unarmed combat and night attacks were ruthlessly exploited. The hills echoed with the detonation of high explosives: bursts of tracer fire flattened the careless patrol – face down in the heather – should they show up against a skyline. In six months several hundred junior leaders had survived the gruelling fortnight course, emerged fitter, more determined to succeed, and with the self-confidence to do so.[2]

The failure rate, however, had been high: 30 per cent of those awaiting their 'trial by selection' at Inverailort failed to complete the course and were RTUd (returned to unit).

It remains entirely possible that, during that winter, March-Phillipps approached Inverailort – and thus, whether he knew it or not, MI(R)/SOE – with his own ideas. He already had an entrée: When Lovat had joined Ampleforth Officer Cadet Corps, March-Phillipps had been his platoon sergeant. In the close world of special forces training in Scotland, that Ampleforth link might have been connection enough. It is also possible that the officers of No 7 Commando simply linked up on the unofficial 'shop' grapevine with their kindred spirits at the STC further up the coast and made the MI(R)/SOE link in that fashion. In any event, Appleyard completed the School of Special Warfare course at Inverailort between 14 August and 6 September. What *is* definitely known is that, at some stage during their winter training on Arran, March-Phillipps made contact with MI(R)/SOE when he sent in a paper on survival behind enemy lines.

During wet weather he had challenged his men to write an essay entitled 'How To Win The War'. Jan Nasmyth – he of the one eye and that
meeting with March-Phillipps on horseback one summer's evening in
Newmarket – had written a paper about self-sufficiency in enemy territory. It hit the mark:

> It was an essay really about the possibility of keeping troops in being in
> enemy territory by making them independent of any form of human life,
> either for food or for shelter and next morning Gus came bursting in in full
> battle order, so to speak, and said to me that my essay described *exactly*
> what he had been trying to think of![3]

Jan Nasmyth's paper with March-Phillipps' endorsement found its way
to Brigadier Gubbins in London – a Gubbins now constantly on the look-
out for suitable material to bring into SOE. To an organisation that was
unable to advertise, word of mouth and personal contact were the best,
indeed often the only, form of recommendation. Gubbins already had
an eye to the future when SOE would be sending its agents into occupied territory – agents who would need exactly the same sort of training
and killing skills now being taught in the western highlands to the newly
formed commandos. Now Nasmyth's unorthodox paper brought the commanding officer and second in command of 'B' Troop, No 7 Commando,
to Gubbins' attention: it appeared that one or two of its officers and men
might indeed have the makings. Between that wet November and the end
of January 1941, both March-Phillipps and Appleyard travelled south and
found themselves in a new role, 'auditioning' for and being interviewed
by an organisation that did not officially exist and which operated under
a bewildering number of cover names, the most usual of which was the
Inter-Services Research Bureau. Evidently, early interviews went well. Both
men were later described by Brigadier Colin Gubbins as 'full of initiative,
bursting to have a go, competent, full of self-confidence in their own personalities, which they had every right to be, and quite determined to get
into the war just as soon as they could.'[4] They would soon have their wish.
But, first, both still had to go through formal vetting and selection.

'SOE was created by government edict in July 1940 when everything
was at its blackest and government was of course searching for any possible way of getting at the Germans to help our main forces while they
reformed', remembered Colin Gubbins after the war:

> Our task was our Charter and was simply to carry out all forms of irregu-
> lar warfare against the Germans that we could possibly devise or think of

– mostly, of course, behind their own lines from a straight-forward act of sabotage of factories or communications right up to open guerrilla warfare.[5]

The SOE files that exist in The National Archives at Kew, London, for March-Phillipps and Appleyard are sparse.[6] It is possible, however, to track their movements from No 7 Commando to the darker, more subtle and secretive world of the Special Operations Executive. SOE ran a security trace on March-Phillipps – now officially part of 3 Special Service Battalion – with MI5 on 19 January 1941 'with a view to employment with this Section [SO2/SOE]'. The all-clear came back four days later with a reassuring 'Nothing Recorded Against' stamped across the file in green ink. Interest in Appleyard followed a similar path. He signed the Official Secrets Act for SOE and by 25 January 1941 there had been 'Nothing Recorded Against' him either. Colin Gubbins recorded in his diary that same day: 'Appleyard reported for duty.'[7]

SOE loved to cloak itself in code-names, ciphers, symbols, aliases and numbers and, on occasion, a stifling air of often unhelpful and impenetrable secrecy. During the war Professor Michael Foot served with Combined Operations and dealt closely with SOE once it had found its feet: 'I got on to somebody in F Section who would answer to three different names over the telephone with the same voice and was inclined to say: "I'm sorry, old boy, we can't help you at all." That was their general line.'[8] Now Geoff became SOE operative No 1441. Later still he would be allocated the SOE symbol MH.1. His SOE file records: 'M advised: 1441 joined the organisation 26.1.41 and will be employed on the operational side as an instructor with Allied Armies.' M was Gubbins. It must all have seemed rather a long way from the Workshops of 'E' Section, Royal Army Service Corps.

March-Phillipps became operative No 1442. And, later, WO1. Then, later still, MH. The day after Appleyard received his all-clear from MI5, March-Phillipps' file records baldly: 'Stated from M: it is proposed to employ 1442 as an instructor for Allied troops.' 'B' Troop and whatever plans and ambitions he might have harboured for his hand-picked volunteers was now, evidently, a thing of the past, which, for him and Appleyard personally, turned out to be a blessing in disguise that may well have saved their lives: their former unit moved to the Middle East in February 1941 as part of Layforce, where it was intended to harry Axis lines of communication in the Mediterranean. Diverted to Crete as German invasion threatened they, along with No 8 Commando, were severely mauled in the mishandled defence of that island after the German *Fallschirmjäger* landings in May 1941. As a consequence, both No 7 and No 8 Commando were disbanded.

In early March another cryptic entry was made in March-Phillipps'
SOE file: '5.3.41: M. Section advised that 1442 is employed on HQ Staff.'
His move to SOE Headquarters in Baker Street may or may not have been
the full story. Inspired by his training on Arran with the men of 'B' Troop
– and especially by the possibilities of foreign-shore insertion that opened
up before him once he started sailing *I'm Alone* – March-Phillipps took
a further plan to Brigadier Colin Gubbins, his new boss: he and a select
group of volunteers – Appleyard, of course, among them – should be
authorised to form a special clandestine maritime unit that would cross
over to enemy-occupied Europe from the south coast of England and
make contact with those who might wish to develop some form of resistance to Nazi rule. They were to meet local patriots, gather information
and then return to Britain. Brigadier Gubbins gave the idea his blessing.

March-Phillipps almost certainly was *not* told that SOE already had a
similar operation elsewhere. Or that his plans, like those at SOE Helford
in Cornwall down the coast, were about to sail into a full gale of troubles.

Those troubles had a number of separate but interlocking origins. The
first of these lay in the stark fact of SOE's sudden arrival in Whitehall in
the urgent, fearful days of July 1940. Gubbins observed after the war:

> The creation of a new and secret organisation with such an all-embracing
> charter aroused suspicions and fear in Whitehall. At the best, SOE was
> looked upon as an organisation of harmless backroom lunatics which, it
> was hoped, would not develop into an active nuisance. At its worst, it was
> regarded as another confusing excrescence, protected from criticism by a
> veil of secrecy. So SOE went ahead rather on its own.[9]

Those suspicions were compounded – most particularly within the SIS – by
a fear of territorial encroachment and a poaching of a role that stemmed
from a lack of mission clarity that had surrounded SOE from its inception:
in the haste and urgency of its creation, no one had thought to delineate
just where SOE's areas of responsibilities ended and those of the SIS began.
They were two sides of the same coin: both agencies would have agents in
the field; both would cultivate contacts in enemy-occupied territory and
both would concern themselves with the gathering of intelligence, a role
that had once traditionally belonged to SIS. Sir Stewart Menzies, the Head
of SIS, had seen it coming. On 4 September 1940 he 'sadly predicted the
difficulties that would follow when two sets of secret agents worked inde-
pendently into the same territory'.[10] They would clash, not simply because
they would compete for results while working on the same side of the street,
but because their methods and *modus operandi* were so diametrically

opposed. SIS believed in stealth, guile and silence; SOE believed that its remit, particularly in the early days, included coastal raiding, sabotage and the creation of general noisy mayhem within German-occupied territory. A paper submitted in August 1940 – a month after SOE was created – envisaged one of SO2's (SOE's) principal tasks as recruiting 'a carefully selected body of saboteurs ... operating exclusively against objectives on or near the coasts ... and at short notice, at widely separated points'.[11] Sir Brooks Richards witnessed the feuding between SOE and SIS at first hand:

> The trouble from SIS's point of view was that SOE, not content to wait for resistance to develop spontaneously, saw itself as a striking force whose blows would help convince opinion in occupied Europe that Great Britain was fighting on and was neither beaten nor cowed. This was why they planned small scale raids on targets accessible from the sea as well as landing agents and cargoes of arms and explosives for subsequent use.[12]

That intention of SOE to carry out small raids of their own – despite the creation of Combined Operations with precisely that remit in June 1940, a month before their own creation – remained in place, despite Gubbins' presence at a meeting with SIS on 16 December 1940 at which the SIS representative stated categorically that his organisation was 'against Raiding Parties as they might interfere with their organisation from getting agents into enemy-occupied territory'.[13] Thus SOE and SIS went together like oil and water, their missions, aims and objectives mutually repellent. Yet both, as Brooks Richards astutely observed, had been mandated 'at the highest level' to pursue incompatible objectives.[14] Only Winston Churchill, perhaps, could afford to take a more pragmatic view, confiding to General Hastings Ismay later in the war: 'The warfare between SOE and SIS is a fundamental and perhaps inevitable feature of our affairs.'[15] Yet, had there been the time and opportunity for deeper strategic thinking when SOE was created in July 1940, it might not have been.

There was a further complication, a restriction, lying in wait for March-Phillipps and his plans to take the war to France by fishing boat, although this would not become apparent for a few months. After the withdrawal from Dunkirk, the Channel was, in effect, an unregulated 'no-man's-water', where a wide variety of units, army formations and shady organisations took it upon themselves to slip across and poke about on the German-occupied shoreline. The commandos had operations *Collar* and *Ambasssador*; SIS had agents to land; SOE had French evacuees they wished to slip back into France: in the absence of a developed air link – which would come later – clandestine passage by sea was the obvious way back to France.

After attempts at liaison with SIS proved unsatisfactory, SOE set up their own man in Helford to requisition French fishing vessels which could blend in with local French fishing fleets and be used to pick up agents and deliver messages, arms and supplies to the French in northern Brittany. The man behind this clandestine delivery and collection service was Gerry Holdsworth, a former advertising executive and Section D agent who had done good work for SIS in Norway before the war and who, since its outbreak, had transferred first to the Royal Navy and then to SOE. Charged by SOE with setting up their own ferry service to France because, as he put it with a characteristic lack of tact 'other people [i.e. SIS] keep letting us down', Holdsworth had anticipated the dangers of the enemy on the far shore but had underestimated those of the enemy closer to home. He was, however, soon to know his name: it was Slocum, Commander, later Captain, Frank Slocum, RN.

Slocum had served with the Grand Fleet in the First World War, become a navigation specialist and then 'retired' from the Royal Navy in 1936 as a Lieutenant Commander. He had then been surreptitiously seconded to SIS before returning to the Naval Intelligence Division of the Admiralty in 1940 in the rank of Commander RN. Slocum's Operations Section at the Naval Intelligence Division was responsible for arranging sea transport operations to France. Faced with the conflicting needs of both SIS and SOE, Slocum, it might be supposed, suffered from divided loyalties. He did not. He was, first and foremost, an Admiralty man who believed in the primacy of the Admiralty, the Royal Navy and SIS, in that order; an Admiralty, moreover, that quite literally ruled the waves and whose august Lordships maintained that no operations at sea could take place without what Michael Foot describes as their 'authoritative assent'.[16] The Admiralty already enjoyed a long-established relationship with SIS and thus had little time for SOE, the upstart organisation suddenly foisted into their midst. As the months went by Holdsworth was to find himself increasingly frustrated by this man related to the famous nineteenth-century voyager who was the first to sail single-handedly around the world. Now Hollingsworth found that this twentieth-century Slocum had the power to send SOE round the houses, to veto SOE's cross-channel missions or, at the very least, place obstacles in their path. And he would do so, moreover, whilst maintaining all the while that he was doing all in his power to help. Robin Richards, Brooks Richards' younger brother, served with the Helford Flotilla in Cornwall and watched these two powerful personalities – Gerry Holdsworth and Commander Slocum – clash head to head:

Holdsworth was a very independent, tough-minded fellow and he regarded Slocum with great distrust and Slocum regarded him as a hothead and with great mistrust. Gerry Holdsworth was a buccaneer, a strong character. Although he was in naval uniform and had a naval rank he was very informal in his methods in the sense that if he wanted anything he would use any method that he could to accomplish it.[17]

But this was wartime and Commander, later Captain, Slocum, NID(C) – Naval Intelligence Division (Clandestine) – and later DDOD(I) – Deputy Director of Operations (Irregular) – was the senior officer and the man with the ear of the Admiralty. In time, the bruising Holdsworth–Slocum confrontations could have only one ending. Gerry Holdsworth and Gus March-Phillipps shared similar traits. Had they met they might have got on, perhaps even compared notes. There is no evidence that they did. There would shortly be evidence, however, that Capt. March-Phillipps and Commander Slocum would cross cutlasses. And here too there could be only one victor.

Reviewing undercover maritime activities in the Channel during this period, it is evident Commander Slocum was struggling to meet a number of different and often conflicting mission briefs from the various clandestine organisations that looked to him for transport to and from the French coast. Between February and August 1941 there were twelve different sea transport operations to the north and west coasts of France that fell within his remit. Two of these were for the Free French and de Gaulle's nascent Deuxième Bureau, seven for SIS and three for SOE. Most important of these perhaps was the SIS Allah mission to set up the '*Johnny*' intelligence network.[18] This was based in Quimper, Brittany, and covered the vitally important new German naval base at Brest. On 21 March 1941 the two German warships *Scharnhorst* and *Gneisenau* had moved there for repairs. That work – and the subsequent break-out date of the two mighty battle-cruisers – was of huge strategic importance to the Admiralty. Weighed against the importance of keeping '*Johnny*' supplied with the agents, wireless operators, stores, equipment and money it needed to ensure that vital intelligence kept flowing back from Brest, anything March-Phillipps might wish to offer by way of a nuisance raid or two across the Channel in spring 1941 was likely to be viewed in precisely that light.

In March 1941, however, Commander Slocum's name was still unknown to March-Phillipps. With Gubbins' authority, he was able to recruit a few men from 'B' Troop together with one or two SOE men he had met during training. He then began to create his as yet unnamed new unit. His mission from Gubbins was to train his men for amphibious duties and to work out ways in which they might raid the enemy shore. So much, then, for SOE sensitivity to the operational concerns of SIS.

Moving to Poole in Dorset on the south coast, only a few miles from the family home in Blandford Forum, March-Phillipps set up a temporary base in the Antelope Hotel in the High Street. The Antelope is an old coaching inn, its brick facade the same as it must have been when Gus first saw it, a life-sized antelope poised to leap into the road below from a first-floor buttressed window set high above the portico. Here he soon made friends with the landlord, Arthur Baker, known to all as 'Pop', who rapidly took Gus and his growing number of recruits under his wing. One of those was then Sergeant, later Major, Leslie Prout, who remembered shortly after the war: '"Pop" treated us with much kindness over our many exorbitant demands. "Pop" remains today a very great friend of all who served under Gus and Apple, and the Antelope is our natural rendezvous for reunions.'[19]

Units that train for amphibious operations need boats to train with and, with *I'm Alone* left astern in Scotland, the need for a boat, or boats, was pressing. March-Phillipps solved his problem with customary directness. A scouting trip took him to Brixham harbour to the west. Here he spotted three ketches – *Maid Honor*, *Tcheta* and *Our Boy*, all of which appeared suitable for what he had in mind. The shipmaster at Brixham 'is particularly anxious to be rid of them and suggests that we requisition them at once and wire their owners'. Typically, March-Phillipps was now in a fever of impatience: 'Upham, shipbuilders, Brixham, is standing by to receive a wire from me to put the sails and running gear aboard and will have all three boats ready for sea in a week.'

Maid Honor, particularly, caught his eye. She was a 55-ton Brixham fishing ketch, built in 1925–6 for a local fisherman and named after his daughter Honor. She was a beautiful, wooden-hulled vessel with planks 4 inches thick. She was 70 feet long and 16 feet in the beam. She carried mainsail, topsail, mizzen, jib and foresail and was, like *I'm Alone*, a real sea boat designed to go everywhere by sail and whose four-cylinder auxiliary had been put in later almost as an afterthought. Gus fell in love with her and rapidly found good tactical reasons to justify her suitability: her reddish-brown sails would offer silent approach to the enemy shore, he reasoned, whilst her hull would not be affected by magnetic mines. He requisitioned her on the spot. You could do that then, in wartime.

He wrote to Colin Gubbins on 11 March 1941:

Permission is asked to wire Upham to start work immediately and to wire the three owners. Authorities at Brixham will co-operate to the fullest extent – both civil and naval ... No 1 Commando is now stationed at Dartmouth. Without giving away any trade secrets, I learned that the Colonel and 2nd in command would fall in with almost any project and, I believe that, if approached, they would attach men and officers with sea experience unofficially to form crews and possible raiding parties. The men could live on board on their extra ration allowance, and it would be very much in their own interest to keep silent ... I talked with many NOs [Navigating Officers] on M.L. [Motor Launches] duty and what I gathered from them of conditions in the Channel made me a great deal more confident of success. It seems that the enemy patrols are keen but very thin and do not operate much in bad weather. I could operate these boats in dirty weather, without undue risk. If given powers and the word 'go' I believe I could have at least one of these boats ready for operations in a fortnight from now.[20]

To March-Phillipps, every day counted. Britain was fighting for survival; he was desperate to play his part in her struggle.

'Having obtained agreement in principle to the proposal of small-scale raids Gus pulled off a feat that only he could have got away with', remembered Leslie Prout:

Although having no authority to proceed, he calmly requisitioned a Brixham trawler whose attractive name was *Maid Honor*. With her he secured her Skipper, Blake Glanville, and sailed her from Brixham to Poole. Safely berthed in Poole, Gus informed an astonished Navy of the requisition who in turn informed an astonished Brigadier [Gubbins], who won the everlasting gratitude of the crew by backing us up through thick and thin.

Blake Glanville, a softly spoken, portly sailor in his fifties, stayed with his ship. He would go on to become the unit's chief sailing instructor and, like 'Pop', become devoted to Gus and his band of would-be young raiders who, in the evenings below decks, would be held spell-bound with his tales of life at sea in the old trawler days – 'I only exaggerate a little, mind'ee!'[21] He would also teach them, as all old sailors should, the business of knots and cordage. 'Always with us was the vast, rock-like and beloved figure of Skipper Blake Glanville', remembered Leslie Prout:

He fathered all of us, and taught us all we ever came to know in the handling of the *Maid*. We all owe a great debt of gratitude to Blake, for the success of his young pupils on the sea was very largely due to the thoroughness of his teaching.

Maid Honor, before conversion to 'Q' ship, could sleep five to eight below decks but, wherever they were to sleep, it could not be alongside at Poole harbour, with the busy town and port just a line's throw off the bows. It was too public. Just as in Scotland, somewhere more private, more secretive was needed; somewhere far from prying eyes. And, just as in Scotland, the answer lay close to hand.

Poole Harbour itself offered 14 square miles of shallow, enclosed water – it was, in effect, a flooded valley – and was one of the world's largest natural harbours. Seen from seaward and from above, it appeared to represent an apple cut in section with the harbour entrance to the south-east being the stalk of the apple and the largest of several islands – Brownsea – slightly above or to the west, representing the apple's core. Across the water from Poole town and jutting out into Wareham Channel was Arne Peninsula, the western edge of which ran down past low water mud flats to the River Frome and Wareham town. Today Arne is an RSPB nature reserve that looks north across half a mile of grey water to a distant rash of gleaming summer chalet homes with, to the east, the moored present-day brown and black camouflaged Landing Craft, *Assault*, of the Royal Marines Special Boat Service at Hamworthy. Back in 1941, Arne was a lonely and secluded wasteland of heathland and heather, of gorse, old oak and silver birch. March-Phillipps moored *Maid Honor* off Russel Quay. Jan Nasmyth remembered it as a place of 'sandbanks covered with heather and a little sandy cliff that we used for a firing range'.[22] Appleyard makes no mention of the firing range. A keen bird-watcher from childhood, he evidently felt completely at home, describing the area where they were moored as 'right out in the wilds, miles from anywhere, up a creek. It is very quiet and lonely, but very lovely. Thousands of all kinds of waders and sea birds all around – especially shelduck, herons and curlews. There is a big heronry nearby.' He later recalled:

> One night, Gus and I sailed the dinghy five miles up the river to Wareham, had a meal at the Black Bear and then sailed back again on the ebb in the late evening. It was a still, warm evening and it was one of the most lovely experiences I have ever had – just 'ghosting' down in the twilight between great reed-beds, sandbanks and mud-flats with the lovely evening light and no sounds at all but the cries of the warblers and waders and the lapping and rustle of the water against the boat. It really was beautiful.

Appleyard's warm, lyrical letters home may have made gentle reading, but did little to allay a family's underlying fears, for they disguised but did not conceal the deadly serious purpose that had brought their son and his particular friend to this remote and beautiful part of Dorset. They were there to train for war. Soon, they knew, the time must come when they would lead the men they had chosen out across the Channel towards the dangers that awaited them all in the darkness beyond the harbour's mouth. Those men were now arriving.

March-Phillipps' formation – still unnamed – would be a small unit with never more than a dozen or so volunteers in its present form. Some would come from No 7 Commando, some from SOE. Not all would be British. There would be three Danes, a Frenchman and a Yugoslav to add spice to the mix and interest to the mess deck. Early on both officers realised the need for another officer, someone with professional maritime experience who could shoulder some of the sea-going responsibilities of navigation and watch-keeping. Appleyard knew just the man. Graham Hayes was a childhood friend from the same village, Linton-On-Wharfe; his family home, Kiln Hill, was less than half a mile from Geoffrey's at Manor House. A skilled craftsman with a talent for working in wood who nurtured post-war ambitions of becoming a sculptor, Hayes had eschewed the family engineering business and served in the merchant navy instead. In 1934–5 he had sailed around the world as a deck-hand aboard the SV *Pommern*, a Finnish-owned, four-masted, 2,376grt, steel-hulled barque on the grain run from Australia, a voyage unforgettably captured in Eric Newby's *The Last Grain Race* in which, as an 18-year-old, he too shipped out before the mast aboard the windjammer *Moshulu* to sail round Cape Horn in 1939. Hayes had served in the Borderers before volunteering for No 2 Commando, the all-commands unit earmarked for parachute training. Now he transferred again, this time to Poole, bringing with him eventually – after a letter, two telegrams and a great deal of wrangling – his trusted 'oppo', Sergeant Major Tom Winter, aged 36. Like Appleyard, Winter had started military service in the Royal Army Service Corps before transferring to No 2 Commando where he had met Hayes. In time, that unit evolved into 1st Battalion, The Parachute Regiment. A paratrooper with more than 150 jumps to his credit, he had enjoyed none of them. 'He is a special protégé of Graham's and the two always work together', wrote Appleyard. 'He is a very good scout, and has seen a lot of different parts of the world and done a lot of tough jobs, and is an expert engineer.'[23]

Leslie Prout was one of the older originals too, a man of 29 in 1941 with 'an adventurous personality', described by Brigadier Gubbins as 'a good, sensible officer, very loyal and steady'.[24] His wartime service with March-Phillipps' unit saw him rise from Sergeant to commissioned Major within four years. There was André Desgrange, aged 30, described by Appleyard as:

my special protégé [and] one of the very finest chaps with whom I have ever had anything to do ... He is a Frenchman, was a deep-sea diver in the French Navy before the war and is also a good engineer ... He is big, strong as a horse and has black curly hair and a perpetual grin! He never gets flurried, and is always cheerful and willing for the hardest and filthiest jobs that are going. He really is a wizard and I feel tremendously fortunate to have such a stalwart with me as my right-hand man.

There was March-Phillipps' diminutive batman, Jock Taylor, nicknamed 'Haggis'; Dennis Tottenham, 24, a tall, experienced seaman; 'Buzz' Perkins, youngest in the unit but very sound, willing and tough, who had an uncle, a major, at SOE Headquarters who had pulled strings to get him into the unit. At just 17 himself, Buzz may have had something to prove on his own account. There was also a ship's cook aboard *Maid Honor*, Ernest Evison, who had trained in France and Switzerland and took a real pride in his work. He was young – only 23 – bilingual and described by Leslie Prout as 'invaluable and unbeatable ... the cook of all cooks', a man with good sea legs whose 'artistry so often made the fastidious Gus wax lyrical over food and was responsible for sighs of utter satisfaction from Apple and Graham, whose appetites had to be seen to be believed!'

There were also, at the outset, three Danes. Two made no particular or lasting impression. The third did. His name was Anders Lassen.

In four short years Anders Lassen would be awarded the Military Cross *three times* and become the only member of the wartime Special Air Service Regiment (the SAS) to be awarded Britain's highest medal for valour, the Victoria Cross. To Danes everywhere he would become the personification of courage and a national legend whose fame in Denmark endures to this day. He would also, under March-Phillipps' command, become an ice-cool, merciless killer. He was a phantom of swift, silent movement, an expert with knife, dagger, cross-bow and longbow – his preferred weapons.

To begin with, he was just another Danish professional seafarer. But Lassen had travelled to England the hard way. Caught at sea when his country was invaded on 9 April 1940, his ship, the 16,500-tonne Danish tanker *Eleanora Maersk*, had sailed on to Oman, the Persian Gulf, Colombo, Singapore, Borneo, Durban and Cape Town. Here his ship turned away from the war, away from Britain. That was not what Lassen wanted. He broke his cadetship contract, paid off and signed on again as deckhand on the *British Consul*, a 10,000-tonne tanker heading directly for Britain. She left Cape Town on 26 October 1940. *British Consul* was par for the course for merchant ships of the period and conditions on board were grim. Norman Fidler, one of the crew, remembered that like her sister ship, *British Councillor*:

they crawled with cockroaches. There was no running water or shower for the crew, but only a hand pump fed from a tank of rust-brown water. We had no freezer but only an ice-box which kept food fresh for a week at best; after that, we lived on tinned and barrelled food such as salt pork. Except for our dry tea and condensed milk, the diet couldn't have been much different from the *Mayflower*.[25]

Lassen took it all in his stride. After two years at sea as cabin boy, dishwasher and deckhand, he had seen worse.

Whatever else she may have been, *British Consul* was a lucky ship that year. She took her chances, sailed due north up the west coast of Africa and on into the stormy North Atlantic before making UK landfall in Oban on Christmas Eve 1940. When Anders Lassen stepped ashore with £19 14s 2d, his two months' pay doubled by war bonuses, he was just 20 years old. Tall, fair-haired and with a disconcertingly direct gaze from eyes that were of the palest blue, Lassen made his way to Newcastle-upon-Tyne where he volunteered for the Royal Air Force: like March-Phillipps and Appleyard making *I'm Alone* seaworthy a little way down the coast at Arran, Lassen burned to avenge his country, to erase the shame of invasion and Danish capitulation. The RAF turned him down for Aircrew: his mathematics was not good enough. On New Year's Day 1941 Lassen headed south, to London. There he joined the British Army. But not before he and fourteen other young Danes, patriots all, had signed their names to a solemn pledge recorded for posterity in the cover of a pocket Bible:

> In the year 1941, on the 25th day of January, the undersigned Free Danes in England swore, sword in hand, to fight with their allies for Denmark's liberation from a foreign yoke.
>
> I hearby swear that I will stay true to my King, Christian X. I also swear that I am ready to serve loyally whatever authority is working against the enemy that occupied my Fatherland. I swear that I will never disclose whatever military secrets are entrusted to me.[26]

The solemnity of that vow appeared, at first glance, to be at curious odds with the casual, silent young man whose neat signature appeared ninth in alphabetical order on the soft cover of that Bible, as their escorting officer, Capt. Werner Iversen, prepared to shepherd his party of Free Danes into the British military machine. For Lassen appeared distinctly unmilitary. He was scruffy, unkempt and, from the very beginning, took no trouble to conceal a total abhorrence of British Army 'bullshit', in all its many triplicated forms; of creased uniforms, polished brasses, burnished toe-caps, drill by numbers and army regulations of whatever description. 'I came to fight, not parade', announced Lassen succinctly and often. By then, he was actually closer to the fight than he realised. Posted with the other Free Danes to Arisaig for commando training, Lassen and his fellows were actually being assessed, not for some line rifle battalion, but as to their suitability for the Special Operations Executive. And SOE did not care about burnished toe-caps. Anders Lassen was passed on with sparing praise: 'A professional seaman. Skilled with weapons. Aggressive enough to lead a boarding party.'[27] They got that right.

One morning in the spring of 1941, Lassen and two of his Danish colleagues, each in loose-fitting, unpressed British Army battledress but with a small red and white Danish flag stitched proudly beneath their 'Denmark' shoulder flashes, caught the early morning train from Market Harborough to St Pancras Station, London. There, amidst the noise and chaos of a dirty, crowded mainline railway station in wartime, they were met by Sergeant Tom Winter, late of 2 Commando, who had collected another soldier, cook Ernie Evison, at the barrier. Presently this party of five were approached by an officer coming down the platform towards them. Winter came smartly to attention. So did two of the three Danes. But not Lassen. He was still smoking. As the officer approached, Winter noticed he was smiling. It was Geoffrey Appleyard.

Presently all six were heading south, out of London – towards Poole, March-Phillipps and a Brixham trawler called *Maid Honor*.

Kayaks and Medals

It was not just Gus March-Phillipps and Geoffrey Appleyard who were eager to get back into action: SOE as a wider organisation also badly needed to make its mark and answer those critics who believed that supporting SOE was little more than a waste of scarce, misdirected resources. Yet SOE's first air operation into France was to pitch SOE into a controversy that struck at the very heart of the arguments about 'ungentlemanly warfare' which had dogged the early days of SOE's existence.

By the end of 1940 the Battle of Britain was over, the Luftwaffe had been repulsed and the Local Defence Volunteers – renamed the Home Guard in July 1940 – had been cheated of their invasion. The Battle of Britain might have been won but, by winter, the killing of civilians and the bombing of British cities – mainly at night – had become a feature of wartime Britain with London, Birmingham, Liverpool, Hull, Coventry and the industrial West Midlands being particularly hard hit by accurate bombing.

In December 1940 the Air Ministry had discovered – almost certainly through the interrogation of captured Luftwaffe aircrew – that most of that navigational accuracy was provided by marker flares put down by Pathfinders of the Luftwaffe's *Kampfgeschwader* 100, an elite Luftwaffe bomber formation equipped with Heinkel IIIs and based at Meucon airfield near Vannes in South Brittany. The Air Ministry approached SOE. *Coup de main*, it appeared, was their line of country: could they perhaps do something about those Pathfinders?

The answer, assuredly, was yes. The SOE plan, formed and developed in January and February 1941, was brutal in its simplicity: it was known – presumably through the sophisticated electronic eavesdropping of POWs at CSDIC, Cockfosters[1] – that the pilots and navigators of *Kampfgeschwader* 100 travelled from their hotels to the aerodrome 9 miles away each night by a commandeered bus.[2] So, SOE would drop agents into France by parachute, who would set up an ambush, block the road, bomb the bus and murder the German Pathfinders' crews while they sat in their seats with grenades and small arms fire and thus put out the Luftwaffe's eyes. That, at least, was the plan. But first they needed volunteers. SOE 'F' Section had no one ready for the mission. After some delay, distrust and prevarication, General Charles de Gaulle finally agreed that five of his men, all trained parachutists who had gained valuable experience in Norway, might be loaned from Free French forces. The perfidious British would supply the aircraft, weapons and a special 'road trap'[3] to halt the bus.

After the attack, the five men of Operation *Savanna* – variously also referred to as Operation *Savannah* or *Savana* – would withdraw south and west to the Golfe-de-Morbihan where they would be picked up and brought home to England by a French fishing boat, the *La-Brise*, operating out of Newlyn, Cornwall, on behalf of de Gaulle's newly formed Deuxième Bureau. One of the agents, Sergeant Joel Le Tac, had some claim to seamanship and local knowledge and, in early March, it was decided that he and an SOE officer should liaise to discuss the outward crossing from Cornwall and the extraction of the five agents from Brittany. That other officer was to be Lieutenant (now Acting Captain) Geoffrey Appleyard, now attached to SOE.

Leaving March-Phillipps with his dozen men in Poole to begin early training and to set about transforming *Maid Honor* into something more than just a simple Brixham fishing trawler, Geoff went down to Newlyn with Joel Le Tac. However, rows and disagreements between SOE and General de Gaulle's Head of Intelligence and Operations, Colonel André Dewavrin ('Passy'), were never far below the surface. One of these now surfaced and, as a consequence, extraction by *Le-Brise* was suddenly no longer an option. There was a change of plan: Appleyard would still be involved, but now he and his right-hand man, André Desgrange, would make the RV from a British submarine. They would paddle ashore in Folbot rubber inflatable canoes and bring the French agents out to the submarine off a beach to the south of Saint-Giles-Croix-de-Vie near Les Sables d'Olonne. Only now there was another problem, another delay. And this time it came, not from the French, but from the Royal Air Force. They wanted the SOE agents to be dropped in uniform. Gladwyn Jebb, Dr Hugh Dalton's CEO, wrote to Sir Charles Portal, Chief of the Air Staff:

Dear Portal

I hear from the Head of SO2, Sir Frank Nelson, that at mid-day today Air Chief Marshal Sir Wilfrid Freeman sent for our Liaison Officer, Squadron Leader Redding, and informed him that operation '*Savanna*' must at once be cancelled owing to the fact that it involved what amounted to the assassination of certain crews of KG.100 ...

What I would like to say here is that our Organisation was definitely asked by the Air Ministry to go ahead with the project and we have, as a result, devoted much time and thought to it during the past few weeks. Certain very brave men have volunteered for the job, even though it is unlikely that they will escape with their lives, and they have gone through a course of intensive training ... we do not, ourselves, wish to have any views on the political or moral issues involved; all we want to do is to carry out any project which may be confided to us by the service departments. We regard this particular project as one put up to us by the Air Ministry and if it is now the Air Ministry's view that we should not go ahead with it after all we can, of course, only call it off. At the same time, I must repeat that from our point of view it would have been considerably more convenient if we had known at a rather earlier stage that there were objections on general grounds to the operation being proceeded with at all ... [4]

Portal replied to Jebb the same day and referred to a meeting between himself, Nelson, Jebb and the Chiefs of Staff on 1 January when the operation had first been proposed:

You will remember that surface [sea] transport was to be used, and that we were told that the men who would do the job were desperate men of the Apache type who were to receive large sums of money if they carried out their work. Two days ago I learned for the first time that the whole nature of the operation had been changed and was now dependent upon RAF aircraft for its execution ... You must therefore not be surprised that I was unable at an earlier date to inform you of my views on the operation in the form now proposed. I think that the dropping of men in civilian clothes for the purpose of attempting to kill members of the opposing forces is not an operation with which the Royal Air Force should be associated. I think you will agree that there is a vast difference, in ethics, between the time-honoured operation of the dropping of a spy from the air and this entirely new scheme for dropping what one can only call assassins. If we are to be used to carry them, my view is that they must be dressed, and must conduct themselves, in accordance with the laws of war. [5]

It would be a distinction that might well have been lost upon the women and children lying beneath the rubble of their bombed-out homes in London, Coventry and Hull. To SOE, Portal's 'laws of war' was a dangerous and irrelevant oxymoron.

Eventually, the objections of Sir Charles Portal and Arthur Harris [not Redding] were overcome, but by the time all was resolved the weather-window for early March had closed. It would be the evening of 15 March 1941 before the five would-be assassins – dressed in civilian clothes – boarded a Whitley bomber and took off for France.

They dropped blind near Elven, 8 miles east of Vannes and 5 from their target. They landed under cover of a light bombing raid on the Meucon airfield. They buried their parachutes and gear and, at dawn, made their way to the target area undetected, only to discover that their mission was now impossible: the Luftwaffe KG 100 Pathfinders had changed their way of travelling to the aerodrome. Now, instead of a bus, they travelled in several cars. Delay, argument and prevarication had cost SOE dear: the opportunity of a single, surgical strike had been missed.

Nothing ventured, the unit split up into a series of reconnaissance missions that would prove almost as useful as the mission itself. This was the first time SOE had the opportunity to discover what conditions were like in occupied France, how General de Gaulle was viewed in his homeland and how the German forces of occupation were controlling everyday life. One agent stayed near Vannes, one went to Brest. Another went to Paris, Nevers and Bordeaux. Their leader, Capt. G. Berge, took the opportunity to slip across the border into the unoccupied zone to present himself to the father of the girl at de Gaulle's headquarters in London whom he intended to marry. That part of the mission, at least, was a resounding success.[6] All five agents were to meet at Les Sables d'Olonne at the end of the month.

In the event, only three of the five got to the beach in time. Flashing the agreed light signal out to sea on the appointed night, there was no response.

HMS _Tigris_ surfaced between 2 and 3 miles off shore to carry out her part of what the Royal Navy knew as Operation _European_. Appleyard and Desgrange launched their inflatable canoes. Paddling strongly to shore, both landed undetected on a rocky shoreline although it was there, according to Appleyard, that Desgrange's canoe was holed on submerged rocks and had to be abandoned. Crawling up and down the beach searching for the flickering torchlight of contact with _Savanna_'s agents, they stayed on enemy territory for an hour but found nothing and nobody. In fact, they had landed on the wrong beach. Disappointed – and paddling now two-up in a single double canoe – they returned to HMS _Tigris_. As agreed, there would be another chance four nights later.

HMS _Tigris_ surfaced a second time on the night of 4/5 April. This time conditions were very different and there was a heavy sea running. Watching from the conning tower of the trimmed-down submarine, Appleyard _thought_ he saw the briefest gleam of torchlight on shore. The signal was not repeated, nor was it seen by anyone else. The captain of the submarine, Commander H.F. Bone, DSO, tried to dissuade Appleyard from attempting to paddle to shore in the heavy swell, but he was adamant: the rescue mission should be attempted.

His father recalled: 'Geoffrey had an inward assurance that the agents were at the appointed place and that he must try to go and bring them off. His request that he should be allowed to make the attempt was finally agreed by the Commander.'[7] The two remaining rubber canoes were brought up on deck and assembled: the idea was that both Appleyard and Desgrange would paddle a double each and bring back two agents on each trip. Before they could launch, however, a rogue wave washed over the casing and carried away one of the canoes. It disappeared into the heaving, wave-flecked darkness and was lost. Now, if he went at all, Appleyard would have to go alone. Despite discouragement, he insisted the attempt must be made. Time and time again they tried to settle him into the Folbot and launch him away from the submarine. Time and again the boat broached-to and capsized, flinging him into the dark, freezing water. Finally, soaked to the skin, teeth chattering with cold, he managed to paddle away from the submarine and strike out for the shore 3 miles away, salt-rimmed eyes searching for that telltale flicker of light. He saw nothing. Landing finally on the shore, Appleyard dragged himself above the surf-line and began casting up and down the beach, searching for the agents who must be waiting. He saw nothing. And all the while, time was slipping by: HMS *Tigris* would dive, regardless, at 0300. Throwing caution to the winds, he ran up and down the shoreline shouting and waving his torch. Finally, at last, there was an answering flash of light and three of the five *Savanna* agents stepped out of the darkness to greet him. But time was running out. Appleyard offered them a stark choice: there could be no second trip, no second rescue before Moonrise. If they wanted to come with him now, then two of the three would have to take their chances and cram with him into the double canoe and brave the waves and rising seas for that 3-mile paddle out into the darkness where the submarine might – or might not – be waiting. The third man would have to stay behind. Sergeant Joel Le Tac elected to stay ashore, holding the canoe's head to sea while Capt. Berge and Jean Forman squeezed aboard. The surf was running too high for a safe paddle out so Appleyard swam the boat out beyond the breakers and then clambered aboard over the stern. Punching out into the dark waves and heaving swell, the frail canoe battled towards the hope of safety with Appleyard paddling hard and both passengers bailing as each dark, looming wave threatened to capsize their frail craft. Finally, through the darkness, they made out the dark fin of the submarine's conning tower. It was 0300. As she had warned, HMS *Tigris* was about to submerge. As they closed the final yards to the submarine, the canoe capsized and all three were pitched into the sea. Swimming to the flank of the submarine they were hauled aboard, exhausted, and bundled below. HMS *Tigris* slid below the surface of the Atlantic. It had been a very close run thing indeed.

On his return to Poole, Appleyard settled back into regular training. The men were now accommodated out on Russel Quay in two pre-war houseboats, *Dormouse* and *Yo'n'Jo*, described by Jan Nasmyth as 'play-things for rich men in the 1930s'.[8] Tucked away from prying eyes, where today only the low-water stumps of an old wooden jetty betray the site of their mooring, March-Phillipps and his men settled down to serious train-ing on both land and sea. Weapon handling and range firing, shore-based navigation theory at the Board of Trade offices in Poole harbour and prac-tical seamanship out beyond Sandbanks and South Haven Point all figured strongly in a rigorous programme of self-devised training to prepare them for operations. But it was personal fitness, above all, that March-Phillipps required and expected of his men. One Saturday afternoon Appleyard ran 32 miles around the head of Poole harbour and over the hills to Swanage. He wrote home of those times:

> Still at Poole, as you see, and likely to be here quite a while longer as there is much work and training to be done. However, we are learning a lot and all continues to go well. Graham [Hayes, his childhood friend from the same village of Linton-On-Wharfe] has arrived – last Sunday to be exact – and is in great form. He suits the job and the job suits him admirably, and he fits in with the party very well. Since he arrived he and I have started having a swim early each morning – at 6.45. Cold, but refreshing, and I need something pretty drastic to wake me up these days because I sleep so soundly.

Something else that woke him up was the award of the Military Cross for his actions supporting SOE's Operation *Savanna* in Brittany. Endorsed by both Gubbins and Dr Hugh Dalton (who initially recom-mended an MBE), the award – ostensibly to an officer still serving with the Royal Army Service Corps and promulgated in the *London Gazette* on 23 May 1941, for 'gallant and distinguished services in the field' – was totally unexpected:

> What an amazing surprise! I hadn't the foggiest idea there was anything in the wind whatsoever! We came into port yesterday afternoon about 4 after a hard eight hours at sea and someone came on board and handed me three

telegrams ... I opened them and found they were of a congratulatory nature and was still baffled until I suddenly saw how they were addressed! But how did you know? I suppose it must have been in the *Gazette* or something but I haven't seen a paper. With your wire was one from 'the Brigadier and the boys at HQ' and many others. It was such an extraordinary surprise that I haven't quite got used to it yet. It all goes to show that the army at present must be pretty hard up for people to give medals too! ... Gus, Tim and I had a night ashore to celebrate. We went to a flick and then had dinner and spent the night ashore, returning here at 1030 this morning, Sunday. Since then we have been at sea all day. We dropped anchor here again at 8.30 pm and it has been a terrific, rip-roaring day. There has been three parts of a gale of wind and torrential rain, so we have had a glorious day of immensely hard work. I am physically quite tired out now, with hands swollen and sore from ropes and water.[9]

Brigadier Colin Gubbins visited Poole – presumably to congratulate Appleyard personally on the award of the Military Cross – on 1 June. He stayed at the Antelope on 8 June and inspected *Maid Honor* on 9 June. Sometime during this period Appleyard finagled his way onto a parachute course at Ringway outside Manchester: 'It's a remarkable business, but I don't think anyone would pretend that actually leaving the plane is enjoyable. I was very frightened each time, but not so much as I have often been before a ski-race.' He completed his jumps without serious mishap: 'I am now qualified for and wearing "parachute wings" on the arm of my uniform. It's rather a nice badge and has been authorised in Army Council Orders.'

As summer wore on, the weather improved and there were occasional days off – and time for reflection:

Last Sunday, two of the crew and I landed on Arne peninsula (our nearest bit of land) and walked a mile over the heath to Arne village where we went to service in the tiny, very old church ... Afterwards I was approached by the 'lady' of the village who offered us the hospitality of her home, hot baths, etc., whenever we wanted one, so doubtless we shall avail ourselves of the offer soon. The weather has mostly been too good for us – hot and calm and a lot of sun. However, today there is half a gale of wind from the west and we have had a really hard day's sailing and training in handling the ship. We are really very happily placed ... In general, at present, our training for the day is just planned according to the weather the day brings forth. We are very busy at all hours of the day and night – but it's such grand work that one doesn't want any time off.

It was not just Appleyard and his men who were preparing for battle. *Maid Honor*, also, was being readied for war, although progress of that sort was not passed on to his family in letters home. In the weeks she lay at anchor at Russel Quay she was fitted out as a 'Q' ship. *Maid Honor* was given a dummy collapsible deck-house made of plywood which hinged down to reveal a two-pounder Vickers cannon; part of her weather deck was armoured and lowered to allow twin heavy machine-guns to fire through the scuppers. Fake crows' nests were added to provide exposed Bren-gun firing platforms above the deck. There would also be four Bren guns, four tommy guns, six rifles and thirty-six hand grenades hidden on board within easy reach. Leaving as little as possible to chance, Lassen shinned 60 feet above the deck to nail a dolphin's tail to the top of the main mast: it was a gift from a well-wisher, he said, and would bring them all luck.[10]

As far as Commander Slocum was concerned, however, the men of *Maid Honor* had enjoyed about as much luck as they were going to get.

Amongst the other weapons secreted about *Maid Honor*, March-Phillipps had taken a fancy to something produced by SOE's very own 'Q' Department of special weapons at Aston House, Stevenage. This was the Spigot, a stumpy, short-range, single shot anti-tank mortar also known as the 'Blackler Bombard'. It was bolted to a steel plate on the deck and lobbed a 5lb finned charge which, it was hoped, would prove both devastating and unexpected to any unsuspecting enemy vessel lured within close range. It certainly proved devastating and unexpected on board *Maid Honor* during trials. Graham Hayes was sitting on the thwart of *Maid Honor*, smoking his pipe, calmly watching proceedings and thinking no evil when the thing was fired for the first time. There was a very loud bang. The blast bowled him over and blew away both pipe and trousers whilst red-hot particles of the charge burned holes in *Maid Honor*'s mainsail. March-Phillipps was not amused. However, they persevered. Working with the Dutch section of SOE, March-Phillipps now devised a plan to sail *Maid Honor* close to a large enemy port. There they would heave to – and wait. Sooner or later, he reasoned, a German vessel would come out to investigate this innocent-looking fishing boat. When that happened, they would drop their disguise – and the hidden Spigot mortar would do the rest. This highly dangerous plan, perhaps surprisingly, won the approval of SOE. But it did not meet the approval of their Lordships in the Admiralty, nor with that of Commander Frank Slocum, RN. Sir Brooks Richards remembered that:

> It became clear that there was a conflict of interest between SOE's naval interests as they envisaged them at the time and those of SIS as they perceived

them. Gus took this boat over [*Maid Honor*] and proceeded with his unit to try her out and fit her out and sail her. And when he was in the middle of this, Captain Frank Slocum, who was head of SOE's effective Naval Section known by the acronym NID(C) and who had overall responsibility for SOE and SIS cross-Channel operations, said to Gus March-Phillipps: 'What on earth are you going to do with that boat you're fitting out?' And March-Phillipps said: 'Well, I'm going to lie off a French port like Cherbourg with her and wait til the Germans come to investigate and then when they get close enough to me I shall sink them because I've got a secret weapon on board.'[11]

Slocum said: 'You're certainly not going to do *that* in the English Channel!' And so poor March-Phillipps was rather crestfallen and there was a haggle between SOE and SIS.[12]

And not just with SIS. One file, reviewing the progress of the *Maid Honor* unit, recalled:

All this [March-Phillipps' preparations] took much longer than expected. The Admiralty refused permission to operate outside coastal waters until a specific operation was put up and approved. When, in June, a specific plan was worked out with the Dutch Section of SOE, it was turned down. In addition to criticising the plan in detail the Admiralty made it clear that they objected to giving information of a secret character to army officers who might get captured ... It was evident that, for the time being at least, *Maid Honor* would not be allowed to operate in home waters at all and the scheme for small scale raiding had to be temporarily abandoned.[13]

Which raised a pressing question: what were they – SOE and March-Phillipps – going to do with *Maid Honor*? The answer lay, not in Poole, but 3,500 miles away – in West Africa.

6

Passage to Africa

For months, the Battle of the Atlantic had been threatening to starve Britain into defeat. With German and Italian U-boats roaming the seas, British merchant shipping losses were rising – and not just in the North Atlantic, but off the coast of West Africa as well: between June 1940 and March 1941, twenty-seven allied merchantmen had been sunk off the coast of West Africa whilst on 21 May 1941 – and while the United States was still neutral – U-69 sank the US freighter SS *Robin Moor* 750 miles west of Freetown. Although carrying no war supplies, her passengers and crew were cast adrift and left to survive for eighteen days in open boats. British Intelligence suspected that U-boats and their supply mother ships might be using the creeks and rivers of neutral and Vichy territory in West Africa to lie up and reprovision before venturing out once more to harry allied shipping. If *Maid Honor* were sent to Africa, ran Admiralty reasoning, not only would she be the ideal vessel to sniff out those German hiding places, but she would also be working far away from the English Channel and those repeated conflicts of interest between SOE and SIS which were causing such friction. All in all, it seemed the perfect solution.

The rationale for such a long, perilous, open-sea voyage into seas watched by a vigilant enemy was supported by a threadbare Admiralty contention that the wooden-hulled, sail-driven vessel would be immune to magnetic mines and inaudible to anyone listening below the surface. 'The theory was that a sailing-ship without an escort would not be worth a torpedo', recalled Jan Nasmyth:

But if a U-boat surfaced to attack with a gun, the *Maid* could give a good account of herself with the machine-guns and cannon. The Royal Navy, it was presumed, kept German surface raiders out of the Atlantic and so the main danger lay in attack by air patrols. That danger seemed very considerable and the Vickers cannon, although a dual-purpose weapon, might have been ineffective as an ack-ack gun through being hemmed in by masts and rigging. I should say the *Maid* was entirely vulnerable to attack by air. One just had to hope that the Germans wouldn't notice her.[1]

Nevertheless, the whole enterprise was heavy with risk. Which may well have been one of the main reasons Gubbins decided to split *Maid Honor's* crew and senior officers, with only seven sailing to Africa while the others travelled by troopship. Appleyard – as second in command – was one of those who drew what he saw as the short straw: he would have to go on ahead by the P&O liner SS *Strathmore*. Once in Africa his job would be to 'discuss questions connected with the employment of the ship and her personnel with the head of the Mission and to make arrangements for her reception with the Naval authorities at Freetown.' Meanwhile, he was responsible for preparing *Maid Honor* for the longest voyage of her life:

Everything is working up well and, barring accidents, the show is definitely on. The Admiralty have given their approval, blessing and full co-operation. The kit, equipment and stores side of things has kept me tremendously busy for ten days and is now well in control ... I am going down to Poole late tomorrow night on a lorry with about three tons of food stores, etc.[2]

Maid Honor was scheduled to sail from Poole on 9 August. Her crew would be Gus March-Phillipps as Capt., Graham Hayes as First Lieutenant, with Anders Lassen, 'Buzz' Perkins and Denis Tottenham and two Danes as deckhands. Her voyage out would be south-west across the top of the Bay of Biscay, then past Madeira and west of the Canary islands and so on round towards the Sierra Leone staging port of Freetown just north of the equator. The voyage was expected to take between four and six weeks.

On the morning of departure, Sunday, 10 August 1941, *Maid Honor* slipped her moorings at Russel quay for the last time and, heavily laden with stores and crew – her armament now had been increased to one 2-pounder and *four* Spigot mortars – singled up to Stakes Buoy. From there the crew went ashore for a farewell lunch provided with all the generosity which wartime rationing could allow by the landlord, 'Pop' Baker, who emerged from the cellar clutching several bottles of champagne. There, seated at the head of the table, and down especially to see them off, was Brigadier Colin Gubbins. Yet not their Brigadier's reassuring presence, nor the dolphin's tail he had nailed to the top of the mast, could lift Lassen's gloom and sense of foreboding at the other end of the table. 'He's mad, our commander', muttered Lassen to Jan Nasmyth. 'We are doomed. I will never see any of you again.' Nasmyth tried to cheer him up by telling him there was always a chance. But Lassen wouldn't have it: 'You don't understand because you have not been to sea in the war. I have, and I know. A ship that drops out of convoy is lost. We are sailing without an escort. We haven't a hope.'[3] But for Lassen, as for everyone else, it was much too late for second thoughts. Now, glasses raised and toasts drunk, nothing beckoned but the open sea. March-Phillipps, by all accounts, was in emotional overdrive at the prospect of action after almost a year's preparation for this moment. 'He was', remembered Jan Nasmyth, 'a bag of nerves.'[4]

With a bottle of champagne put aside to broach when they rounded Old Harry Rocks, the party decanted to the pilot boat and watched as *Maid Honor* sailed out to keep her rendezvous with history. But it was not all plain sailing. Jan Nasmyth remembered:

> He had the engine going full blast but that wasn't enough. He wanted the topsail up too. Graham Hayes, the best seaman aboard, was in charge of that complicated operation but made some mistakes and got into a tizzy. Appleyard, who never allowed himself to panic, was amused by seeing Graham get it wrong and I heard Gubbins saying something caustic like 'He's going to pile it up.' The three of us were on board watching these operations but said goodbye when the topsail was raised at last. We climbed into the pilot's launch at Poole Bar Buoy and watched the *Maid* sail out round Old Harry.[5]

Leslie Prout remembered watching Blake Glanville, the man who had taught them all to sail but who, with a wife waiting at home and with his age against him, elected not to accompany his boat to Africa: 'With many waves and exhortations the *Maid* gradually disappeared behind Old Harry, watched by a silent Blake, who never took his eyes off his beloved ship until she was out of sight.'[6] One of those watching and waving 'again and again' from the shore at Sandbanks was Gus' aunt. Concerns about security, evidently, did not extend to the next of kin of the autocratic unit commander.

Maid Honor turned away into a strong wind and battled her way westwards through heaving seas. Most of the crew were seasick. At Dartmouth March-Phillipps put ashore two of the passage crewmen, a Danish navigator whose work was not up to scratch and another Dane he described as 'a chronic puker'. He also carried out repairs to the ship's two-pounder, although why these were necessary so soon after departure when everything should have been in perfect working order remains unclear. *Maid Honor* departed Dartmouth two days later. Her new, blue, cloth-bound 'Log Book

For Yachts' recorded: '12 August 1941. Left Dartmouth at 6 pm, covered thirty miles, average speed five knots.' They were on their way.

The two Danes joined Appleyard and Lt Leslie Prout at Oban where they boarded SS *Strathmore* for speedy passage under naval escort to the British colony of Freetown, Sierra Leone, West Africa, arriving there at the height of the wet season at the end of August 1941.

When they arrived Appleyard and his small team began preparing the main camp for the rest of the party. Freetown itself – with a rainfall of 9 inches a day just before he arrived – was 'very one-eyed, ramshackle, and quite an outpost of Empire'. Nevertheless, he appeared to have soon found an ideal, secluded site for their camp on Lumley Beach 9 miles outside Freetown at the end of Cape Sierra Leone. There, cooled by a sea breeze, free from mosquitoes and in a tropical bay with clumps of palm, coconut and banana trees nearby, they put up a few canvas bell tents and persuaded the Royal Navy to erect some wooden huts for the stores and more explosive supplies that were now en route aboard *Maid Honor*. Appleyard even arranged for the officers to mess with the local Royal Artillery unit. By the end of September he was in Lagos further around the coast towards the Equator where, one may presume, he made contact with SOE's local agent and Head of Station Lt Col Louis Franck. While he was there:

I got the best piece of news I have ever had in my life, that is, that Graham and M-P and the others have arrived in Freetown after an 'excellent' voyage. Not having seen any of them yet (they arrived two days after I left Freetown) I don't know any more about their voyage than that. But I was enormously thrilled and literally shouted with joy![7]

Appleyard hurried back to Freetown:

It was grand to arrive here and find Graham and Gus and the others. They had a magnificent trip with no particular excitements and a great deal of interest. Gus had found Graham a magnificent First Mate and was full of praise for his tireless energy and his seamanship. They were very warm at times, their record temperature being when the thermometer in the galley went off the scale at 135 degrees F! However, in spite of such things they were pretty comfortable, fed well and had plenty of drinking water, and a lot of flying fish which landed on board each night.

The first week out from Devon they had battled strong winds and big seas with *Maid Honor* leaking continuously. As the seas eased down on 18 August, March-Phillipps recorded in their newly purchased Log: 'Time to clear ship and dry everything. Much needed.' A few days later he added: 'Monday, August 25 (after 1, 267 miles by patent log) sighted Madeira. Good landfall.'[8] Here they put in for water, fruit and eggs. Fresh trade winds then pushed them south and, in the first five days out of Funchal, *Maid Honor* sailed 2,000 miles in her first twenty days at sea before the trade winds began to ease down. Then, on the edge of the Doldrums, it was found that the engine had rusted solid with seawater and had to be stripped down. The hero of the day was 'Buzz' Perkins, who earned this accolade from his exacting, short-tempered Skipper. The case of the engine appeared hopeless but he removed the cylinder heads, fitted new gaskets, reground the valves with home-made valve paste, and unstuck the pistons, which had rusted solid in twenty-four hours, by removing the big end bearings and reassembling the engine, again all in a heavy swell and with a temperature of 120°F in the engine room. He has proved the most reliable man on the ship, even though the youngest by several years.'[9]

'Buzz' Perkins – saddled with the nickname from childhood because his sister pronounced 'brother' as 'buzzer' – was just 17 years old. His technical triumph was short-lived for shortly thereafter they were plagued by further engine problems. Their progress south slowed to a miserable 1,000 miles in sixteen days and at one stage left them dangerously becalmed 300 miles north of the Cape Verde Islands. Dangerous, because it was near Vichy-controlled Dakar in September 1940, during Operation *Menace*, that General de Gaulle and the British Royal Navy had conspicuously failed in their attempt to occupy the port. Shots had been fired, British battleships and cruisers damaged, and Vichy French ships sunk before the British withdrew. It was the second time British units had fired on their erstwhile allies: in July the Royal Navy opened fire on French ships anchored at Mers-el-Kabir off what was then French Algeria to prevent French warships falling into German hands, leaving 1,300 Frenchmen dead. The Royal Navy had not been forgiven, and nor had the allies. If *Maid Honor* had been spotted and then intercepted by the Vichy French off Dakar, she could have expected a most hostile reception. However, she slipped past, silent and unnoticed, to arrive in Freetown on 20 September, six weeks and 3,185 miles after leaving England. They had been lucky: at no time had they seen, or been seen by, an enemy aircraft, submarine or surface vessel. The only vessel that had ordered them to heave to had been a Royal Navy battleship, HMS *Barham*, which had taken part in Operation *Menace*, the thwarted attack on Dakar almost exactly a year earlier. Now she was living on borrowed time. In less than two months 841 of her crew of 1,184 would die in a spectacular explosion after three torpedo strikes fired at close range by U-321. With no way of guessing the fate that awaited her, on this occasion she stopped abeam *Maid Honor*, guns trained, and sent over a boarding party. Having established who they were, and then offered hot baths, fresh fruit and good wishes, they had sent *Maid Honor* on her clandestine way. When she had first appeared, unrecognised, hull down on the horizon, *Maid Honor* cleared away for action. Had HMS *Barham* been the enemy, then *Maid Honor* and her crew would, quite literally, have gone down with all guns firing. Standing Order No 5, written in longhand by March-Phillipps when Hayes assumed temporary command of *Maid Honor* during March-Phillipps' absence, stated: 'Avoid a fight if humanly possible, but *resist capture to the last* [author's italics].' Now he wrote pithily in the ship's log shortly after meeting HMS *Barham*: '4.30pm. Hove to. Boarded and questioned. English. D.G.' The last two letters are Latin: *Deo Gratias* (God be thanked). If that warship had been the enemy it would have been a slaughter. And March-Phillipps knew it.[10]

The remainder of Maid Honor Force, who had neither sailed with March-Phillipps nor come out aboard the SS *Strathmore* with Appleyard and Prout, arrived quietly in Freetown, dressed in civilian clothes, in early October after completing the SOE sabotage and explosives course in the Western Highlands. That brought the full complement of Maid Honor Force to thirteen. Unlucky for some.

Maid Honor may have sailed triumphantly into the still waters of Freetown harbour and rattled out her anchor chain quarter of a mile off the camp at Lumley Beach, but around her there now swirled undercurrents of significant political turbulence and sensitivity. Their origins lay in a matter of simple geography: the British Crown Colonies of Sierra Leone, the Gold Coast, Nigeria, British Cameroon and the Proctorate of Gambia rimmed the Gulf of Guinea and the eastern South Atlantic and were surrounded by the French colonies of French West Africa and French Equatorial Africa to the north and east. Most of that vast territory now owed at least token allegiance to pro-Nazi, Vichy France, although French Equatorial Africa had declared itself for de Gaulle and the Free French. There were Spanish territories nearby also. If Vichy France and Franco's pro-German Spain were to enter the war, then Britain's much smaller African territories – including the vital staging port of Freetown – would become immediately threatened. Any incident, large or small, could be enough to trigger an end to the fragile non-belligerent status of both Spain and Vichy France. The British Admiralty and the Foreign Office recognised the need to handle the region with kid gloves. Both senior officers in theatre concurred: there were to be no 'big bangs' and neither army General Sir George Giffard, Commander-in-Chief West Africa, nor Vice Admiral

Algernon Willis, the Royal Navy's Command-in-Chief, South Atlantic, would encourage or support anything which threatened the precarious political balance. Giffard, indeed, had imposed what SOE referred to as a 'ban on bangs'[11] and took precisely the same view of SOE's proposed activities in West Africa as SIS did of SOE's ambitions for the English Channel. In West Africa, however, SOE's anger and frustration glowed like a flame in the dark. An undated Most Secret memo of that time states:

> It is felt that the G.O.C.-in-C should be asked to justify his attitude towards SOE … He has enunciated and through his right of veto, applied a policy of passivity which conflicts with that of H.M.G. in sending an SOE mission to West Africa and authorising it to take action along certain lines. [...]
>
> It is clearly necessary for SOE to work in the closest harmony with the military. The idea that the price of harmony should be a complete negation of SOE functions is farcical. It is no doubt reasonable that Giffard should hope to preserve absolute calm within the borders of the four colonies. SOE however is an aggressive organisation which fails in its purpose when the overriding consideration is passivity and passive defence.[12]

Yet SOE *did* have plans to disrupt that comfortable status quo in West Africa. Soon after he arrived at SOE Headquarters in November 1940, Brigadier Colin Gubbins had set up 'W' (West Africa) Section based in Lagos, the capital of the British colony of Nigeria. Its head of station – a Belgian named Louis Franck – flew out to Lagos in December and set to work. His target area was all of those Vichy French territories to the north and east of Nigeria. His mission? To do what he could to support the Free French: to change the loyalties of the people who lived there and to swing their allegiance away from Pétain to General de Gaulle. At his disposal was propaganda, coercion, subversion, blackmail and the use of 'ungentlemanly' warfare – sabotage – those 'bangs' so recently vetoed by General Giffard. Franck was 32, married with children and a former banker. He spoke fluent English, French, Dutch, Flemish and German. Recruited by the War Office in May 1940, he had been sent to Dunkirk as a special courier to the King of Belgium.[13] Like March-Phillipps and Appleyard, he had shortly afterwards been evacuated through Dunkirk and returned to England where, unsurprisingly, he had come to the attention of the fledgling SOE. Franck was now also code-named 'W' after his station and began feeding information back to London by wireless. Some of this involved the tiny volcanic island of Fernando Po (now called Bioko), a part of Spanish Guinea tucked away in the Bight of Biafra (now the Bight of Bonny). Some 20 miles from the mainland of what is now Equatorial

Guinea, and just 44 miles long and 20 miles wide, Fernando Po boasted a shallow-water harbour, Santa Isabel. It was this port – and its contents – that warmed the air waves between Lagos and SOE Headquarters in London during that summer of 1941.

One of those who Louis Franck relied upon for information was the British Vice Consul in Fernando Po, Colin Michie. His office overlooked the port. On 10 June 1940, Italy had entered the war on the side of Germany. That same day an Italian cargo liner of 7,651grt, the *Duchessa d'Aosta*, had sought sanctuary in Fernando Po's harbour, ostensibly because her master feared capture on the high seas by their new enemy, the Royal Navy. She had been moored there, 50 yards from the western end of the quay, ever since. Her master had been recalled to Spain but her crew of forty to fifty men – and one woman, a 55-year-old stewardess – remained on board, incarcerated in port.

Michie sent a series of detailed intelligence reports back to Lagos for onward transmission via Franck to SOE in London. He managed to obtain details of the cargo manifest[14] – wool, copra, hides, copper and coffee – and reported that her ship's radio still appeared to be working, suggesting that she appeared capable, at least, of sending reports of British shipping movements back to Italy and Germany. Rumours that she might also be carrying armaments were fuelled by the acting Chief Officer's refusal to produce for inspection the top page of the cargo manifest. If there was nothing to hide, ran the argument, why not produce the missing page? It did not appear. By January 1941 Michie was reporting back to Franck that two small German vessels had also now sought shelter in Santa Isabel, the *Likomba*, a German tug, and the *Bibundi*, a German diesel-driven barge. At the end of August 1941 Lagos cabled London that Michie had found it impossible to bribe the Captain or the crew of the *Duchessa d'Aosta* and 'it was therefore suggested to send a "Maid Honor" party with a canoe at night to immobilise the ship and at the same time to try to bring back the tug. An attempt would be made to put the blame on anti-Axis Spaniards.'[15]

In London, Michie's news and Franck's stream of reports caused interest and not a little consternation. Setting aside the missing page of cargo manifest and the possibility, however remote, that the *Duchessa d'Aosta* might be carrying armaments and using her radio to transmit shipping movement details to Italy, her very presence in Fernando Po represented, to SOE London, both a challenge and a threat. A challenge because, though she lay at anchor within a neutral harbour, both she and the German tug *Likomba* represented valuable trophies of war that, if seized rather than sunk or immobilised, could augment Britain's rapidly depleting shipping fleet. And a threat because, although she sheltered under Spanish 'neutrality' laws and should by international maritime law remain impounded for the duration of hostilities, that Spanish 'neutrality' was extremely lopsided: the Spanish Governor of Fernando Po, Capt. Victor Sanchez-Diez, was known to be 'violently pro-Nazi', reported Michie.[16] Were *Duchessa d'Aosta* to decide to up-anchor and sail – perhaps to support German or Italian U-boats out in the South Atlantic – it was almost certain Spain would do nothing to prevent her leaving. It was equally clear that there was little that Britain could do to stop her ... or was there?

By early January 1941 Brigadier Gubbins, 'Caesar' – Lt Col Julius Hanau, his deputy on matters relating to West Africa – and Head of Lagos Station 'W', Louis Franck, had begun considering ways in which the potential threat posed by the Italian passenger liner might be countered, especially as it appeared that the Spanish authorities in Fernando Po were increasing both the armaments that overlooked the harbour and the size of the Spanish garrison committed to defend it. Options included simply blowing her up or boarding her in port at night, capturing her crew, starting her engines and simply steaming out of harbour into international waters. In May SOE sent a further four officers out to West Africa to support the Franck mission in the field and to train black African recruits in the demolition and sabotage skills devised and perfected in the SOE special schools in the misty highlands of Scotland. In the following weeks there were more detailed reports from Michie in his office overlooking the harbour: the tug *Likomba* had been noticed taking fuel on board – perhaps she was getting ready for sea; the *Duchessa d'Aosta* was taking on fresh drinking water; she had painted the top of her funnel red; her radio was not prevented from transmitting and had been sending messages to a German/Swiss shipping company in Las Palmas. Straws in the wind. All these little signs could presage departure – or nothing at all. In London, SOE formed the view that all three vessels in Port Isobel – the *Duchessa d'Aosta*, the German tug *Likomba* and the German barge *Bibundi* – now represented what they considered a 'supply fleet in being' and asked 'W' – Louis Franck in Lagos – for his ideas as to how they might move against all three ships. He replied on 12 July that, given the present situation and the ramping up of readiness amongst the Spanish garrison, 'action was almost impossible'.

That same day, 12 July 1941, Gubbins met March-Phillipps in London and the two had lunch together. There was a further meeting two days later after which Admiral John Godfrey, the Director of Naval Intelligence, agreed to the relocation of *Maid Honor* from Poole to West Africa to 'undertake subversive operations on both land and sea'. Twelve days later Godfrey's proposal that the now named 'Maid Honor Force' should be detached from Poole and sent to West Africa on SOE duty was endorsed by the Admiralty. Five days after that and ten before *Maid Honor* sailed from Poole for Dartmouth, Admiral Godfrey sent a signal to Admiral Sir William James, Commander-in-Chief Portsmouth, stating that *Maid Honor* was to be detached from his command and sent to the South Atlantic to 'carry out such sabotage operations as may be ordered by SOE ... No definite project is yet in view, but plans are at present being drawn up for her.'[17] In fact, Gubbins had given March-Phillipps 'a general direction'[18] that the crew should be made available for whatever purposes 'W' (Franck) might wish, provided always that a reasonable crew was kept available for her at the shortest notice. It was further requested that C-in-C South Atlantic, Admiral Willis, 'afford this ship any assistance she may require. At the same time, SO2 [SOE] would like to place Maid Honor at the disposal of the Admiral to carry out any operations he may think fit.' No mention at this stage, then, of any cutting-out operation involving an Italian merchant vessel moored in neutral waters.

Reading between the lines, it appears likely that the Admiralty gave their approval to Admiral Godfrey's proposal, not because they supported possible plans to attack enemy shipping in a neutral harbour – such an idea was still in its early stages and unlikely to have been brought before their Lordships in embryonic form – but because his proposal removed the troublesome *Maid Honor* to distant waters. There may indeed have been discussions as to what she might do when she arrived, but sanctioning a long, slow 3,000-mile sea voyage to West Africa was not at all the same thing as sanctioning clandestine attacks in a neutral port when she got there. It was a distinction that may perhaps have been lost on March-Phillipps in the flurry and excitement of imminent departure.

It is extremely likely, however, that Gubbins, during those meetings with March-Phillipps on 12 and 14 July, briefed him, not only on the possibilities of using *Maid Honor* to search out possible U-boat supply bases along the coast, but also about the two tempting targets – the *Duchessa d'Aosta* and the *Likomba* – in neutral Fernando Po that he and the saboteurs aboard *Maid Honor* might one day, Admiralty permitting, be sanctioned to attack. It is also extremely likely that something else was drummed into the impatient, impulsive army subaltern seconded to SOE and now Captain of a commandeered Brixham trawler about to sail to Africa: that this was a Top Secret, disavowed mission. He and his men were on their own. If discovered, they would be disowned. There could be no back up, no admission of ownership, no rescue mission. They would travel, work and fight in civilian clothes. From their masthead they would fly the flag of Sweden. If captured, they could expect to be executed as spies.

Now, perhaps, despite expectations, *Maid Honor* had arrived safely in Freetown. What she needed was a reason for being there: a mission. London cabled Lagos on 25 September: 'News of safe arrival Maid Honor causes us to occupy our minds with problem her suitable employment.' The same signal went on to suggest investigating possible German radio stations or submarine bases that might – or might not – be within *Maid Honor's* striking range. London concluded: 'We invite your suggestions with a view examination and authorisation this end and preparation all information regarding targets you may have in mind.'[19]

Lagos had already put up the first considered plan for an attack on the vessels at Fernando Po at the end of August. 'W' had also proposed another attack on axis shipping elsewhere: two German ships, the *Wamaru* and the *Wagogo* lying in Lobito in Portuguese Angola, another neutral colony further south. All that he – and *Maid Honor* – needed now was official sanction from the Admiralty and the Foreign Office, but in that regard there was nothing but a lengthening silence. *Maid Honor* was left to swing around her anchor for three long weeks as London stalled. Her crew spent their days swimming, spear-fishing, sun-bathing, replenishing their ship's supplies from a parsimonious Naval Stores and keeping fit: 'I get a half-mile swim and a half-mile run every day before breakfast. Also, I am again very brown and thoroughly acclimatised to the sun and immune to sunburn. We wear nothing all day (aboard and ashore) but bathing trunks and sand shoes.' It was an idyllic, welcome interlude – just so long as it did not go on too long. Writing home Appleyard admitted: 'Really this camp is for us a sort of holiday and rest camp.'[20]

On 29 September 'W' signalled SOE Headquarters in London. He poured cold water on their target suggestions and then returned to the proposed Fernando Po mission: 'This scheme is being endangered by delay and will require several weeks after approval by you for preparation ... If not approved and as long as prohibited bangs against Vichy ship maintained utility of vessel nil.'[21]

On 30 September 'Caesar' signalled bad news from London. The Fernando Po plan was NOT approved. A follow-up signal the next day confirmed that the Admiralty, when pressed, had expressed 'complete indifference'[22] at the prospect of an attack on the *Duchessa d'Aosta*. Given the climate of enthusiasm for the entire Fernando Po proposal, the seizure of the *Likomba* – the Admiralty was 'ignorant existence [*sic*] this tug' – had not even been mentioned. Despite support from the Ministry of Economic Warfare, SOE's parent body who were 'interested'[23] in the immobilisation of the Italian liner, there was thus no prospect of action on the immediate horizon for the sun-tanned, battle-fit men impatiently awaiting orders in Freetown. Sweltering in the heat, Appleyard's thoughts turned to England and home:

> I suppose autumn is well on at home now and the trees and leaves must be in their finest colouring. It's a lovely season. What is it Keats says: 'Seasons of mists and mellow fruitfulness, close bosomed friend of the maturing sun.' The harvest too will all be in now I suppose and ploughing will be in progress. I wonder what sort of fruit season you had at home. And the evenings will be drawing in, with a feeling of frost in the air. And I suppose you will be getting the first of those strange evenings when the sun drops to the horizon with a bank of mist and is just a red disc, and there is a vague mistiness everywhere and a strange quietness. And celery for tea! What a lot of character a country like this misses because there are no seasons – no time of growth, no autumn and no dead winter when the trees are bare.[24]

On 10 October, with the situation no clearer and the whole Fernando Po operation in danger of stalling, *Maid Honor* left Freetown on her first clandestine mission. Grudgingly authorised by Vice Admiral Algernon Willis after repeated orders from London – the Admiral felt, frankly, that *Maid Honor* would be better off turning round and sailing home – they were ordered to snoop along the coast from the Gulf of Guinea to neutral Liberia looking for secret submarine bases or supply dumps. They sailed from Freetown with even more hardware than they had brought with them. March-Phillipps had managed to procure four depth charges, just in case they met German U-boats. He was aware, however, that the blast from his depth charges would not discriminate between friend and foe: 'If we can't knock a sub out any other way, we shall heave these into the ocean. The sub will then proceed to perdition, closely followed by ourselves.'[25] That first trip lasted five days and – if the log is to be believed – they *did* see a German U-boat; possibly: 'Sunday, October 12. Sighted shape like a submarine which disappeared suddenly. Reported by wireless. Engine failed.'[26]

Most trips lasted longer than just a few days as they slipped into a routine of operational patrol followed by rest, recuperation and refit back at Lumley Beach. *Maid Honor* would sail along the coast, investigate creeks, lagoons and deltas, send a scouting party ashore, perhaps investigate a promising estuary by Folbot canoe. On one of these recces of the Pongo River, begun on 7 November 1941, March-Phillipps and Appleyard launched their canoe whilst *Maid Honor* was still ten miles offshore.[27] They paddled to land and then spent three days, plagued by mosquitoes, lying up in the mango swamps by day and playing chess in the sand with twigs to pass the time in the sweltering heat before paddling up river at night looking for signs of the elusive enemy they never found. One night, with Appleyard in the bow, March-Phillipps accused him of slacking when progress slowed to a crawl: 'Come on, Apple. Do your bit',[28] he hissed. The reason for the slow progress became apparent: a crocodile, jaws agape, white teeth gleaming in the moonlight, was straddling the bows of the frail canoe, slowing their progress. A swipe of the paddle by Appleyard dislodged him and the pace immediately picked up. Dangerous times in mosquito, shark and crocodile-infested waters.

But no sign of a U-boat. Tom Winter, one of those aboard *Maid Honor*, recorded : 'Gus's nightly prayers surely included one for a U-boat to surface and ask the *Maid Honor* for some fish. If one did, he was prepared to sink her with the hidden depth-charges or to blow a hole in her with the spigot mortar ...'[29] A small ship offers no place to hide. Faults and strengths are exposed to all. Aboard *Maid Honor*, Appleyard continued to be impressed by his childhood friend, Graham Hayes:

> Graham is in great form and invaluable. He has an enormous capacity for work and is about the finest chap you could have with you. Gus, too, flourishes and is as full of drive as ever, which is one of the reasons for my saying we are not likely to be here much longer as, with the prospect of things slackening, Gus is already pushing for a move to 'fresh pastures'.

In all, *Maid Honor* completed three clandestine reconnaissance missions to the African shore: the first 'submarine patrol' on 10–14 October, the second to the Liberian coast on 23–30 October and the third to the Pongo River on 7–10 November.[30] Those missions were not entirely fruitless: two full 50-gallon oil drums in good condition were found – allegedly washed ashore – and there were persistent rumours of an earlier visit by two Germans who arrived at Baffu by boat from Monrovia. There was no sign of them during the *Maid Honor* patrols and March-Phillipps felt it safe to assume the Germans were making a reconnaissance with a view to establishing their own refuelling points.[31] But such patrols – and their slender gleanings of intelligence – cut little ice back in Freetown. Had their presence in West Africa been welcomed by officialdom, there might well have been more patrols. But it was not and, consequently, there were not.

In Poole it had been Commander Slocum who had frustrated March-Phillipps' intentions. Here it was the Commander-in-Chief, South Atlantic, Vice Admiral Algernon Willis. Returning on 11 November 1941 from their latest patrol in search of those elusive U-boat bases, March-Phillipps learned that there would be no more reconnaissance missions along the coast. Their forays into neutral territory made them too risky, too danger-ous. *Maid Honor* and her crew spent the next three weeks at Lumley Beach waiting for news from London. There was nothing else to do.

Even while they had been at sea, *Maid Honor's* long-term future had hung in the balance – for a while there was the very real possibility that, unwanted and with no further specific role in West Africa, she might simply return to England. In London, SOE was reviewing its own brief-ings to March-Phillipps in the event of the 'fiasco' that might surround the decision to order *Maid Honor* back to home waters:

> March-Phillipps could not have had any illusions regarding the employment of his ship and crew on the coast. He had been informed that there was a possibility that the crew might be used for land operations and to satisfy a request from Franck for additional sabotage experts. March-Phillipps had expressed his complete agreement with these instructions. Major Hanau ['Caesar'] did not think that March-Phillipps, even if the despatch of the Maid Honor proved a fiasco operationally, would regret the trip.[32]

Now, a month on, London was still stalling. With the Fernando Po attack on the horizon there was now a 'definite prospect'[33] of work for *Maid Honor* and her crew. They should sit tight and await further instructions.

SOE Headquarters, meanwhile, were working hard to break the deadlock. Louis Franck, back in London on timely leave, had taken the opportunity to refine the plan of attack for the ships at Fernando Po and had enlisted Gubbins' help to press his case with both the Foreign Office – code initials ZP – and the Admiralty, which gave Admiral Willis his orders. Now, instead of simply blowing up the passenger liner in a raid that would rely on crude 'bangs' which could not fail to antagonise the Spanish authorities, the intention would be to break the liner out of her anchors and tow her quietly out of harbour at dead of night: it was a classic interpretation of what today has become the motto of the Royal Marines Special Boat Service, based at Hamworthy, 2 miles across Poole Harbour from *Maid Honor's* secret summer anchorage at Russel Quay: *By Strength and Guile*. If the mission were successful, the *Duchessa d'Aosta*, her cargo and the *Likomba* would become valuable prizes, not just rusting hulks littering the shallow bottom of a neutral harbour. And – better yet – if they played it right, then both vessels would be gone, leaving no trace of those who had stolen them. There would be *suspicion*, most certainly. But, without *proof*, Britain's hands would be clean. It was a persuasive argu-ment. At the eleventh hour, it appears, Louis Franck and Brigadier Colin Gubbins had carried the day. Both the Foreign Office and the Admiralty had been persuaded to authorise the raid on Fernando Po. Signal from SOE London to 'W' Station Lagos, 14 November 1941:

ZP AND ADMIRALTY HAVE AUTHORISED SHIP PROJECTS AT FERNANDO PO AND LOBITO. TAKE NO ACTION PENDING FURTHER INSTRUCTIONS.[34]

The mission was about to become reality. As such, it now warranted a code name. One was duly allocated: Operation *Postmaster.*

With Friends Such As These ...

The men of Maid Honor Force broke camp and set sail for Lagos, 1,300 miles down the African coast, on 30 November 1941. The provisional date for Operation *Postmaster* was 22 December. With March-Phillipps were eleven of his thirteen men – two were held back by malaria – all of whom were sent on their way with the good wishes of the fellow gunners of the Royal Artillery unit whose mess they had shared. They presented the ship with a special gift to mark their happy association on the warm sands of Lumley Beach: 'Seen off by Gunners', wrote March-Phillipps in the ship's log soon after *Maid Honor* got under way. 'Presented with silver mug. Jolly good send off.'

The voyage to Lagos should have taken seven days. In the event, recurring engine breakdowns and light winds turned the journey into a slow and wearying fortnight, their dawdling progress enlivened only by the harpooning by André Desgrange of a 9-foot shark that was hauled alongside and then shot through the head by Graham Hayes with his .45 automatic. It was, wrote Appleyard, 'a filthy brute and as ugly as sin and stank like a sewer.'[1] They cut off its fin and nailed that to the bowsprit to replenish their store of good luck. *Maid Honor* made her way into Lagos harbour on 14 December.

The *Maid Honor* SOE support team waiting in Lagos had much to plan and discuss before Operation *Postmaster* could be passed up the line to London for approval. Time, meanwhile, was slipping by and, in the prolonged absence of both March-Phillipps, Maid Honor Force Commanding Officer and Appleyard, his second-in-command, the three men who would do so much behind the scenes to make Operation *Postmaster* a success began to refine their own thoughts as to how the raid's objective – the seizure of both the *Duchessa d'Aosta* and the *Likomba* – might best be accomplished. The three were Colin Michie, the British Vice Consul at Santa Isabel, Major Victor Laversuch (W4), of SOE's 'W' Section, and Lt

Leonard Guise (W10), formerly of the Nigerian government service who had been seconded to SOE in March 1941. It says much for the intelligence, foresight and painstaking tactical appreciations conducted by these three undercover civilians that, when March-Phillipps and Appleyard finally arrived in Lagos on 14 December to run their professional and operational slide rule over their proposals, they adopted them virtually piecemeal. Sergeant Tom Winter, one of the original *Maid Honor* party who took part in Operation *Postmaster*, recorded: 'Great credit must also be given to those nameless few who "prepared the ground". Without their efforts the operation could never have succeeded, and at considerable hazard they were responsible for enabling plans to be made that reduced risk to a minimum.'[2]

The final operational plan for *Postmaster* would ultimately have to be submitted via London to both General Giffard, the local army commander, and Admiral Willis, his naval counterpart. Before that could be done, however – and following the swift postponement of that 22 December H Hour after *Maid Honor*'s late arrival made it hopelessly impracticable – the men in Lagos determined to secure London's formal agreement to a list of operational principles they drew up together. These were submitted and agreed by London on 20 December.[3] The 'given' between London and Lagos was that both target vessels would be seized simultaneously by *coup de main* and towed into international waters, not simply blown up or disabled in Santa Isabel harbour; that the assault on both ships must take place at night; and that each target ship must be allocated its own towing tug whose professional master and crew must also take part in the operation.

Sitting there, making their plans, all were aware of the mission's potential for failing in spectacular fashion. Covert reconnaissance over many weeks by the shore party had established the size of the local Spanish garrison and the number of heavy weapons, including 6-inch guns and machine-guns that could be brought to engage the raiders if they were detected during the approach – the *Duchessa d'Aosta* was moored less than 60 yards from the end of the quay. And, even if the raiders reached the deck of both ships undetected in the darkness, their problems were by no means over. Unless taken by complete surprise, the crews of both vessels – there might be as many as thirty Italians aboard the merchant vessel, some of whom could be armed – could offer the potential of a prolonged and costly below-decks gun battle that could bring death, injury, exposure, mission failure, disgrace and political humiliation to the men of Maid Honor Force, the British consulate and the Foreign Office in distant London. If they *were* to succeed, ran SOE's reasoning in that signal to London, then more fighting men were needed, men who could be recruited locally. Force might well have to be used and there would be explosions as charges of plastic explosive went off to sever both target vessels from anchors and moorings. All involved conceded that Spanish *suspicion* of British involvement was unavoidable. What was absolutely vital, however, was to ensure that suspicion was not bolstered by the smallest shred of evidence. A new date was set for the raid during the next moonless period: Operation *Postmaster* would now be mounted on the night of 14–15 January 1942.

Matters now began to gather an exciting momentum: Governor Sir Bernard Bourdillon and the Nigerian government readily offered the loan of two tugs based in Lagos: the large government vessel *Vulcan*, which would be used to tow out the *Duchessa d'Aosta*, and the smaller tug *Nuneaton* – together with their officers and crews. The seventeen extra men needed for the actual attack, it was anticipated, would be provided locally by the regular army commander, General Giffard.

†††

In Lagos, the men of Maid Honor Force found themselves surrounded by friends – and by enemies. Yet both were on the same side.

SOE agents, friends and members of the consulate staff had already helped plan the raid. Some had gone considerably further: Vice Consul Colin Michie persuaded a local aeroplane pilot to take him up joy-riding, with the result that he was able to present London and March-Phillipps with invaluable aerial photographs of the harbour showing the precise location of each vessel and its proximity to the shore; it is believed Michie was also responsible for arranging photographs of a rather different kind.[4] These were of the pro-Nazi Spanish governor, F.L. Soraluce, bathing naked with his African mistress. After these were brought to the Spanish governor's attention, his enthusiasm for ordering continuing close surveillance of British activities on Fernando Po decreased markedly.

Another SOE Officer sent to the island in May 1941, Capt. Richard Lippett (W25), had been given the vital task of luring ashore the ships' officers of both the *Duchessa d'Aosta* and the *Likomba* to a dinner party on the night of the raid. Major Laversuch told Lippett that 65 per cent of the raid's chances of success rested upon his ability to ensure that *all* the two ships' officers were his dinner guests ashore and so seated that they would, quite literally, be looking the other way when March-Phillipps and his men swarmed into action. No pressure, then.

Major Victor Laversuch, however, had pressures of his own. He had decided to couple his request for the loan of seventeen troops from General

Sir George Giffard with the detailed briefing of the operation to which Giffard, as General Officer Commanding, West Africa, was entitled. Their meeting, however, did not go well.

From the outset, 55-year-old Giffard had objected to SOE's presence on *his* patch of West African soil, telling London back in May 1941: 'To be candid, the trouble with the SOE representatives [of W Section] was that (a) they did not know enough French and (b) they had not the knowledge of what will get under the skin of the African. In general, these SOE representatives are very able, but they are not round pegs in round holes.' Now the obstinate, hide-bound General proceeded to place Operation *Postmaster* in real jeopardy. Victor Laversuch (W4) signalled London on 22 December 1941:

1. A snag has arisen at Postmaster Operation owing to attitude GOC West Africa who is at present Lagos.
2. At interview W4 had with him this morning he expressed concern at reaction Spanish authorities.
3. He also hinted operation might jeopardise other possible plans he had in mind and could not -
   (a) Give us his blessing
   (b) Loan us personnel until he had communicated with C-in-C Freetown which he is doing by cable this morning.
4. We informed him operation in principle had been approved by ZP [the Foreign Office], Admiralty, HE Governor Nigeria and that it was evident ZP had carefully considered point raised by him regarding Spanish reaction before giving their approval.
5. He has promised to give definite reply before December 25.
6. If you can assist your end please do. In meantime we are going ahead with preliminaries.[5]

Records show that the Foreign Office authorised the attack as far back as 14 November.[6] The Admiralty offered the mission full support on 25 November and sent an appropriate signal to C-in-C South Atlantic, Vice Admiral Algernon Willis, with the request that he would 'afford them all assistance possible'. SOE Lagos had received notification of mission approval in principle 'by the appropriate authorities' in signal No 43 despatched on 28 November 1941.[7]

Almost a month later, on 23 December 1941, the War Office felt obliged to signal General Giffard once more, reminding him the Foreign Office had authorised the raid. In his turn General Giffard was now requested – but not ordered – to give 'any assistance possible' to the Fernando Po project.

That signal was authorised, sent for transmission – but not despatched. Christmas festivities, it has since been presumed, overcame military efficiency and the vital signal languished in some out tray. Laversuch, however, was cabled on Christmas Eve, wished Happy Christmas and told, incorrectly, that the message had been sent. Ergo, reasoned Laversuch and his SOE colleagues, Giffard would now come on-side. The sense of relief in Lagos that ensued, however, was to be short-lived.

On Christmas Eve Giffard met Admiral Willis and shared his concerns. Willis, it appears, was a kindred spirit. His priority also was to maintain the *status quo* and thus minimise what he saw as the threat to British colonial interests. Encouraged by Giffard, Willis sided with the army in opposing Operation *Postmaster* and sent London the following signal. It was despatched at 2305 and arrived in time for Christmas Day:

HUSH MOST SECRET

GOC (? In) Chief West Africa is much against seizure of Axis ships in Fernando Po in view of:

(a)War Office instruction to examine (corrupt group) capture of this island

(b)   Fact that origin of operation must become known whether successful or not and this will have bad effect on Spanish attitude.

(c)Operation is unnecessarily provocative unless value of ships considered or to offset repercussions.

2. I concur with G.O.C. in C *and have suspended operation* [author's italics] pending further instructions.[8]

Admiral Willis' signal went directly to London. In Lagos, SOE's Victor Laversuch (W4) was still awaiting that promised response from General Gifford by 25 December. He would later claim it never arrived.

Maid Honor Force, meanwhile, believed their mission was now definitely ON. They were spending Christmas up-country in Olokomeji, staying in the former holiday home of the Governor of Nigeria, firing their weapons in the bush and testing their plastic explosive charges against sample lengths of anchor chain. Again, this was a tactical secret Appleyard chose not to share with his parents:

[we] had three nights there. It was a delightful change and really felt like a Christmas holiday ... We had some rifles with us and shot some small game but saw nothing bigger than gazelles ... However, we shot quails and guinea-fowl with some success. They were excellent eating. We dynamited fish twice – great sport and yielded a big catch of about 40lbs each day ... We had luscious fruits there which we picked straight from the forest trees – oranges,

grapefruit, coconuts and tangerine as big as grapefruit, no pips and full of juice – one of the loveliest fruits you could wish for! There were nine of us up there for Christmas – all men, except for the wife of the present occupier of the house. We had a very jolly Christmas Day ... and a grand Christmas dinner at night'[9]

Yet, even as Appleyard and his friends enjoyed their unexpected Christmas festivities, the mission for which they had trained so hard and travelled so far still hung in the balance. And there was another, more personal question mark that also hung over the viability of Operation *Postmaster*. The question of command, of leadership. It was a question which had lain there, unresolved, for some time.

Station Head Louis Franck had met March-Phillipps and was not completely reassured by what he saw. The man with the stammer and explosive, short-fuse temper lacked, in his view, basic common sense.

There is a file in the National Archives at Kew, London, that records Franck's reservations and is marked in pencil – presumably by Gubbins himself: 'For our records but not for circulation.' The file is a record of a conversation in Gubbins' office held on 21 November 1941, four days before the Admiralty swung behind Operation *Postmaster* and sent Willis the signal he either chose to ignore or failed to receive. The meeting was attended by Gubbins, 'Caesar' – Lt Col Julius Hanau, Gubbins' West Africa deputy – and one other. Franck began by stating that, although he found all the Maid Honor Force personnel involved 'admirable in their own way' he feared that the team 'did perhaps not have the necessary qualifications of leadership for the successful conduct of an operation of this kind which required a good deal of planning and special leadership'. March-Phillipps, he felt, whilst possessing qualities of courage and enterprise, lacked common sense and was therefore 'not a suitable leader for this job'.

Brigadier Gubbins heard him out and then added his own view. Which was that, with Appleyard's assistance to work out the details of the operation, he felt March-Phillipps was quite capable of leading the operation successfully. And there, for a while, the matter rested. Yet, in time, events both off the island of Fernando Po and later, on the beaches of Normandy, would show that both Gubbins and Franck, in their own way, were right. And that Louis Franck's instincts, his gut-feelings of reservation about some of the personal qualities that drove March-Phillipps to court an impulsive, quixotic death in battle, were not misplaced.

On 26 December, just over a month later, 'Caesar', in London, followed up with another memo to Gubbins. Describing the *Postmaster* plan as 'sound' he concluded: 'We should be interested to know who is in command of Postmaster. You will recollect that W. [Franck] expressed certain misgivings about W01 [March-Phillipps] on temperamental grounds and felt that it might be hazardous to put him in charge.'[10] The files reveal that, despite Gubbins' apparent support for March-Phillipps, SOE London had assumed that Major John Eyre, their senior man in Lagos, would command the raid.

Now SOE Lagos – including John Eyre – sprang robustly to March-Phillipps' defence. Major Laversuch signalled London two days later:

A) We feel strongly that W01 must be in command for the following reasons.
1. His seafaring and general experiences which are most valuable in an operation of this nature.
2. Personnel of M.H.[*Maid Honor*] are backbone of whole party and they have utmost confidence and trust in him.
3. W29 [Major John Eyre, Senior SOE Officer, Lagos] volunteered to act under command of W01 in any capacity.
4. In view of above we submit it would be fundamentally wrong to change specifically at this late stage of preliminaries.

London was quick to capitulate and cabled back: 'In view of your representations we agree that W01 will be in command.'[11]

On 27 December, the day after Boxing Day, despite his promise, there appeared to be still no word to SOE from General Giffard. Major Laversuch cabled London:

1. Despite the urgent cable sent by Headquarters at Lagos to G.O.C. in C who is now Accra no reply received.
2. Question most urgent and unless we have decision at once our plan will be upset and success of the operation jeopardised.
3. Please request War Office cable urgent instructions G.O.C in C.
4. We also understand reason for delay in reply from G.O.C. in C is due to the fact that he in turn has not had reply from Commander in Chief Freetown.
5. Please also therefore arrange Admiralty signal urgently to Commander In Chief Freetown.[12]

SOE Headquarters slammed back a reply that same day:

A.   Fully realise urgency of position.
B.   Admiralty expected signal shortly. Am now working on War Office.[13]

Laversuch's urgent plea for higher intervention seems to have worked. Yet there appears to be confusion as to the timing of these important messages between Lagos and SOE Headquarters in London. After claiming righteously that General Giffard had ignored his promise to let him know where things stood by 25 December, a Christmas Day signal to London from Lagos reveals that Laversuch had indeed heard from General Giffard by that deadline. For Laversuch himself cabled London that day:

FROM W4. MOST SECRET. DECYPHER YOURSELF.
WE HAVE JUST RECEIVED FOLLOWING MESSAGE FROM GOC IN C. BEGINS:
FOR W4. HAVE CONSULTED COMMANDER IN CHIEF SOUTH ATLANTIC WHO DOES NOT REPEAT NOT AGREE OPERATION SHOULD TAKE PLACE AT PRESENT. ENDS.[14]

It might be supposed that General Giffard was getting Admiral Willis to do his dirty work for him. Operation *Postmaster* appeared stalled – dead in the water. Shielded by the impersonal jargon of encrypted communications, by distance and, perhaps, by festive administrative incompetence, this was a direct challenge to its authority that London could not ignore. It did not. Four days later, on 29 December 1941, and in language that neither General Giffard nor Admiral Willis could misconstrue, London restated the position: SOE's Operation *Postmaster* was to go ahead and he, Admiral Willis, was to help make it happen. The Admiralty, too, threw some of their weight behind SOE's request for urgent co-operation, salting – either wittingly or unwittingly – a little untruth into the stream of telegrams flowing between London, Freetown and Lagos. Referring to the signal sent to General Gifford on 13 December which 'it is regretted was not repeated to you', the Admiralty, a little disingenuously in view of the London cable sent the very same day, reassured Admiral Willis: 'These instructions are for examination of the project only *and there is no repeat no intention of implementing them in near future* [author's italics] ...' Is it possible that, at this late stage, the Admiralty did not realise the raid itself was imminent? It seems unlikely. Their cable continued:

Activities against Axis interests will always arouse suspicions. Proof of these suspicions must be avoided ... Possible political repercussions are acceptable provided collusion of our forces or authorities is not apparent. If present plan is unacceptable to you in this respect, you should have it recast. Shipping involved is of sufficient value to be worth obtaining if possible. War Office concur. Pass to G.O.C. in C West Africa [Giffard].[15]

Now the word came back to Lagos from Admiral Willis in Freetown who, knuckles rapped, still attempted to salvage a little pride: although he still disliked the idea of *Postmaster* he was prepared to discuss it. Laversuch and March-Phillipps hurried to Freetown. They arrived on 4 January and saw Admiral WIllis twice on the evenings of 4 and 5 January. Finally, after much discussion at a level of detail that must have sorely tried March-Phillipps' short-fuse temper, Willis allowed himself to be persuaded: the plan as outlined might well work and, if it did, one of his Royal Navy warships, the corvette HMS *Violet*, would be tasked to intercept *Duchessa d'Aosta* on the high seas after the cutting-out operation had been completed successfully.

One down, one to go. Laversuch now requested a meeting with General Giffard: he still needed seventeen fighting men from the General's command. Laversuch recorded afterwards:

The proceedings were exceedingly brief and the following conversation took place:

Laversuch: 'I was informed by the C-in-C South Atlantic that you had agreed in principle to the operations taking place, for which we are grateful.'
Giffard: 'I have agreed, but I tell you frankly I do not like the scheme, and I shall never like it.'
Laversuch: 'I am very sorry to hear this, but thank you for having given your consent. There is a question of personnel. Could you assist us on this subject?'
Giffard: 'No – most definitely – no. The only thing I can offer you is my best wishes for the success of the operation.'
Laversuch: 'Thank you very much, Sir. Goodnight.'[16]

March-Phillipps was also at that brief and unhelpful meeting, though his reaction outside the general's office is not recorded – perhaps it is just as well. Both men hurried back to Lagos, from where Operation *Postmaster* would start. With departure to Fernando Po scheduled for 11 January, time was extremely short. And they still needed seventeen men.

Help, however, was at hand in the form of the Governor of Nigeria, Sir Henry Bourdillon – no friend of General Giffard – who immediately invited Laversuch and March-Phillipps to select seventeen potential volunteers from his own Colonial Service. Civilians all, they selected men from the police, education, public works and administrative branches of the Service, many of whom had previous military service. All of the seventeen men selected, described as 'the toughest individuals in the public service in Nigeria', were approved by the Governor and each was then sent a telegram by March-Phillipps inviting them simply to take two weeks' authorised holiday and 'come to a party' at 12 noon on 10 January at 32, Cameron Road, Lagos. Conjecture was rife. Some thought they would be required to trek hundreds of miles through the bush and had been busy breaking in thick-soled walking boots.[17]

At Cameron Road they were given a general and non-mission-specific briefing by March-Phillipps about the sort of work that might be involved. He did not mention long treks through the jungle but did invite anyone having second thoughts to step down. No one did. SOE agent Lt Leonard Guise (W10) recalled afterwards:

> The situation on 7 and 8 of January was not too good ... the question of manpower looked serious. Owing to intense enthusiasm from His Excellency and the Deputy Chief Secretary, Miles Clifford, the entire matter was solved in some twenty-four hours, and at midday on 10 January, as choice a collection of thugs as Nigeria can ever have seen was assembled at 32, Cameron Road.[18]

A champagne toast followed, after which each volunteer was kitted out with dark clothing and plimsolls.

Small, inconspicuous groups of volunteers left Cameron Road that evening and made their way to Apapa Wharf in Lagos harbour where the two tugs loaned by the Governor, *Vulcan* and *Nuneaton*, lay quietly moored side by side. Stores were already loaded and the men – some of whom had enjoyed perhaps rather more of Cameron Road's hospitality than was strictly wise – embarked: 'By midnight the decks of the *Vulcan* vibrated with snores and 560 lbs of the Administrative department were fast asleep on *Nuneaton*'s sun deck', recorded Leonard Guise.[19] At 0530 on 11 January 1942, and with *Vulcan* towing *Nuneaton*, Maid Honor Force with 41 men set sail south-east for Fernando Po. Zero Hour – the assault on *Duchessa d'Aosta* and the tug *Likomba* – was scheduled for 2330, 14 January 1942.

At last, after days of uncertainty, confusion, obstruction, objection and administrative incompetence, Operation *Postmaster*, an act described by one author as 'flagrant piracy in a neutral harbour'[20] and by one of those involved, SOE's Leonard Guise, as 'a cut-out operation. In other words, simple theft' had begun:[21]

MOST IMMEDIATE. [SOE headquarters to SOE Lagos]: [Sent 10 Jan 1942]
From Brigadier Gubbins to W4 [Laversuch] FOR W01 [March-Phillipps]
from M:

GOOD HUNTING. AM CONFIDENT YOU WILL EXERCISE UTMOST CARE TO ENSURE SUCCESS AND OBVIATE REPERCUSSIONS. BEST OF LUCK TO YOU AND ALL MH [Maid Honor] AND OTHERS.[22]

Gubbins' 'am confident you will exercise utmost care' may have smacked a little of their chief whistling nervously in the dark, but it mattered little. For March-Phillipps and Appleyard particularly, actually casting off and heading out into the soft light of an African dawn with the unequivocal prospect of coming to grips with the enemy at journey's end must have come as something of a relief. March-Phillipps replied to Gubbins back in London:

GREATLY APPRECIATE YOUR GOOD WISHES WILL DO OUR BEST[23]

8

Assault on a Duchess

Aboard the tug ST *Vulcan*, Capt. March-Phillipps distributed his core unit of men who had come out from England as part of Maid Honor Force. with him, targeting the merchant ship *Duchessa d'Aosta*, were Capt. Appleyard, second-in-command; Anders Lassen; Denis Tottenham; Ernest Evison, the cook; André Desgrange; 'Haggis' Taylor, March-Phillipps' batman; and Leslie Prout. With Lt Graham Hayes would be Tom Winter and 'Buzz' Perkins, the baby of the party. Their mission was the seizure and towing out of the smaller German tug *Likomba*. The remaining men aboard both vessels were allocated their place in one of five different teams: cable party, engine-room party, boarding party, back-up boarding party and towing party.

Nuneaton was towed alongside as far as the bar at the mouth of Lagos harbour and then slipped astern on a long tow. As both vessels crossed the bar, the ebb tide met the swell of the open sea and:

> the heavily laden tugs wallowed like pigs. This was most unfortunate for the volunteers, most of whom were not accustomed to small craft, and some of the poor fellows took fully two days to recover from their agony. As for the crew, if any of them had felt bad they would not dare have shown it, for the wrath of Gus would have descended upon them like an avalanche![1]

Leonard Guise (W10) was also aboard. He recalled:

> *Vulcan* wallowed slowly along with *Nuneaton* dancing along behind like a naughty puppy on the end of a lead ... By midday Nuneaton's crew were *hors de combat* ... *Vulcan* was having her own troubles. The ship's movement was not so bad but at least 2/3rds of the volunteers were extremely ill.[2]

That evening March-Phillipps relented and allowed the crew of *Nuneaton* to board *Vulcan* where the movement was less nauseous. The following day sunshine, easing seas and good food from Evison improved everyone's spirits. The *Nuneaton*, however, was still being towed. That same morning, whilst the recovering crew were having tommy-gun practice on *Nuneaton*'s sundeck, she suddenly lurched onto her side and threatened to capsize. Still being dragged through the water on the end of her long tow by *Vulcan* and with her bilge keel now plainly visible, stores were jettisoned into the sea and men rushed to the port side and prepared to abandon ship as the Skipper, up to his neck in water in the wheelhouse, fought to keep his ship afloat. As screams of fear came from the flooding engine-room below, Lassen, the only professional seaman amongst the *Maid Honor* crew, leapt to the stern of *Vulcan*, grabbed an axe and, without waiting for orders, severed the tow. No longer being dragged through the water on her side, *Nuneaton* slowly righted herself and the crisis was averted. 'Undoubtedly', recalled Leslie Prout:

> Andy's prompt action saved Graham's tug from total loss. Graham [Hayes] and Tom [Winter] swam about retrieving their previous provisions and cases of beer, heedless of sharks or barracuda. Eventually, reprovisioned from the large tug, and with her engine again in action, Graham's vessel got under way and the voyage was resumed.[3]

The tow was not reconnected and both ships now proceeded eastwards under their own power.

Each member of the boarding parties was issued with a cosh – a foot-long metal bolt sheathed in rubber. March-Phillipps ordered at one of his briefings: 'When possible – intimidate. If not, use force. Speed is essential.' Too right it was. Whilst Bren gunners were instructed to 'deal with any boats. Shoot across bows. No useless slaughter',[4] the thought would have occurred to the more perceptive amongst the raiders that, if the operation degenerated into a straight shot and shell fire-fight, then the game would be as good as over. And that it would take more than a few judicious bursts of Bren to cover their escape and withdrawal.

On the Tuesday, weapons were cleaned and all ranks – including the volunteers – practised with tommy guns and Brens as they emptied magazine after magazine into the heaving ocean. Michie's air photographs of the harbour, the *Duchessa d'Aosta* and the *Likomba* were studied, ships' plans memorised and explosive charges assembled. March-Phillipps briefed each team on their precise role in the coming attack and, after boarding ledges had been fixed on the bridge deck of *Vulcan* to simplify the swift and silent movement from ship to ship in groups of four, all boarding parties, dressed for action and carrying weapons, practised their response to the call to Action Stations and the strict order of their assault.

They had sailed from Lagos in the early hours of Sunday, 11 January 1943. On Tuesday evening *Nuneaton* stopped and put two Folbots over the side with orders to creep up on *Vulcan*: 'This was highly successful, the Folbots approaching within a few yards without being seen', March-Phillipps reported.[5] Wednesday was spent steaming slowly into position out of sight of land. The plan of attack was minutely adjusted and there was another briefing from March-Phillipps while 'Explosives were made ready on both ships and a cold lunch was served on *Vulcan* because the galley stove was occupied by an earnest figure boiling and moulding plastic [explosive]. Torches, pistols and Tommy-guns were issued and that afternoon when the island was sighted everything was ready.'[6]

It was at this point, as *Vulcan* and *Nuneaton* were moving quietly into their final pre-attack positions, that disaster nearly overtook Operation *Postmaster*. The approach into the mouth of Santa Isabel harbour and the attack on the two vessels themselves were supposed to coincide with the town's midnight, power-saving blackout which plunged the town and harbour into all-enveloping darkness. But Fernando Po, being Spanish, kept to Spanish time in Madrid – whilst Lagos and March-Phillipps had their watches set to Nigerian time, one hour ahead. Maid Honor Force had arrived early. And the lights were still on.

March-Phillipps' formal after-action report makes no mention of his own conduct thereafter, or what actually happened next. Leonard Guise, however, was more forthcoming.

At 2200 both vessels lay about 4 miles north of the harbour of Santa Isabel, the town lights still showing clearly. At 2315 *Nuneaton* moved ahead and very slowly crept closer to the harbour. Guise reported afterwards:

Some dismay was felt aboard her when an excited and well-known voice came bellowing through the darkness: 'Will you get a b-b-b-bloody move on or g-g-g-get out. I'm coming in.' As Zero Hour was 12pm and the whole scheme swung on the extinction of the town lights which it was known would occur at that hour, this demand was resented.[7]

He remembered later:

Gus was all teed up and he wanted to go in and there was for one moment a rather sticky little scene when we on *Nuneaton* could hear Gus quite loudly disclaiming that he'd every intention of going in and to hell with it. Gus himself struck me as completely intrepid, almost to the point of overdoing it because … this was not really a military operation. It was a burglar's operation and burglars don't go in shooting. But Gus gave the impression that he much preferred to do a job when he did go in shooting.[8]

The captain of the *Nuneaton*, Lt Goodman, had heard enough. Taking matters into his own hands he simply swung *Nuneaton*'s bows across *Vulcan*'s path and stopped dead. Leonard Guise recalled: 'After some furious comments from each ship, common sense prevailed and *Vulcan* sheered off into the darkness to wait.' Perhaps Louis Franck's reservations, expressed in London to Colin Gubbins that previous November, held some merit after all.

At midnight local time – 0100 by March-Phillipps' watch – both ships were about 200 yards outside the rim of harbour lights. *Nuneaton* was ahead with *Vulcan* astern and to starboard. Ashore, in Santa Isabel, and right on cue, the lights went out: 'What had been a well-illuminated display became utter darkness.'[9]

There was no moon. Ahead, through the darkness, they could just make out the dark gleam of the *Duchessa d'Aosta*. The *Likomba* lay unseen, her position noted. *Nuneaton* moved slowly ahead and then stopped 40 yards inside the two flashing lights that marked the harbour entrance to lower her two grey-painted Folbot canoes. One headed off in the wrong direction before being frantically recalled, the other made her way silently towards *Likomba*, both two-man crews paddling silently in the darkness as they closed in on their quarry. Lt Graham Hayes and Sergeant Tom Winter were in the first canoe and two volunteers – District Commissioners William Newington and A.F. Abell – were in the second. *Nuneaton* restarted her engine – 'with a honk that could have been heard for miles'[10] – and swung away into the darkness around the west of the harbour to bring her up alongside *Likomba*. As she did so *Vulcan* swept past between the two harbour lights, heading around the east side of the bay in a gentle curve that would place her port side alongside the starboard side of the *Duchessa*.

On *Vulcan* the boarding parties formed up fully armed, packed together on the mess deck as they waited to take their place on the boarding planks run out over the tumblehome of *Vulcan*'s sides. There was a stern light on the *Duchessa* and one or two lit cabin portholes attested to people aboard. As they swung round closer, engine stopped but still under way, figures could be seen on the after-deck. But there were no shots and no shouts as *Vulcan* closed the last remaining yards, her armed boarding party clustered tightly together on the boarding platforms. Just seconds to go now. March-Phillipps was in front.

Nearby, Graham Hayes and Tom Winter closed in on the *Likomba*. As they did so 'we were amused to see a lighted window in which the light was dipping and flashing, mixed up with which we read the repeated signal OK, OK.' It was, said Tom Winter later, 'The most ancient of spy signals, a blind raised and lowered at a lighted window by the docks.'[11] Graham Hayes reported: 'The work done by our agents ashore had been very thorough which probably accounted for the absence of the two officers from the *Likomba* when the canoe parties boarded.'[12]

Indeed it did. Reminded by Major Victor Laversuch that 65 per cent of the success of Operation *Postmaster* rested upon his ability to lure away the officers of both *Duchessa d'Aosta* and *Likomba* to a shore-side dinner party, SOE Officer Capt. Richard Lippett (W25) had not failed his friends. He – using as local cover a sympathetic anti-Falangist, Don Abalino Zorilla – had organised a 'dry-run' party just after Christmas which had been attended by *most* – but not all – of the German and Italian officers aboard *Duchessa d'Aosta* and *Likomba*. Thanks to the depth of SOE's coffers, the drink had flowed particularly freely and the party had been judged a great success. So successful, indeed, that the German officers aboard *Duchessa* had felt compelled to extend a return invitation to a party aboard ship on 6 January. That too had been a success. Now Lippett had countered with a second invitation. And this time all eight *Duchessa* officers – including the Acting Captain Umberto Valle and the officers of the *Likomba*, including Capt. Specht – had accepted. Now, as *Vulcan* and *Nuneaton* eased quietly into position on silent engines, as nervous men fingered their weapons and bunched together on boarding ramps, as four men in double Folbot canoes dug their paddles deep into dark water and moved in on their targets, all those officers were seated at the Casino Restaurant above the port, their backs to the harbour, their night vision conveniently wrecked by the considerable lighting of Tilley lamps that had been provided to keep the party going as soon as the town lights had been doused at midnight.

Meanwhile, in the harbour below, the attack on the officer-less *Likomba* was already underway:

> The watchman on the *Likomba* challenged and flashed a light as the canoe came alongside the lighter (a barge which was secured along the starboard side of the *Likomba*). Non-commital noises were made in reply and the watchman came forward to help with the painter as he was under the impression it was the Captain coming back on board. A letter was proffered and intimation made that it was for the Captain. The watchman said that both officers were ashore.[13]

For the second time that evening the second canoe, manned by District Commissioners Abell and Newington, set off to attack the wrong ship. Realising their mistake in time, they swung away from an empty Spanish launch, paddled alongside and boarded *Likomba*:

> The first and more professional of the two [canoes] were challenged by a native from the *Likomba* but he took no immediate alarm when asked for his master in pigin English. As however the visitors came aboard he became unhappy, and when a second canoe followed and the chains blew, he and two of his mates went sprinting down the long deck and went popping over the side into the sea like performing gymnasts over a horse.[14]

They were not the only ones discomforted by the explosion. A third team of two from *Nuneaton* were boarding just at the moment the charges went off. Their task was to secure the tow between *Likomba* and *Nuneaton*:

> As the two figures clambered over the side loaded with Mills bombs, Tommy-guns, hatchets, torches and the towing hawser, a somewhat Australian voice roared 'Get out you ...! I've just blown!' He certainly had. Both the climbers were blown into the air and landed, one on the sundeck, the other on a bollard back aboard *Nuneaton*. The first had his Mills bomb blown unexploded from his hand, and the second received a cracked rib. Then the stern moorings, after one misfire, went off and the *Likomba* was adrift and still completely divorced from *Nuneaton*. A second attempt to board from *Nuneaton* went well and though *Likomba* was fast turning, the hawser was made fast and the party was over.[15]

Aboard *Vulcan*, it was the closing moments. In the van was Lassen, cosh at his waist, a length of thin messenger line over his shoulder coiled and ready to throw. As *Vulcan* passed the rope ladder leading to the cabin deck, he leapt aboard. *Vulcan* touched and March-Phillipps and the first wave of five raiders crossed to the *Duchessa*, their moment of maximum danger and commitment covered by two Brens on the roof of *Vulcan*'s bridge. *Vulcan* had hit hard. Now she recoiled, touched again. Another six raiders jumped aboard followed by a final party which included a doctor with medical supplies, who found that *Vulcan* had now moved too far forward to trans-ship and had to cross on an 8-foot bamboo ladder thrown across a dark abyss. All reached the *Duchessa* without mishap.

March-Phillipps and 'Haggis' Taylor made their way straight to the bridge whilst Lassen looped his messenger line around a bollard on the *Duchessa* and flung the coiled line back to Robin Duff aboard the *Vulcan*:

'Pull!' yelled Lassen. 'Pull, Robin! Pull like fuck!' Duff pulled. First the light messenger and then the heavy towing hawser came aboard, hauled in by Lassen on his own. Meanwhile, SOE's Desmond Longe (W30) was following March-Phillipps and 'Haggis' as they hurried to the bridge:

> We ran up the little ladder from the well-deck on the promenade of the merchant ship, chased along the gangway. By this time we had a knife in one hand and a pistol in the other. The first thing I knew was something between my legs and I went for a burton and I thought it was a panicking Italian, or something or other. In actual fact it was a pig because the Italians had two or three pigs on the deck at the back.[16]

Like the *Duchessa*'s days at anchor, those of the pig were also numbered. As boarding parties hurried through the ship, herding startled and unresisting prisoners ahead of them to cluster under armed guard in the after saloon, the explosives teams made their way to stem and stern of the *Duchessa* with their primed charges: Appleyard to the bows, Eyres and Long to the mooring cables astern. 'There was no resistance worthy of the name', reported March-Phillipps afterwards. '... the whole operation, from entering to leaving the harbour, went according to plan.'[17] And, so far, though the middle-aged stewardess aboard *Duchessa* had fainted at the sight of the boarding party, not a shot had been fired. 'Only one blow was struck, and that was when one of the volunteers found an enemy officer "looking aggressive". The poor wretch did not look very aggressive after a tap with his assailant's "persuader".'[18] Other Italian crewmen were struck a little later after showing a reluctance to lie down on the deck: 'Their sick heads were due to having no English ... a large Public Works Official had to take to his persuader and play a quick *arpeggio* on their heads. The wounds were not very grave, and the casualties served a very good breakfast next morning.'[19] The original plan had stipulated that *Duchessa*'s charges would be blown first. Only then would Graham Hayes and his men blow the restraints holding *Likomba* at anchor. It didn't work out that way: 'As the *Nuneaton* had given doubtful proof of her abilities on the way to Fernando Po, it had been decided to blow the cables on the *Likomba* as soon as ready', reported Graham Hayes.[20] The charges blew, *Nuneaton* picked up the tow and *Likomba* with another vessel lashed to her side began to move steadily towards the mouth of the harbour. The second vessel, the yacht *Bibundi*, was added as something of an afterthought. Hayes' first instinct had been to cut her adrift: 'Take her, Graham, because of these', urged Tom Winter, shining his torch over snapshots he had found in the cabin. These showed a woman – perhaps the owner's wife – posing against a swastika flag flying from the *Bibundi*'s jackstaff.[21] Expensive snapshots. Now *Bibundi* too was a prize of war.

From *Vulcan*'s engine-room, Leslie Prout reported:

> the Chief and Second Engineers were waiting for the clang of the telegraph and every ounce of steam and every evolution they could coax out of the 2,000 h.p. engines. In the stokehold I was telling the sweating stokers the tale as I had never told it before, and promised them a big 'dash' if they worked well. My powers of persuasion were considerably assisted by a tommy-gun and a Colt .45.[22]

His presence there – and his powers of persuasion – were vital: the *Vulcan* was planning to pull out an 8,500-tonne inert merchant vessel with no power from a cold, standing start. She would need every ounce of strength she could gather. As *Nuneaton* slid past *Vulcan* with her two tows astern on the way to their rendezvous 200 miles away in the safety of international waters, March-Phillipps, waiting impatiently on *Duchessa*'s bridge, received the news he had been waiting for: the ship was his. He gave the signal: a long blast on his whistle and 'with a titanic roar and a flash that lit up the whole island the Duchess lost the principal lace to her stays'.[23] But she was not yet free.

Below decks on *Vulcan*:

> The telegraph clanged in the engine room of the tug and the Chief opened the throttle wide. The powerful engines shook the tug as she strained and pulled at her huge burden and the water was churned up into a phosphorescent race by the thrash of her propellers. The liner did not move. In the silence that followed the explosions Apple's clear voice was heard 'I am laying another charge.' One of the forward charges had failed to ignite and Apple, realising that the whole success of the operation depended upon him, rushed forward and laid another charge with a short fuse on the huge anchor chain. After what seemed like an eternity Apple's voice rang out again: 'I am going to blow!' Unable to get back to proper shelter he crouched behind a nearby winch. A blinding flash and a huge explosion followed immediately, the tug's propellers thrashed again, and the huge liner lurched and began to slide forward. A mighty shout rang from the bridge: 'My God, she's free!'[24]

March-Phillipps reported afterwards:

> *Vulcan*'s performance was almost miraculous. She gave the *Duchessa* two slews, one to starboard, one to port, like drawing a cork out of a bottle, and

then without the slightest hesitation, and at a speed of at least three knots, went straight between the flashing buoys to the open sea, passing *Nuneaton* and *Likomba* a few cable lengths from the entrance. This operation, the most difficult in my view, was performed with amazing power and precision ... The estimated time taken from entering the harbour to leaving with both tows was thirty-five minutes ...[25]

The severing of the anchor chain after the explosives' misfire had been *the* critical movement in the cutting-out of the *Duchessa*. Appleyard, once again, had proved his mettle. After successfully attempting that 8-foot leap across the widening gulf between *Vulcan* and *Duchessa* – a feat attempted by no one else that night – he had, by his quick thinking, risen to match his moment. His actions that night – and, indeed, throughout the entire *Postmaster* operation – would win him his second Military Cross, the citation of which concluded: 'These operations were performed with complete disregard of his own personal safety, and the cutting out of the liner was ensured [sic]'

And, meanwhile:

Pandemonium reigned ashore. Immediately after the detonations were heard the anti-aircraft guns went into action and blazed into the sky, the explosions having been mistaken for bombs from raiding aircraft. It was not until daylight that it was realised on the shore that the steamers had gone in the night ... It was as well that the 6 in. guns covering the harbour had not opened fire because the most powerful gun aboard the tug was a Bren.[26]

March-Phillipps remembered later:

Bugles were sounding on the shore and there was much activity near the pier head, which ceased very suddenly at the sound of the explosions. Shouts of 'Alerta!' could be heard and it is presumed that those on shore believed an air raid to be in progress. No attempt was made to board either of the two ships.[27]

The town lights had come on after the explosives on *Likomba*'s anchor chains had detonated and several cars had rushed down to the quay: 'One makes no aspiration on Spanish gallantry' recorded Leonard Guise, warming to the telling of a successful tale he must have been aware could not fail to delight and amuse his superiors:

but the fact remains that after the first of the Duchessa's rather louder performances a number of cars were seen to be rushing rather faster in the opposite direction. Bugles were blown, but bugles blow all day in Fernando Po and never have very much effect. The Italian captain was seen on the quay waving his arms and appealing for light, for an explanation, for his ship. Nobody replied.[28]

His ship was long gone.[29]

A Very Proper Lie

By 0100 on 15 July the *Duchessa d'Aosta* was a mile or two out of the bay and the Bren guns, sited by March-Phillipps on the boat deck to deter small-boat pursuit, could be stood down. March-Phillipps kept the prisoners under guard and told them to behave. It was hardly necessary: 'it was apparent that they wanted nothing better than to leave Fernando Po … The elderly stewardess driven nearly dotty by the explosions was sent to bed after treatment from the doctor and, with guards posted, some of Vulcan's crew got a little sleep.'[1]

No one was getting much sleep aboard *Nuneaton*. She was towing both *Likomba* and the seized private yacht *Bibundi*, both of which were connected, one to another, by a 50-yard hemp hawser. Now, as the vessels plunged and strained through the swell in the darkness, the tow rope began to fray. Once, long ago in Scotland during SOE survival training, Lassen – 'lithe as a cat' in his mother's phrase[2] – had astonished his fellow SOE course members when, on foot, he had stalked and killed a fine, big stag armed only with a knife. Now he was about to astound them again. Without, again, waiting for orders, he tied a line around his waist and, in the darkness and heaving seas, swarmed across the fraying rope to *Bibundi*, the strain of the tow tossing him alternately high into the sky or down into the sea. Somehow, he hung on. Swinging onto the vessel, he then, on his own, hauled in the replacement heavy hemp tow-line, made it fast to the bitts in the light of torches shone from *Likomba* and, after five minutes' rest, came back hand over hand down the tow-line back to *Nuneaton*. It was, remarked Leonard Guise 'what seemed to the onlookers one of the bravest things they had seen'.[3] Like Appleyard, Lassen too had risen magnificently to the challenge of live operations. Appleyard's reward would be a Bar to his Military Cross. Lassen's would be different: 'I should like to recommend Lassen for a commission' stated March-Phillipps simply in his post-action report, 'for I consider that his work on the ship has been [of] exceptional quality, and he has shown great ability in handling men.'[4]

With *Bibundi* now safely under tow, the little convoy of vessels – *Vulcan* towing *Duchessa d'Aosta* and *Nuneaton* towing *Likomba* and *Bibundi* – made its way across the heaving darkness on a westerly course leaving Fernando Po in its wake. As the *Duchessa* wallowed along behind *Vulcan* making best speed towards that rendezvous with HMS *Violet*, March-Phillipps wrote in the *Maid Honor* log taken aboard his prize vessel: 'Boarded, captured and towed out D'Aosta, cutting out went according to plan.'[5] Behind the sparse words, March-Phillipps, the Elizabethan buccaneer born into the wrong age, was on fire with patriotic fervour: 'Tremendous patriot, tremendous patriot. Almost to ... to the point that one sort of looked at him and wondered whether he was really true' remembered Desmond Longe. 'I remember Gus saying to me on board the ship: "This is a wonderful thing for the old c-c-c-country, you know." As far as I was concerned it was a wonderful thing to be alive.'[6] The rendezvous with HMS *Violet* was scheduled for 1400 hours on 15 January, the day after Operation *Postmaster*. It was to take place at 4 degrees 10 minutes north, 8 degrees, 20 minutes east. HMS *Violet* would approach on a course of 298 degrees.

Early on the morning of 15 January the unreliable *Nuneaton* developed further engine trouble and dropped astern. With the time for the rendezvous with the corvette fast approaching, March-Phillipps, aboard *Vulcan*, decided to press on ahead. In the event, he need not have hurried. Once on station, the time of the RV came and went. HMS *Violet* was nowhere to be seen. March-Phillipps decided he needed to retrace steps, and find out what had happened to *Nuneaton* and her prizes. To do that he had to transfer from the bridge of the *Duchessa* to the smaller *Vulcan* now alongside. According to one account, March-Phillipps then took a rash and impatient decision that almost cost him his life. Without waiting to rig a bosun's chair or bothering to tie a line around his waist, he simply leapt across the gap between the *Duchessa* and the smaller tug but, instead of landing on the plank, he mistimed the roll of the tug. There was:

a gasp of horror from all spectators as he landed on the forward end of the plank which acted like a spring-board, flicked Gus up into the air above the spectators then, spinning like a top with arms and legs out-stretched, he fell between the two vessels. Down he went into the ocean and the two craft bumped together and, as the tug bounced off the Duchess, Gus bobbed up like a cork and in a flash Prout and the African crew, with the aid of a boat-hook, had him out of the sea and on board the tug, shaken and bruised, but protesting that he was not hurt.[7]

March-Phillipps now left Appleyard in charge aboard *Duchessa d'Aosta* and, under overcast skies, *Vulcan* slipped her tow and reversed course 15 miles to chase up *Nuneaton* and her two wallowing charges. They found *Nuneaton* dead in the water, her engine stopped. Graham Hayes felt she was in danger of drifting back towards Fernando Po, still visible on the eastern horizon. He asked for a tow up to the rendezvous with HMS *Violet*. As Leonard Guise remembered, his request fell on deaf ears: 'At 3pm Vulcan came over the skyline and, after what seemed like a somewhat meaningless exchange of courtesies, pushed off again.' Afraid of missing the drifting, powerless *Duchessa* in the soon-to-be gathering darkness, after what experience had shown would be a slow and lengthy operation, March-Phillipps handed over food and water, told Hayes he would send HMS *Violet* back to support *Nuneaton* as soon as she arrived and then headed back once more towards *Duchessa*. Whereupon: 'a slightly sour Nuneaton sadly saw Vulcan disappear into the sunset.'[8]

Approaching the *Duchessa* once more, March-Phillipps flew into one of his characteristic rages. In his absence the high-spirited cutting-out crew had nailed a Jolly Roger to the masthead: 'When the skipper came back we all got a rocket and we were told we weren't to fly the Jolly Roger with a red duster and so we hauled it down immediately. He was a great stickler for etiquette, old Gus', remembered Leonard Guise.[9]

Vulcan would not make contact with HMS *Violet* until Sunday, 18 January. The 11-month-old corvette would be three days late for her important rendezvous and her excuse for such tardiness would be as embarrassing as her timekeeping: HMS *Violet*,[10] Pennant K35, (Temporary) Lt Frank Reynolds RCVR Commanding, had run aground in the mouth of the Niger. In the event, she would not be refloated until the morning of 19 January.[11]

Embarrassment aboard HMS *Violet*, certainly. A range of different emotions, however, on the island of Fernando Po as dawn the morning after *Postmaster* revealed a harbour curiously empty of shipping. For 18 months the dark hull and white superstructure of Italy's *Duchessa d'Aosta* had dominated the small, horseshoe-shaped volcanic bay. According to Vice Consul Michie, the morning after the raid many Spaniards showed open amusement and admiration for the manner in which both ships had been whisked away from under the noses of their party-going officers. German shipping agent Heinrich Luhr was reported to have said that, if Germans had been responsible for the taking of *Duchessa d'Aosta*, each man would receive the Iron Cross.[12] There was suspicion of British involvement certainly – but, critically, no evidence. That first morning rumour was king around Santa Isabel harbour with the Free French, Vichy France, America and Britain 'all equally possible culprits', especially after the convenient discovery of Free French caps floating in the harbour.[13]

The night before, Michie had made sure he had a grandstand view of the unfolding excitement as Operation *Postmaster* swung into play. He and another Briton, SOE agent B. Godden (W51), the Deputy Consul on the mainland, were in the Consulate looking down onto the harbour from the centre of the horseshoe:

> At 11.33 we could discern the noise of the tug's engines: then silence. Soon we saw torches being flashed on the deck of the DA. We heard what sounded like a challenge in Italian, followed by a gruff 'Keep 'em up.' At about 11.30 two lovely bangs which woke Sta [sic] Isabel up and incidentally brought the Collinson's dining room glass candelabra down ... Two more bangs and then a few cars appeared ... Then we heard very plainly from the DA 'we are laying another charge' in an ultra Mayfair or West-End accent. Nobody appears to have heard this as far as we know yet. The other charge went off with a terrific detonation. Just before midnight we saw DA glide out of the harbour. Down in the square, trying to look dazed, we asked passers-by what was happening. Nobody had the remotest idea ... Spaniards and Africans alike were highly amused by the incident to judge by the laughter and excited chattering that came from the Plaza below.[14]

Anticipating a vigorous German anti-British reaction to the cutting-out operation, Michie and his colleagues had wisely destroyed every scrap of incriminating paperwork long before *Vulcan* slid alongside *Duchessa d'Aosta*. It was just as well. The German shipping agent Heinrich Luhr may have felt that those responsible for the raid deserved Iron Crosses, but then it had not been his command that had been stolen, his pride that had been dented. The Captain of the *Likomba*, Herr Specht, took a different view. He had been one of the guests being lavishly distracted in the Casino restaurant while his boat was being seized. Now, although clearly very drunk, he had no doubts at all who was responsible, or that he had been duped. Rushing round to the British Consulate, he broke down the door:[15]

> Specht was very drunk and very quarrelsome. He was told to get out. In reply he struck me in the face which gave W51 (Godden) and myself the excuse we wanted. Between us we knocked the stuffing out of him. My steward boy then handed the dilapidated Specht over to the Police.[16]

On 16 January Godden cabled London:

(1) No official reaction yet … As far as we can ascertain nothing tangible revealed.

(2) General impression seems satisfaction departure these vessels and recognition of efficient operation which was complete surprise.

(3) Many now say W25 [Lippet] and J [sic] am fully aware of operations but I do not regard too seriously as many wild rumours current.

(4) Captain German launch entered consulate 0130 hours 15th lubricated started fight was ejected then arrested. We have Police protection day and night. Behaviour Chief Police friendly helpful.[17]

Word of the successful cutting-out operation in Santa Isabel harbour spread like wildfire. By 17 January Sir Samuel Hoare, British Ambassador in Madrid charged specifically with keeping Spain out of the war, was reporting back to London his receipt of an inaccurate account of Operation *Postmaster* which the Spanish would later refer to as 'an incident of exceptional gravity':[18]

Arriba publishes today a leading article voicing a violent protest alleging action of a Free French destroyer in entering the harbour of Santa Isabel Fernando Po and seizing three 'enemy' merchant vessels which they 'towed out of harbour' after 'dropping depth charges in order to break moorings and killing crew'. 2. Use is being made of this alleged incident in order to stir up feeling against Great Britain as ultimately responsible. I should be glad to know if there is any truth in it.[19]

The Foreign Office replied to their man in Madrid on 20 January:

For your own information, although no British or allied warship was concerned, operation was carried out by SOE with our approval. Every precaution has been taken and it seems reasonably certain that no evidence can be traced to our participation in the affair. One of the ships concerned carries an extremely valuable cargo and is herself a valuable modern liner … Please burn this telegram after perusal.[20]

That same afternoon HMS *Violet* finally closed with *Duchessa d'Aosta*. She had been ordered to sea with a prize crew, ostensibly to bring back another vessel. Once at sea her captain had opened sealed orders which detailed the true reason for their mission.[21] At 1500 *Vulcan* spotted HMS *Violet* steaming up towards their starboard beam. Her Captain, Tom Coker, remembered: 'A shot was fired across our bow at the same time a string of bunting was hauled aloft. Identified as "STOP. HEAVE TO.

DO NOT ATTEMPT TO ABANDON OR SCUTTLE YOUR SHIP." This caused quite a laugh between us.'[22] HMS *Violet* came alongside *Duchessa d'Aosta* and sent aboard a young sub lieutenant and a boarding party of four ratings armed with rifles. Security on board HMS *Violet*, evidently, had been watertight. After a ludicrous exchange between the autocratic Capt. March-Phillipps and the junior naval officer who had not the slightest idea with whom he was dealing, the young sub lieutenant signalled back to his Captain aboard HMS *Violet*: 'Captain of the Italian ship wishes to speak to the Captain of Violet. Italian Captain speaks good English.'[23] Quite so: March-Phillipps had actually written books on the subject. He crossed to *Violet*'s bridge and presently the situation was made clear.

All resolved, the vessels got under way once more and presently *Duchessa d'Aosta* made her triumphant way into Lagos harbour, surrounded by a swirl of immaculate Royal Navy motor launches sent out to escort her in. She arrived at 1800 on Wednesday, 21 January. *Nuneaton* and *Likomba* had made the safety of Lagos port two hours earlier. Plagued by continued troubles with her engines, *Nuneaton* had been hailed by a passing vessel the day before. It transpired the captain of *Nuneaton* knew the master of SS *Ajassa*, who promptly offered a tow to the tug and her charges. Once approaching the harbour:

> We had a tremendous reception. The old General himself [Giffard], who was against us, came down and looked upon us as his chaps having pulled off a successful operation and we got all sorts of telegrams from the Cabinet and from the Foreign Office and so forth, congratulatory, and then, of course, the jitters set in on the part of the authority. They thought 'My God, what have we done in a neutral harbour?' and we were all dispersed to the far corners of the earth.[24]

The safe arrival of all three prize vessels in Lagos was topped off in fitting style by His Excellency, the ever-supportive Governor Sir Bernard Bourdillon, who stood at the end of his private landing stage with many of the SOE home team, cheering loudly, whisky and soda in hand.[25] It was a stylish finale to a skilfully executed and audacious piece of piracy. Major Victor Laversuch's signalled London:

LAGOS.
FROM W4 [Laversuch] FOR C.D. [Gubbins]: 22.1.42
MOST SECRET DECYPHER YOURSELF.
1. ALL POST MASTERS ARRIVED HERE 2000 TODAY.
2. CASUALTIES OUR PARTY ABSOLUTELY NIL.

3. CASUALTIES ENEMY NIL WITH THE EXCEPTION OF A FEW SORE HEADS.
4. PRISONERS GERMANS NIL. ITALIANS MEN 27, WOMAN 1, NATIVES 1. ALL LEAVING TOMORROW NIGHT FOR INTERNMENT CAMP 150 MILES IN INTERIOR AND WILL BE KEPT ENTIRELY SEPARATED FROM OTHER INTERNEES.
5. OUR PARTY ALL WELL AND COLONIAL GOVERNMENT VOLUNTEERS BEING DISPERSED TO THEIR RESPECTIVE POSTS TOMORROW UNDER COMPLETE SEAL OF SECRECY.[26]

This triggered a fusillade of congratulatory responses including one from Brigadier Colin Gubbins himself:

To W4 FROM CD:
SO [Hugh Dalton] AND ALL RANKS HERE SEND BEST CONGRATULATIONS TO ALL CONCERNED ON COMPLETE SUCCESS OF A WELL THOUGHT-OUT CAREFULLY PLANNED AND NEATLY EXECUTED OPERATION.

'Caesar' followed up his telegram of congratulations with this letter from London dated 21 January:

The extent of our satisfaction and pleasure at the success of this jolly little venture will have been clear to you from the telegram which was sent to you by me and W Section yesterday, and I should just like to add that everybody at London HQ from the Chief right down to the messenger is frightfully pleased and proud of this marked SOE success.[27]

From Lagos, Major Laversuch forwarded to Brigadier Gubbins one particular telegram which must have touched a particularly pleasant chord with the triumphant raiders. It was from that old obstructionist, General George Giffard:

DEAR W4.
FOR REASONS WHICH I WAS UNABLE TO EXPLAIN TO YOU I FELT I HAD TO OPPOSE YOUR PROJECT. IT DOES NOT LESSEN MY ADMIRATION FOR SKILLED?[28] DARING AND SUCCESS WITH WHICH YOU HAVE SUCCEEDED. I SEND YOU ALL MY HEARTY CONGRATULATIONS AND HOPE IN THE EVENT OF SIMILAR PROJECTS IN FUTURE, CIRCUMSTANCES MAY PERMIT ME TO ASSIST AND NOT OPPOSE.

YOURS SINCERELY
GIFFARD[29]

Not all telegrams to do with Britain's flagrant breach of Spanish neutrality on Fernando Po were quite so warm or conciliatory. The British Ambassador in Madrid, Sir Samuel Hoare, the former War Cabinet's Lord Privy Seal and the man sent to Madrid by Churchill expressly to keep Spain out of the war, was still busy fielding irate diplomatic communiqués. Earlier the Admiralty had eased matters a little – but not by much – when they issued a communiqué of their own, stating that one of their patrols had simply happened to intercept *Duchessa d'Aosta* and the tug *Likomba* off the west coast of Africa and that 'it appears that these ships were endeavouring to reach the Vichy port of Contonu to take on sufficient fuel to enable them to continue their voyage to a port in German-occupied France.'[30]

By the middle of February, Sir Samuel Hoare was able to send the Spanish authorities his government's measured response to the very *suggestion* that Britain might have been in any way involved in the seizure of Axis shipping from within a neutral Spanish port. After the usual hollow pleasantries, during which Sir Samuel emphasised that he was writing on the instructions of Foreign Secretary Anthony Eden, he continued:

> His Majesty's Government in the United Kingdom have had under consideration the Spanish Government's communication regarding certain events which are alleged to have taken place in the harbour of Santa Isabel in the island of Fernando Po on the 14th January, before the interception of the Italian vessel *Duchessa d'Aosta* by His Majesty's Ships.
>
> His Majesty's Government's action in connection with this vessel was confined to operations of British Naval and Air Forces reported in two communiqués issued by the Admiralty ... These communiqués, copies of which for convenience are enclosed herein, clearly show that it was owing to the information obtained from the German broadcasts that the British Commander-in-Chief in the area concerned despatched five patrols to cover the area in question. As a result the Italian vessel *Duchessa d'Aosta* was intercepted, captured, and sent into a British port together with the two minor enemy vessels.
>
> In these circumstances His Majesty's Government cannot accept any protest of the Spanish Government in regard to this incident. They feel indeed compelled to express their surprise that the Spanish Government should so readily have assumed that His Majesty's Government were concerned with any events which may have taken place in Santa Isabel or on the *Duchessa d'Aosta* prior to the vessel's departure from the harbour ...

His Majesty's Government, *being in no way responsible for what happened prior to the capture of the enemy vessels on the high seas* [author's
italics], are not in a position to provide an explanation of the events that
have occurred in the harbour of Santa Isabel ...

In all the circumstances His Majesty's Government do not perceive any
grounds on which they could be called upon to take steps to restore an
enemy vessel which was captured on the high seas in accordance with the
accepted rights of belligerents.[31]

The Rt Hon. Anthony Eden, His Majesty's Secretary of State for Foreign
Affairs, was lying through his teeth.

Medals, Marjorie and Marriage

Yet *still* word could get out, the story leak. With the Italian prisoners moved to a remote inland internment camp and colonial government volunteers scattered back to their different stations, it was only the original Maid Honor Force that now remained to be dispersed far away from Lagos and the scene of their illegal triumph of violated neutrality. March-Phillipps and Appleyard were ordered back to England: both were needed urgently for the debriefing and caught the first available passenger liner back to England. The others were permitted to take a more leisurely route home. Lassen and a handful of others stayed in Nigeria, others headed south to Cape Town for a fortnight's leave before – eventually – returning home to England. *Maid Honor* herself, Blake Glanville's pride and joy that had carried them all safely from Poole to Africa but not onto the raid itself, was abandoned with regret in West Africa. Stripped of her 'Q' ship armament and surprises, *Maid Honor* was sold on in Lagos and ended her days as a simple fishing smack working out of Freetown, Sierra Leone, her un-sheathed bottom-planking riddled with teredo worm. Her bones lie there still.[1]

Before *Duchessa d'Aosta* set out for England she was thoroughly examined, her cargo meticulously inventoried. One of the justifications for her seizure had been the possibility that she too was a 'Q' ship and that her radio was being used to pass information which might harm British interests. The fear proved groundless. A Most Secret signal sent to the Admiralty flatly stated: 'No evidence yet found of vessel having given assistance to the enemy. No W/T message sent since Italy entered the war transmitter sealed. This is confirmed by W/T Operator and feel confident is the truth.'[2] Now, with Maid Honor Force dispersed and on the way home, it hardly mattered. What *did* matter, however, was the fact that, at a time when SOE in London was under great pressure to produce results to reassure Churchill and its many critics that SOE was, indeed, a force of real worth manned by competent, courageous officers, March-Phillipps and his men had stepped up to the mark. The success of Operation *Postmaster*, as SOE's first historian recorded after the war, was simply 'manna in the desert to SOE in its early lean years'.[3]

Hugh Dalton, SOE's chairman, describing *Postmaster* as a 'good show',[4] lost no time in writing to Churchill, the prime minister he admired but who disliked him, enclosing in a three-page letter not simply a full account of the raid and its potential political repercussions but generous thanks to the other agencies – excluding General Giffard – who had assisted SOE along the way. He too was in the business of building bridges:

> I should like to express my high appreciation of the attitude of the Foreign Secretary in allowing the operation to proceed in spite of the political risks involved, and my gratitude to the Admiralty and to the Governor of Nigeria for their invaluable assistance. Great credit, I think, also attaches to SOE West Africa, who planned the operation in minute detail and successfully carried it out.[5]

In time, there would be medals: a Distinguished Service Order for Gus March-Phillipps for his leadership of an operation of 'a most delicate and difficult nature', during which he displayed 'military qualities of a very high order'. He was also promoted to Major.[6]

Appleyard, as already stated, received his second Military Cross for leading the explosives' party aboard *Duchessa* and for carrying out the setting and firing of explosive charges 'with complete disregard of his own personal safety'. His childhood friend from the same village, Graham Hayes, the man whose after-action report heaps praise upon everyone but himself, also received the Military Cross for leading the attack on *Likomba* and for fighting another endless battle – that with the troublesome tug *Nuneaton*. He too was promoted, from Lieutenant to Captain.

Anders Lassen got his commission: 'Put your pips up, Andy', ordered March-Phillipps. Lassen did so, by-passing all the recognised channels of selection and officer training. His commission as Second Lieutenant was confirmed later that May.[7]

SOE's men in West Africa were also remembered in December 1942, with Guise and Lippett being awarded the MBE and Laversuch, Michie and *Vulcan* tugmaster Thomas Coker receiving the OBE. *Nuneaton*'s Captain, H.M. Goodman, received a much-deserved MBE. Brigadier Colin Gubbins pushed the additional awards to his civilians through the Colonial Office. 'They would be informed officially through the Colonial Office but if Laversuch could do so without endangering security he should congratulate them heartily from SOE. Laversuch replied that he could do this without endangering security and added that the awards had greatly pleased the Governor.'[8]

With March-Phillipps and Appleyard on the way home it was left to Lt Col Julius Hanau, SOE's 'Caesar' and Gubbins' West Africa deputy, to reflect upon the real success and lessons to be learned that had been left bobbing in the wake of Operation *Postmaster*:

> The operation not only achieved more than its material object, but it achieved it in such a way that the task of the Foreign Office and the Admiralty in meeting the political and legal aftermath has been reduced to a minimum.
>
> We hope that SOE will be permitted to demonstrate that what was possible in Fernando Po is possible elsewhere: perhaps on the next occasion, it will not be found necessary to preface twenty-five minutes compact and decisive action by over four months of prolonged and desultory negotiation.[9]

Touché.

Burned the colour of teak by the African sun, March-Phillipps and Appleyard returned to a drab, rationed, stone-cold England in early February 1942. They were debriefed by Gubbins personally on Thursday 12 February and Monday 16 February. Much time had been spent on the journey home discussing plans to expand Maid Honor Force into something larger, harder hitting, more substantial. March-Phillipps took their ideas to Brigadier Gubbins, a man now favourably disposed to listen to his newly decorated champions.

March-Phillipps planned the creation of a small scale raiding force of 50–100 men equipped with a couple of motor launches and a few 'Goatley' assault boats. The task of these raiders would be to slip across the Channel at night by gunboat, kill sentries, seize prisoners,[10] lift documents to order and steal interesting bits of German military kit for the other fighting services. Above all, his idea was to broaden the base of front-line experience for selected personnel, tie German troops to the coast and generally undermine any German sense of shoreline invulnerability. His idea for a lightweight strike force independent of the cumbrous complexities of higher-echelon planning or air support received, we are told, 'immediate support'[11] from Combined Operations and went forward over the next month to the Chiefs of Staff for their rubber-stamping of the creation of yet another small 'private army'. Other accounts suggest the idea was Mountbatten's own,[12] but the original idea of what would shortly become known as the Small Scale Raiding Force came, almost certainly, from the newly promoted and decorated men of Operation

Postmaster. Those other accounts suggest Lord Louis Mountbatten, the newly appointed Chief of Combined Operations, approached the Chiefs of Staff himself on 19 February with what *he* thought was an interesting idea: to form a permanent group of fifty men as an 'amphibious sabotage force' who would, naturally, operate under his command.[13] The Men of Maid Honor Force, he considered, would be ideal.

But Maid Honor Force came under SOE, not Combined Operations. A certain amount of negotiation took place, after which it was decided that the new force, while still administered and financed by SOE, would come under Mountbatten's operational control. As mentioned, it would be known as the Small Scale Raiding Force and would operate under the cover name of No 62 Commando or, to SOE, 'Station 62'. It was all part of Mountbatten's 'new broom'. Under Admiral Keyes there had been no centralised European raiding system: raids on the enemy shore were the responsibility of the army commander-in-chief defending the English territory opposite, with the Channel itself seen as a sort of First World War no-man's-land. The poorly thought-out theory was that the army would obtain the assault boats they needed for each raid through the local naval commander-in-chief who, in turn, would ask for the boats from Combined Operations. It didn't work. Now, with Mountbatten at the helm of a newly centralised, reinvigorated system, raids across the Channel became more numerous.

As his proposal worked its way swiftly through the various layers of Higher Command within SOE, Combined Operations and the Chiefs of Staff, there was now another distraction that took March-Phillipps' eye off the dangerous business of planning to raid the enemy coastline. Her name was Marjorie Stewart.

One evening at SOE Headquarters in Baker Street, a discreet little party was held to welcome home the *Maid Honor* heroes of Fernando Po. One of those invited to attend to add glamour to drab khaki was SOE agent-in-training Marjorie Stewart, an attractive actress who had volunteered for SOE the year before. About to go away on parachute training to Ringway, she had met Gus earlier in the day – in the Baker Street lift in Norgeby House on her way to her desk at the Polish and Czech Section of SOE. When he asked her later what she did she replied she was the lift girl. Baker Street, after all, was a house of duplicity and many secrets:

> I had no idea who this rather eccentric but highly characterful and bright-coloured figure I met was ... He was very brown, very sunburned and he had high colour and the whites of his eyes were startlingly blue ... and although he was dressed in a uniform which is khaki, he had britches and rather beautiful boots and a bush hat and the boots naturally were beautiful

leather because he always made a great fuss about having his boots made at Maxwell and so they were beautiful horse-chestnut, wonderful colour ... In the evening I was going to a party and Gus's sister Diana had come into our office and said they were having a party for the Maid Honor people and would I go ... I'd heard about it because everybody was talking about Maid Honor when I first joined SOE and I didn't understand what they were talking about for a long time because I thought it was *May Donna*, and then I eventually saw papers about it and realised it was *Maid Honor* and I'd heard about it and I'd read the report ... and it was an interest and an excitement to everybody that they'd done very well and they were coming safely back ... and then we went on to the party for the Maid Honor people at Nell Gwynn house and I arrived rather late with Alfgar [her escort] and Gus [said] almost immediately: 'Are you married to that man?' And I said no I wasn't ... He said 'I've seen you before' and I said: 'Yes, indeed you have. I took you up in the lift this morning. I work the lift at 74 Baker Street.' He believed for quite a long time that I *was* the lift girl. And it was a very splendid party and very chatty then we went on to dinner at the Gargoyle and I remember dancing with Gus ... Yes, I liked him. He was a very attractive personality to meet: good looking and quick and I suppose he did stammer although I didn't notice his stammer for ages ... it was sort of inevitable. I'm trying to think what happened then ... Oh, yes: he asked me to go and have dinner with him so we went and had dinner at the *Ecu de France*. And I can remember – again, one always does – exactly what I wore and it was a very nice dress and I thought I looked splendid and so fortunately did he! But, anyway, we went and had this splendid dinner at which he asked me to marry him. So I said that was ridiculous and he didn't know anything about it. That I think was the third time we met.[14]

Impatient as always, March-Phillipps was in no mood to take prisoners. He launched his unremitting amorous assault from within the offices of SOE Headquarters: 'There was also an occasional visitor', remembered SOE agent Patrick Howarth:

a tall man with a sun-tanned complexion, a stammer and a generally distinguished appearance of the kind most readily described as soldierly. This was Major Gus March-Phillipps. It soon became apparent that his visits were mainly for the purpose of seeing Marjorie Stewart, and I began to feel my presence was something of an embarrassment to them. In this I was right.[15]

'He was a man of quick decisions, certainly', Marjorie remembered:

And we chatted and had a splendid time and that was all very enjoyable and very nice and very exciting and I suppose he wanted probably to find someone to be attached to and I always felt the whole thing was completely inevitable ... it literally just happened. I can remember saying, rather pompously, perhaps: 'Oh, you don't mean you want to marry me, all you mean is I'm an attractive young woman. You've come back from a wearing time that's gone very well ... all you want to do is go to bed with me.' 'Not at all, not at all, shouldn't dream of it. Sharn't until I've married you.'[16]

For all, it was a time of sudden passions, of whirlwind courtships and quick marriage in which each day might be the last. Thirty years on, and the memories remain undiminished:

I saw a lot of him for a few days. You have to remember that, in a war, everything was speeded up ... He came with me to look at Aldford Street, my cousin's house where I was going to go and live and we had the most wonderful Saturday afternoon. *Piercing* cold it was at that time – bitter, bitter – and we had a lovely look at this shut-up empty house with gleams of very cold wintry sun coming in and he was enchanted by the house which was a very pretty one where you [Henrietta March-Phillipps] were born ... and then we went for a lovely walk in St James's Park. He certainly didn't mind breaking rules. The lake was frozen, so we just didn't see the notice saying nobody was to go on the ice and had the most exciting, lovely walk round the island in the lake. But it was thick ice and we walked across the ice rather rapidly not to get caught by stray keepers and had a wonderful exploring walk round the little island in the lake. It was a *heavenly* afternoon altogether.[17]

Gus and Marjorie were married on 18 April 1942 at the church of Our Lady of the Assumption, Warwick Street, London W1. The reception was held afterwards at the house they had visited that cold February afternoon at 2, Aldford Street, London W1. Colin Gubbins' private diary recorded simply: 'Marjorie and Gus. 2 o'clock.'

†††

Although March-Phillipps' plans for a significantly expanded Maid Honor Force had still to be ratified by the Chiefs of Staff, it appeared from an early stage that approval would be something of a formality. Accordingly – and with Gubbins' support – March-Phillipps and Appleyard set out from London to find a suitable base for their secret new raiding force.

They headed first of all back to the Antelope Hotel in Poole harbour, scene of their departure to West Africa and Operation *Postmaster* six months ago. It seemed like a lifetime: 'We stayed in Poole at the old Antelope Hotel which was our shore HQ last summer' wrote Appleyard. 'They gave us a great welcome.'[18] Landlord Arthur 'Pop' Baker, it seems, remembered his friends. From there they set out to explore the local countryside. March-Phillipps already knew much of it well: he had lived at Bere Regis, just a few miles away, before the war when he had been making a living as a novelist. Luck, providence or local contacts led him now to a sixteenth-century manor house.

Anderson Manor

Anderson Manor nestles in rich, rolling Dorset farmland in a fold of land slightly north of the main road between Bere Regis to the south-west and Sturminster Marshall to the east. It is approximately 10 miles north-west of Poole Harbour and within rumbling lorry journey of Portland, Poole and Gosport, the likely ports of embarkation for the raids March-Phillipps and Appleyard hoped would soon follow. Privately owned, Anderson Manor is an imposing, Grade 1 Listed building dating back to 1622. It is a quadrangular, brick-built house with stone dressings and quoins, seven large rooms and a huge, walk-in arched fireplace in what was once the original kitchen. The main house of three stories has a symmetrical front with projecting gable wings at each end, and the roof is topped by two groups of four tall, octagonal-shaped brick chimneys, one for each of the master rooms below. Several floors boast mullioned and transomed windows with lead lights. Served by a wide staircase and gleaming wooden panelling up to the echoing, oak-floored bedrooms above, the property also supports a range of out-buildings, kitchen gardens and ancient walled flower beds. There is even a moat that dries out in summer, fed by the Winterborne River running across the front of the property. The main entrance has a heavy oak, iron-studded door with ancient inset spy-hole. There are formal gardens and even a private place of worship, the twelfth-century St Michael's Chapel and family graveyard on the edge of the Manor's grounds.

Tucked away from prying eyes at the end of an arrow-straight, tree-flanked driveway, March-Phillipps and Appleyard saw immediately that Anderson Manor would make an ideal headquarters for SOE's No 62 Commando. Possessing neither running water nor electricity, the Manor reeked of history and the precious jewel that was the England March-Phillipps and his men felt they were fighting for. Better yet, Gus realised he had a slight acquaintance with the owner, Major Cholmondeley. Negotiations followed, reassurances were given about troops' respect

Shining youth: Geoffrey Appleyard as a pre-war schoolboy with the world at his feet. (Appleyard family)

Freshly minted: Geoffrey Appleyard as a newly commissioned second lieutenant in the RASC, 1939. (Appleyard family)

Captain Geoffrey Appleyard MC, photographed in the garden of the Manor House, Linton-on-Wharfe, 1942. (Appleyard family)

Country seat: Manor House, Linton. Home as Geoffrey Appleyard knew it. (Appleyard family)

Captain Gustavus March-Phillipps in Gunners' (RA) uniform. A pose he adopted, he claimed, to frighten the Germans! It was March-Phillipps' drive, inspiration and fervent patriotism that led to the formation of both Maid Honor and the Small Scale Raiding Force. (The National Archives)

Graham Hayes with family. Graham, aged 14, is fourth from left with his arm around younger brother Malcolm's shoulders. (Malcolm Hayes)

Kiln Hill, Linton. Graham Hayes' family home a few hundred yards uphill from that of his childhood friend, Geoffrey Appleyard. (Annabel Grace Hayes)

Graham Hayes and 'Grip', his tame jackdaw. (Annabel Grace Hayes)

The Hayes brothers, from left to right: Malcolm, Denis, Graham (with dog) and Austin. Malcolm, a Halifax bomber pilot with 295 Squadron, was killed over France in February 1943. (Malcolm Hayes)

Wetherby Rugby Club, 1932–33. Graham Hayes is in the back row, third from right. (Annabel Grace Hayes)

The crew of *Pommern*. Graham Hayes is in the back row, third from right. (Malcolm Hayes)

Tall ships and furled sails. Picture taken by Graham Hayes from the stern of *Pommern*. (Annabel Grace Hayes)

Graham Hayes as SSRF knew him. (Appleyard family)

Men of 7 Commando working on *I'm Alone* at low tide, Isle of Arran. Gus March-Phillipps (?) before mast, Geoffrey Appleyard (?) ashore beside boat's leg. (Maggie Higham)

The Antelope Inn, Poole, Dorset. First Headquarters of Maid Honor force and scene of early planning and celebration dinners. (Author's collection)

Maid Honor at sea. Geoffrey Appleyard in swimming trunks. Gus March-Phillipps bending forward astern. (Appleyard family)

The Brixham fishing ketch *Maid Honor*. Built in 1925 and 70 feet long, she was requisitioned by March-Phillipps in 1941 and converted to a 'Q' ship. Intended to lure German ships to their doom in the English Channel, she ended her days on the African coast. (Lt Col David Owen MBE; artist: John Turk of Brixton)

The Arne Peninsula, Poole harbour, where *Maid Honor* was moored and the early volunteers for what became the Maid Honor force lived aboard ship. Today's SBS base at Hamworthy lies on the far shore. (Author's collection)

St Nicholas Chapel, Arne, where Geoffrey Appleyard and crewmen came to pray. (Author's collection)

Clandestine photograph taken of *Duchessa d'Aosta*, Fernando Po. (The National Archives)

Marjorie, from her portfolio

Marjorie Stewart. The strong-willed West End actress who went on to train as an SOE agent. When they met at SOE in Baker Street, she led Gus March-Phillipps to believe she was the lift girl. She did her early SOE parachute training unaware she was pregnant with Gus March-Phillipps' daughter, Henrietta. (March-Phillipps family)

Marjorie Stewart on the day of her wedding to Gus March-Phillipps, 18 April 1942, with her younger brother David. Brigadier Colin Gubbins, SOE's Director of Training and Operations, attended the wedding. (March-Phillipps family)

Anderson Manor, Dorset. Home and secret headquarters to the select band of men who formed 62 Commando – the Small Scale Raiding Force. (Author's collection)

St Michael's Chapel at Anderson where Tony Hall and Gus March-Phillipps sought strength before Operation *Aquatint*. (Author's collection)

Lt Freddie Bourne. A frequent visitor at Anderson Manor, Bourne took part in seventeen operations with SSRF for which he was awarded the DSC. Skipper of MTB 344 on the ill-fated Operation *Aquatint* to what was to become *Omaha* beach on the Normandy coast. (Chris Rooney)

MTB 344 at speed off Beach Head, Sussex. Also known as *The Little Pisser* because of her small size and turn of speed, MTB 344 was the carrier of choice for the men of SSRF on their raids across the Channel. (Chris Rooney)

Dory training for the men of SSRF on the Dorset coast. Graham Hayes is at far left. (Chris Rooney)

Dawn, Omaha beach, Normandy. The French plaque to Operation *Aquatint* is on the sea wall in the foreground and marks the place where Gus March-Phillipps and his men are believed to have come ashore. Then there were no flags, no sea wall, no beach-set monument to American D-Day casualties – just the same vast, empty beach offering nowhere to hide. And an alert, waiting enemy. (Author's collection)

The French plaque to Operation *Aquatint* overlooked by the vast majority of visitors to 'Bloody Omaha'. (Author's collection)

The grave of Major Gus March-Phillipps in the village cemetery at Saint-Laurent-sur-Mer, flanked by the men who died with him: Private Richard Lehniger (left, serving as Private Leonard) and Serjeant Alan Williams (right). In the foreground, incised in marble, is Gus March-Phillipps' poem 'If I Must Die …' (Author's collection)

British war graves in the Cimetière Communal de Viroflay on the outskirts of Paris. Most of the British war dead were RAF bomber crew. Captain Graham Hayes' grave is nearest camera. (Author's collection)

The grave of Captain Graham Hayes MC, at Viroflay. The freshly watered single rose was taken from his mother's grave nearby and offered by a Frenchman after he was told Graham's story of evasion, betrayal and execution. (Author's collection)

Patrick Dudgeon, St Anthony's House, Oundle School, 1938. Patrick is third from right, second row. (Steven Forge, Oundle School)

Captain Oswald 'Mickey' Rooney of 12 Commando, pictured here in service dress. He was seconded to SSRF after the disaster of Operation *Aquatint*. (Chris Rooney)

Night ops: MTB 344 at work close inshore, Brittany. (Appleyard family)

Working rig. Captain Rooney, left, that 'powerfully built, self-confident officer who knew his men intimately and commanded their implicit obedience'. A good man to have on your rope. Note the commando dagger slung beneath his throat. To his left, training on Beachy Head, is J. Barry. (Chris Rooney)

Inset: Sgt James Edgar, 1945. (James Edgar)

Pointe de Plouézec, Brittany. The ascent to Operation *Fahrenheit*. (Chris Rooney)

James Edgar in 2007. (James Edgar)   Horace 'Stokey' Stokes. (Peter Stokes)

Geoffrey Appleyard's medals. Reading from left to right: DSO (Distinguished Service Order), MC (Military Cross) and Bar, 1939–45 Star, Atlantic Star, Africa Star, Italy Star and 1939–45 War Medal. (Lt Col David Owen MBE, Royal Corps of Transport Medal Collection, Surrey)

Linton Memorial Hall, near Wetherby, Yorkshire. (Author's collection)

The memorial in Linton Memorial Hall, made with the oak laid down by Graham Hayes. A skilled wood carver and cabinet-maker, he planned to work on this after the war. Here are inscribed the names of Linton's fallen including Geoffrey Appleyard, Malcolm Hayes – and Graham Hayes himself. (Author's collection)

Closing moves. J.E.A. and Geoffrey Appleyard playing chess together in the Manor House, Linton-on-Wharfe, Christmas 1942. It was the last time father and son were to enjoy such times together. In July 1943 Geoffrey would be posted Missing, Presumed Killed in Action. (Appleyard family)

for private property and, after protective boarding was tacked over the ancient oak panelling, a generator was installed to provide lighting, a pump was set up to provide water from the well and Anderson Manor was as ready as it would ever be for this latest invasion of heavily armed troops. Appleyard remembered their first visit:

> During the Friday's house hunting we located an eminently suitable and magnificent house about seven miles from Wareham and ten from Poole. It is a large and very beautiful Elizabethan house and is in every way ideal for our purpose ... The house is very much in the country, in a training area and with beautiful gardens. The head gardener is staying on and in our waiting times of which, I suppose, there are bound to be a great deal, we shall, when not training, give a hand in the grounds and gardens. The house, after the owners go, will be almost fully furnished ... Dorsetshire was looking lovely – a really spring-like day. In the woods we found primroses and lovely scented purple violets, and the gardens were full of crocuses.[1]

That same day – 21 March – March-Phillipps sent a secret signal to Brigadier Gubbins urging him to give him the authority and financial sanction to press ahead, and reviewing progress to date.[2] All was moving ahead most satisfactorily: the Chiefs of Staff had by then authorised the creation of a special raiding force under joint SOE and Combined Operations control.

SOE's role would be to provide the men for the raiding parties themselves, some 40 per cent of whom would be foreign nationals whose secondment would also provide a ready pool for Combined Operations to draw on for other missions without breaching security by having to approach governments-in-exile directly for their loan. SOE would be responsible for providing the operational and training base (Anderson Manor), its administrative staff and transport and whatever specialised low-profile approach craft the unit might need. SOE was also to be responsible for providing arms, ammunition, explosives and what were euphemistically referred to as 'special stores':

> Combined Operations were to provide two Motor Launches, their crews, maintenance and the equipment that would carry the raiding force off-shore to their target area. Actual operations and target selection would be controlled not by SOE, but by Combined Operations. It was a plan, evidently, that had Gus March-Phillipps' approval. He urged Brigadier Gubbins: 'This whole project undertaken by us in conjunction with Combined Operations is of major importance and it is incumbent upon us to put everything we

know into it. Undoubtedly the Chief of Combined Operations [Lord Mountbatten] will take the greatest personal interest in it and also the Chiefs of Staff. We must, therefore, make every effort to get our part of the bargain carried out by the agreed date.'[3]

Anderson Manor was ready for occupancy in late April. The old team reassembled as the men of Maid Honor Force, scattered to the four winds for security reasons on the heels of Operation *Postmaster*, gradually filtered back to Dorset, where they were reunited with friends whose trust had been earned on live operations. Initially there would be about thirty men under training living at Anderson Manor: 'nearly all officers', observed Appleyard. The high proportion of officers was deliberate policy by March-Phillipps, who wanted to have to hand the nucleus for rapid expansion: he planned to double his force from 50 to 100 within three months. Among these early arrivals were Anders Lassen and André Desgrange, both of whom had found themselves seconded briefly after *Postmaster* to the SOE mission's training school in Lagos.[4] March-Phillipps himself lost no time in settling in, writing back to his soon-to-be wife in London:

This is the first letter I have written to you, so it's rather a great event. I wonder if it's a record. Apple thinks it is. I wish you were here. It's really a marvellous place, and the weather is perfect. Every morning I ride out through woods full of primroses and bluebells and violets with the dew still on them, and the sun shining through the early morning mist. I think that when the war is over we must settle down here, perhaps in this house if we're very great people then, and spend a lot of time in the garden. It's one of the most perfect gardens I've ever seen. Take great, great care of yourself for me, and I will do the same for you. And one day we will have peace and really get to know each other.[5]

In the meantime, however, there was the business of war and the training for war.

Lt Sparks, RNVR, was appointed senior Motor Launch Commander and began taking over the two designated motor launches, 347 and 297, that were lying at Portland and converting them for silent, clandestine use. Major J. Wynne, the newly appointed Planning and Intelligence Officer attached to SSRF, made contact with the Intelligence Departments of both Combined Operations and Home Forces and submitted a first list of potential targets at the end of that same month.

Anderson Manor very quickly earned a local reputation as somewhere top secret: 'I was the telephonist at Bere Regis during the war' Ethel Brown remembered. 'I did the night shift from 10pm to 6am. I remember the Anderson Manor lines were the top row on the board and all calls were scrambled so that we couldn't hear the conversation. Anderson Manor was something to do with the Home Office and was closely guarded.'[6] Closely guarded, most certainly. And nothing whatever to do with the Home Office.

Amongst those who joined the new unit at Anderson Manor was Peter Kemp, former fighter in the Spanish Civil War and ex-member of the abortive Operation *Knife* team that never made it to Norway. He had completed SOE's rigorous training in Scotland, after which nothing particular seemed to excite his attention. Cruising the SOE Baker Street offices in February and looking for interesting work, Colonel Munn, one of his instructors at Inverailort in 1940, advised him: 'You had better join my old friend Gus March-Phillipps. He is recruiting officers for a scheme of his which should be just up your street.'[7] It was. The introduction to both March-Phillipps and Appleyard was to change his life:

> However overworked and misapplied the words 'personality' and 'genius' may be, it is difficult to avoid their use in a description of these two remarkable characters ... [B]y religion a deeply sincere Roman Catholic, by tradition an English country gentleman, [Gus] combined the idealism of a Crusader with the severity of a professional soldier. He was slightly built of medium height; his eyes, puckered from straining against tropical glare, gave him an enquiring, piercing and even formidable expression, only slightly mitigated by his tendency to stammer. Despite an unusually hasty temper he had a great sense of fairness towards his subordinates. In battle he was invariably calm. He was intelligent, without any great academic ability. Above all, he had the inspiration to conceive great enterprises, combined with the skill and daring to execute them; he was also most fortunate in his second-in-command. Of calmer temperament but similarly romantic nature, less impetuous but more obstinate, Appleyard combined a flair for organisation and planning with superb skill in action and a unique ability to instil confidence in time of danger.[8]

March-Phillipps outlined his plans to create a raiding force that would take the fight to the enemy shore: 'As I listened to the details of this plan and realised its enormous possibilities, the clouds of frustration that had hung over me during the last few months vanished.'[9] Before he left the office in Knightsbridge, Peter Kemp and his friend John Burton were both on the strength of the Small Scale Raiding Force. It would be some weeks, however, before Anderson Manor was ready for occupancy. What would they like to do in the meantime, asked Gus, democratically? The answer, they decided, was to get really fit for the raiding work that lay ahead and brush up their knowledge of fieldcraft and demolitions. So back they went to the Western Highlands for more commando training, this time at Inverailort. It was the usual stuff, refined and honed to a new intensity through the sweat, hardship and experience of countless courses:

> Carrying tommy-guns and fifty-pound rucksacks, we tramped across the hills in mist and darkness, trying to find our way by compass, stumbling over invisible obstacles, sinking into bogs and falling into gullies and ravines … within three weeks we were thoroughly fit, competent at demolitions and accurate with pistol and tommy-gun.[10]

Peter Kemp went back to London in time for March-Phillipps' wedding on 18 April 1942 where he met both Graham Hayes – 'a quiet, serious-minded young man with great personal charm, courage and strength.' – and Anders Lassen – 'a cheerful, lithe Dane with a thirst for killing Germans and a wild bravery'.[11]

The operational personnel started moving in to Anderson Manor on 24 April. Arrangements were made for experts in explosives, small arms and knife fighting, security and escape and evasion to visit Anderson Manor once training had begun. First operations, it was hoped, would take place in the middle of May but would depend upon the time it took to arm and fit out the two MLs. At this stage, the strength of SSRF stood at eighteen officers and five other ranks.[12] The new unit plunged immediately into a period of intensive training. It was commando Scotland all over again, but without the midges.

Another new volunteer was Capt. Francis Howard, Baron Howard of Penrith, known to all as 'Long John' because of his height:

> Appleyard was doing the interviewing and decided to take me on, despite my age being rather above the average [he was 38] … There were rather more officers than men and our training was probably fairly standard … We trained with plastic explosives, gelignite and so on. We did grenade throwing, pistol shooting. There were ranges all round the manor. We did some exercises with live detonators stuck in potatoes which we threw at each other; one had to duck out of the way or risk being hurt … It was a very pleasant unit in which everyone got on extremely well, and there didn't seem to be much difference between the ranks. It was an extraordinary happy experience, in a way. There was a cherub in the garden and there was a slightly dangerous practice of letting off all our guns at his navel![13]

Within the grounds of Anderson Manor they built a covered 'double-tap' pistol range and an assault course with ditches full of barbed wire. They turned the old butler's pantry into their armoury. Explosives were kept in an air raid shelter outside; the ancient moat, filled with barbed wire, had to be jumped; a Nissen hut was erected for close quarter gutter fighting *a la* Sykes and Fairbairn – the two Shanghai policemen turned SOE killing instructors whose double-edged, needle-pointed, custom-designed daggers each man now carried. Ropes were slung high in the ancient limes lining the driveway and these had to be climbed up and then crossed in full equipment. There were also night compass exercises across country. Sergeant Tom Winter recalled:

> We did a lot of compass training in the local area. Whether we got back to where the transport was waiting depended on the accuracy of our compass work. If we didn't get back to the transport in time, it would leave without us. We would then have to make our own way back to Anderson … I remember one training scheme doing astro-navigation, using the stars, around Bovington tank training area. Desgrange and I were challenged by a sentry at Bovington camp, who thought we were spies, especially since André Desgrange, who was a Free French Naval Petty Officer, couldn't speak a word of English. Because of the secret nature of our work, we didn't carry identification and couldn't say where we were based. All we could do was give them the London telephone number of SOE and ask them to confirm who we were.[14]

There were also numerous exercises in individual initiative: troops would be paraded early and ordered to reassemble at a precise location a hundred miles away the next morning. How they got there was up to them. After conversations with his son, Ernest Appleyard remembered: 'The men were trained to value comradeship and friendship … Punishments were avoided. If a man did not make the grade he left the Troop and that was all – very few ever left.' In between night stalking exercises, rock climbing on the Dorset coast and much hard marching with weapons and full equipment in all weathers, the unit practised living off the land. Appleyard wrote to his parents:

> We have had some interesting training schemes to fill the time up and all last week were out on Exmoor and the north Devon coast on a special living-out scheme. We were entirely independent and living solely on a very concentrated special ration and sleeping out under hedges, etc … The aim was to see if we could march 30 miles or so a day without packing up. Quite a

holiday, except for carrying a 45lb pack and the rations ... It was a scorching week but really was great fun. My party and I walked 120 miles in four days – Exeter, Lynmouth, Lynton, Ilfracombe, Barnstaple, Exeter. Mostly over rough ground and tracks.[15]

Captain The Lord Howard remembered the same exercise rather differently:

We were paired off together and, after being set down somewhere between Anderson Manor and Lyme Regis, had to walk to Lynmouth in North Devon about sixty miles away. We had sleeping bags on our backs and hard rations, we had a little tea and some chocolate in our pockets. We slept out on Exmoor under the stars and arrived in Lynmouth so very hungry that we went down to the sea and began eating winkles and molluscs that we prised off the rocks with our knives.[16]

One of those Captain The Lord Howard paired up with was Anders Lassen, the Dane who had excelled during Operation *Postmaster*. Now, at Anderson Manor, he continued to impress:

I feel that being in the same unit as Andy Lassen was rather like serving with Achilles. For Andy did easily what nearly everyone else found difficult. Other people were very good on the assault course. They were all so fit but Andy, without seeming to take any trouble, was much the best. He just floated everywhere, up the ropes and then along them ... And if there was considerable risk, Andy enjoyed it all the more. It was wonderful to see him. When everyone else was straining and making an effort or pulling themselves together, he'd just enjoy himself and do the assault course better than anybody.[17]

He excelled at knife-fighting, too:

A knife would be dropped between two men, who would make a grab for it. The one failing to pick it up would have to defend himself against his armed opponent. Lassen earned a reputation for being almost impossible to disarm when he had the knife.[18]

He was developing into a formidable enemy: 'He had a real hatred for the Germans, much more than most of us had. I've always wondered about Andy's hostility to the Germans', mused Lord Howard after the war. 'Was it simply that they had invaded Denmark? Andy was very nice, not a frightening man – but when he said that he'd like to kill Germans, I believe that he meant it.'[19]

Lassen had formed a particular bond with March-Phillipps: 'There was an affinity between Gus and Andy. I think that the combination of dash, pride, distain and immensely serious purpose attracted Andy to him', recalled Marjorie March-Phillipps. She visited Anderson Manor two or three times:

> It was a beautiful house and the weather was always lovely. I can still see Andy Lassen by the balustrades of lawn alongside the river. Straight yellow hair, a high complexion that was also sunburned, and a rather gappy grin because a lot of front teeth had been bashed out. Andy behaved impeccably while I was there but you could see he was wild. One of the wildest of the lot, I'd say. Gus was pretty wild himself, but not like Andy.[20]

Lassen's obsession was pistol shooting, knife throwing and hunting with bows and arrows. The author has been shown the attic door jamb into which Andy Lassen used to fire arrows from a 20-yard range whenever someone entered the room, delighting in missing them by the narrowest of margins. How delighted they were is not recorded.

A very great deal of their training was done at night: darkness and periods in which there was no moon would be their chosen *milieu* of operations over on the other side. With time, practice and training, darkness became their ally, their friend:

> On our first night exercises we were all very uncertain and noisy, but in a surprisingly short time we became accustomed to the work; within two months we were able to find our way in silence over unknown country at a surprising speed, to crawl noiselessly under barbed wire and to stalk sentries on our stomachs ...[21]

They were learning the skills that would soon save their lives.

There was particular emphasis on boat work, the means by which they would both reach their target and exfiltrate afterwards. At first, Combined Operations had given them those two motor launches – MLs 347 and 297 – but these proved too slow for their needs, were mechanically unreliable and had to be returned to their makers with engine heating problems, resulting in further delays.[22] In time, both were replaced by MTB 344, a small, fast motor torpedo boat with a top speed of 33 knots, which they christened *The Little Pisser* because of its size and turn of speed. Stripped of its torpedo tubes and armed only with two Vickers machine guns either side of the bridge and a couple of drum-fed Lewis guns aft, *The Little Pisser* carried an upturned Dory or flat-bottomed, canvas-sided collapsible Goatley assault boat lashed upturned on her after-deck. She would rely upon stealth, silence and speed to ensure her survival and evasion of marauding German E-boats. Commanded by Lt Freddie Bourne and based at Gosport, Portsmouth, MTB 344 was destined to become their means of transport to and from the enemy coastline on most of their raids.

Post-war, Freddie Bourne remembered the impact the two SSRF officers with their contrasting styles made upon him from the outset; he used to go up to Anderson Manor for briefings and remembered how, on operations, March-Phillipps used to slip a long cook's knife down his trouser leg:

He [March-Phillipps] was a tall, well-connected person. He recruited his friends. [Appleyard] was his First Lieutenant. A University man. Charming. Again, very brave. But whereas March-Phillipps had all the dash and flare and the outgoing signs of a Commando, Appleyard was much more the thinker. I don't say [he was] the brains of the operation but he gave a great deal more detailed thought to what the men were going to do when March-Phillipps set up the inception of the scheme.[23]

It was agreed between them that MTB 344 would close the enemy shore on silenced engine, and then let go an anchor on a grass line. The dozen raiders of the SSRF would then transfer to the smaller Goatley or Dory for the silent, nerve-wracking paddle or row ashore. That approach and the extrication afterwards across open water was recognised from the outset as the time of maximum vulnerability: 'We practised in every kind of weather, under all sorts of conditions, until we had perfected our training in disembarkation, landing and re-embarkation', Peter Kemp remembered. All kinds of boats and canoes were used to develop landing techniques and increase water-confidence. 'We also did a lot of practice at sea because the whole of Poole harbour was at our disposal as well as most of the coast', recalled Captain The Lord Howard:

The beaches were supposed to be mined but we got through the wire and used all those wonderful beaches and sandbanks. We had a large rowing boat for hard, difficult work against the tides; we also had canoes in which we went up the rivers and round the harbour as far as Bournemouth ... Training was designed to accustom us to the sea, particularly rough seas. Sometimes they were too rough. I once made a canoe party pull under the cliffs at Bournemouth because we were getting swamped. We then dried off in an empty house. We tended to do that. If there was an empty house, we'd use it. During training our discipline was extremely strict. March-Phillipps and Appleyard demanding the highest standard of efficiency from everyone.

There were no punishments, nor were any necessary: we knew that the lives of us all would depend on the skill and competence of each. Off parade relations between officers and other ranks were easy and informal, almost casual. We were a very happy unit.[24]

March-Phillipps insisted all men were up and about by 6am. Between then and breakfast he did not mind what they did – they could run, walk, shoot – just so long as they took some form of early morning exercise before the training day began.

The men of No 62 Commando were entitled to wear the green beret,[25] but only once they had attended – and passed – Achnacarry. March-Phillipps encouraged all ranks to wear civilian clothes off duty and off base, particularly when travelling the few miles down the road to the thatched pub *The World's End* at Almer outside Blandford. Here officers and other ranks mixed freely, though not without raising an eyebrow from a senior officer attached to the Royal Tank Corps at nearby Bovington: 'He complained to Gus that his staff car had been held up by a crowd of us, men and officers, spread across the road on bicycles and holding each others arms as we rode away from the pub', Ian Warren, one of the newer recruits, remembered. 'Gus lectured us saying: "This has to stop. Here, ranks don't matter. Outside, you comply with military discipline."' It was a discipline that did not stop either March-Phillipps or Appleyard scrawling their names on the pub ceiling. Their names remained there until the thatched roof of the pub was destroyed by fire after the war.

It wasn't just the members of this secret unit who found themselves swept up in an atmosphere of mutual support and quixotic enthusiasm for the dangerous task that lay ahead as the quiet summer weeks of training slid by. Head gardener Reg Mullins also relished the informality engendered by March-Phillipps: 'Always called him Gus, you know. There was no Army at Anderson. No army regulations. We were just a happy little band.'[26] Lt Tony Hall, ex-London Scottish and Intelligence Corps, agreed: 'He [March-Phillipps] was a very reasonable man and he had a complete contempt for small regulations that sometimes make life in the army tiresome and uncomfortable. As long as a man did his job properly on training and on operations it didn't really matter what he did outside.'[27]

Tony Hall, aged 30, joined SSRF in April 1942. In peacetime he had been a successful writer and radio producer. Perhaps a little more sensitive than most, he was one of those who found that Anderson Manor soon came to embody something of the spirit that shaped the way they wished to fight their war:

It seemed so mad that there was this wonderful house, this charming, small manor dedicated in its way, in its surroundings, to peace. The mulberry tree, the nuts, the kitchen garden and all the rest of it – and yet this was being used for war. It had everything. If you are in a house like that, and you know that here is the England that you're fighting for ... He [Gus] was creating a world of people who loved the idea of doing a thing honourably and this sounds, I know, another piece of chi-chi, but it's not. If you had Gus as a leader you would know that nothing would ever be done that was of evil intent.[28]

By early June, unit strength stood at twenty-four officers and fourteen other ranks with one further officer and four other ranks about to join. Training by day and by night, ashore and afloat, was refined and intensified. The weeks came and went and *still* there was no mission, nothing in the wings to repay all that training, boat work and weapon handling, although one raid, submitted to Combined Operations, had been cancelled 'owing to the intervention of C [SIS]'.[29] Peter Kemp described this time as 'a disheartening period of frustration and delay' during which SSRF personnel at Anderson Manor were broken down into two groups: one for mission-specific and one for general training. Meanwhile, they waited. Delays were officially put down to problems with the MLs, to bad weather, to periods of full moon, or even to what became known as 'convoy nights', when whole areas of sea were closed off to let convoys move up or down the Channel: 'Keyed up as we were, standing by night after night, sometimes setting out on a raid only to turn back after an hour or so, we all found this period of waiting a heavy strain on our nerves. For March-Phillipps and Appleyard it must have been nearly intolerable.'[30]

Bad weather and 'convoy nights' may only have been part of the problem. More probably, perhaps in light of what we know now and that 'owing to intervention of C' quoted above, it may well have been simply another example of the aggressive needs of SOE rubbing up against the greater passive strategic requirements of SIS, a recurring problem earlier identified long before Operation *Postmaster*. It had got no better during *Maid Honor*'s convenient and time-soaking deployment to West Africa the summer before. During that early June of 1942, for example, three SSRF missions were cancelled because they ran contrary to the operational needs of SIS: Operation *Starboard* was planned to destroy a watch post on Île de Batz, off Roskoff, Brittany; Operation *Statement* was to attack a similar isolated watch post on Île Milliau; Operation *Syncopation* was to attack a lighthouse and its tiny garrison on Île de Bréhat. All three – and the meticulous and detailed planning that went into each one – came to nothing. Each was listed simply as 'Cancelled C-in-C Plymouth owing to interference with SIS.'[31] In all, nine raids – including Operations *Hillbilly*, *Mantling*, *Promise*, *Underpaid*, *Weathervane* and *Woodward* – would be worked up and then cancelled at the last moment because of this irreconcilable clash between SOE/CO and SIS. Each of these pin-prick raids would have involved the stealthy approach to an isolated Observation Post or watch-tower followed by the capture and/or killing of the German garrison.

At least one senior naval officer put the delay in large part down to March-Phillipps' administrative incompetence and his apparent inability to work through proper naval channels. Commodore John Hughes-Hallett RN, a strict, unmarried disciplinarian allegedly known to his subordinates as 'Hughes-Hitler' was, in spring 1942, Mountbatten's naval adviser at Combined Operations Headquarters. Later that summer he would become Naval Force Commander for the ill-fated Dieppe raid in August 1942. Hughes-Hallett was later to claim that for some weeks, after providing SSRF with the boats they required, 'nothing happened'. He added:

As far as I know, the chief difficulty before had lain in the inability of the Small-Scale raiders to produce an operation order in a form which would inspire reasonable confidence! ... We did find it necessary to go into considerable detail in connection with navigational problems and escort and cover, and it was not in the least surprising that SSRF should have failed to achieve anything so long as they were entirely independent.[32]

Condescending to a fault, Commodore, later Vice Admiral, Hughes-Hallett RN and the unconventional men of the Small Scale Raiding Force were to clash again later that summer.

Meanwhile, Appleyard was becoming increasingly frustrated, not simply by the continuing absence of any raids to chalk up on a personal tally-board, but by the penny-packet thinking further up the command chain that lay behind the original concept that passed for raiding policy. Echoing March-Phillipps' idea of a series of nightly raids along the whole coastline of enemy-occupied Europe, carried out by an ever-expanding chain of small scale raiding groups that would force the enemy to redeploy their forces in Europe and thus take pressure off Russian allies on the Eastern Front, Appleyard wrote home: 'Personally, of course, I still feel strongly that at the present time our contribution to the European situation ought to be in the nature of a vast number of small raids up and down the length of the European coastline.'[33] He expanded upon his ideas later that summer in a further letter to his father:

Every single little operation you go on helps. Every time you get that tight feeling round your heart and the empty feeling in your tummy, you are mentally and nervously tougher than the time before and so are better fitted for real continuous military action ... No, it is not spirit we are lacking, but experience ...

Well, I think I've burbled on long enough. You must be very tired of reading it!

God bless, Dad.

Very much love,

Geoff.[34]

June became July and July eased gently into August. It was time – and past time – for their first mission, their first pin-prick into the flank of the slumbering enemy. Now, at last, they were to have their chance. Their first raid took place on the night of 14–15 August 1942: Operation *Barricade*.

Raiders

It would be tempting to suppose that Gus March-Phillipps' Small Scale Raiding Force was the only unit dedicated to raiding the enemy shoreline. That would be incorrect. Partly because of the original haste and confusion in which the role of raiding was conceived and allocated, many other units were also now sharpening their knives, oiling their weapons and waiting impatiently for the opportunity to take the fight to the enemy across the Channel. Amongst these were Gerald Montanaro's No 101 Troop, Special Boat Section of No 2 Commando and the men of Nos 4, 9, 10 and 12 Commando, whilst as far back as February 1942 Major John Frost's men of 'C' Company – it would later become 2 Para of the British 1st Airborne Division – had scored something of a coup by pulling off the successful Operation *Biting* against the German Wurzburg, short-range radar station at Bruneval on the French coast near Le Havre.

Operation *Barricade* was a second-hand raid originally intended for someone else; the subject of countless aerial reconnaissance sorties, it had been on the books for months, certainly since before the creation of the Small Scale Raiding Force. Since early summer 1942 the Germans had been building ship-locating stations along the Channel coast. Combined Operations' Search Committee in Richmond Terrace – the group in COHQ responsible for choosing targets for Combined Operations' raiders – decided that the locating station on Cap Barfleur, high on the top right-hand corner of the Cotentin peninsula due east of Cherbourg, would make a suitable target. Early in June the RAF flew three photographic reconnaissance missions and began building up a target dossier. As initially envisaged, the raid was to be anything but small: 'not more than 120 men'[1] were to be carried to the target area by an Infantry Assault Ship. They were to recce the area between Barfleur and St Vaast to the south. As originally conceived, the aim of the mission was to kill and capture German troops and destroy military installations, including a direction-finding station, anti-aircraft gun site and machine-gun nests approximately 800 yards from the beach. They might encounter perhaps as many as a company – 100 men – of German troops billeted at the nearby hamlet of Jonville to the north of St Vaast inland from Pointe de Saire. British forces, landing in eight assault craft carried to within 10 miles of the beach objective by HMS *Prince Albert*, would be supported by five gunboats as close escort and, during the withdrawal, by Intruder aircraft from No 11 Group. In addition to the fighting men from the East Yorks, who were scheduled to spend 'not more than 76 minutes ashore', there would be a Beach Gradient party, a representative of the Royal Engineers to report on the DF station and, finally, a gentleman of the press. In concept this might not be a large raid, like Dieppe or St Nazaire. But it was hardly small, either. Operational orders for this conspicuous, front-door attack on Hitler's *Festung Europa* were issued as late as Friday, 17 July 1942.

And then, quite suddenly, Operation *Barricade* as originally envisaged simply disappeared, cancelled at the last moment by C-in-C Portsmouth, ostensibly because of the ever-present threat of interdiction by German E-boats. Now, instead of 120 men from a Yorkshire Infantry Regiment storming ashore from eight landing craft supported by Royal Navy gunships as they charged head-on into the teeth of waiting German machine-guns, there would be Major March-Phillipps and ten hand-picked men from Anderson Manor. They would slip ashore in silence from a single canvas-sided Goatley assault boat, powered only by wooden paddles that would be delivered close to the enemy shore, in darkness, by *The Little Pisser*. Sometimes, less really is more.

Operation *Barricade*, evidently, had been downgraded, its mission reduced to just three lines: 'To carry out a reconnaissance raid on the French coast NW of Pointe de Saire and to capture and kill enemy in A.A. gun-site.'

March-Phillipps picked his men. One of those left behind – cliff-scaling might have been involved and the man's clumsiness on cliff-work had been noticed – was Peter Kemp: 'With envy and anxiety we watched the party set out in the dusk for Gosport, each of them festooned with tommy-gun, Colt .45 automatic and hand grenades.'[2]

The eleven men of the Small Scale Raiding Force embarked at Gosport and set sail at 2045 in calm, cloudy weather. MTB 344 set direct course for Point de Barfleur. The engine broke down three times during that lonely passage and, even though they travelled at an average 18 knots, such delays while they lay dead in the water put them more than a hour behind schedule. There was another problem, too. MTB 344 carried no hand-bearing compass. Consequentially, every cross-bearing on the approaching coastline had to be taken by immovable ship's compass after slowing *The Little Pisser* to point her bows directly at the land. Meanwhile, the ship drifted helplessly in the tidal set. 'The provision of a hand-bearing compass with light is strongly recommended for MTBs employed in such work' March-Phillipps observed afterwards. 'They are supplied by O.M. Watts.'

Three miles east of Barfleur the starboard engine was cut and the silent engine started. They then moved in to the drop-off point fighting a 2½-knot current. The Goatley was lowered over the side and the raiders clambered in for the three-quarters of a mile paddle to shore. With four men working on each side in absolute silence, wooden paddles dipping in silent rhythm to the dark sea, the approach took twenty long and exposed minutes. Passing between great outcrops of rock, the Goatley hissed at last up onto a gently shelving, sandy beach.

It is a mistake easily made when navigating at night both on land and at sea to make a mistake and then compound that error by forcing the land to fit expectations. Which is what happened now. Unbeknownst to March-Phillipps, the powerful current had set them almost a mile further north up the coast towards Barfleur. It was a navigational error whose importance would not be realised until they examined air photographs back at base once Operation *Barricade* was completed.

They had landed on a falling spring tide. Leaving the Goatley pulled up well below the high water line and with one man left behind to guard their only means of retreat, the remaining ten raiders set off briskly through the fields that bordered the shoreline. Then, suddenly, just beyond a low stone wall they ran into a barbed wire fence. There seemed to be a house beyond, but that was all. Cutting the wire carefully, they moved forward, cautiously aware that, if only by estimating the distance they had covered on foot, the enemy must now be very close. There were grazing cows tethered in the grass, moving restlessly as the intruders approached. The men thought they had perhaps been placed there to give warning of just such an advance. Then came another barbed wire fence with another house beyond, more sensed than seen in the darkness. Then they realised that the object in front of them was not a house at all but some military instrument, or wagon, even, covered with camouflage netting and that the second apron of wire covered an encampment of considerable size. Evidently, they were nowhere near their primary target, the anti-aircraft gun emplacement: 'The head of a sentry, near what appeared to be a guard hut, was plainly visible and an assault was made immediately on the wire fence with the intention of attacking the encampment and destroying as much of it as possible. But the fence proved a formidable obstacle and at least fifteen minutes elapsed while the first half was being cut through.'[3]

British issue single-handed wire-cutters proved inadequate for the task, but they persevered. It was all they had: now the party divided and one section moved up [to] the fence with the intention of getting through it and attacking what seemed to be a large house further away to the right. This section returned with the report that the hut was the size of a hanger and it was then that the true size of the encampment was first realised.

> It was still thought possible, however, to attack at any rate a section of it, and renewed efforts were made to cut a way through the fence but the noise was now attracting attention and the sentry was seen to go into the guard hut and return with other men. Finally, four men made a detour round the guard hut and approached the attacking party down the inside of the fence.
>
> It was getting dangerously late by this time, and for this reason and because of the size and toughness of the fence it was decided to deal with the guard and return as quickly as possible to the boat. The party accordingly crawled towards the guard who was advancing very silently with rifles at the ready.[4]

The Germans approached and challenged once in a low voice. There was no response. The challenge was repeated, twice. Still no response. Now, the Germans' slackness, their cautious movement towards an unidentified, underestimated threat with weapons which were not cocked, was to cost them their lives: 'The guard had not got rounds in the breeches of their rifles, as when the challenge remained unanswered, rifle bolts could be heard being drawn back.' They would have no more chances. The order was given to open fire as the bolts clicked back:

> three plastic bombs landed right in the middle of the enemy together with a volley of tommy-guns and automatic fire. The effect of the plastic bombs was devastating. Altogether some five pounds of explosive went off within a few feet of the enemy and not a sound was heard afterwards but a few strangled coughs.[5] Fire was then opened on other parts of the encampment which showed signs of activity and a retreat was made at the double to the boat.[6]

Apart from firing white Verey lights and the occasional rifle and pistol shot – no automatic weapons opened fire – March-Phillipps and his men made their way back to the boat on the beach without interference from the garrison they had ambushed. They had been ashore less than an hour. They made their way out to sea towards where they imagined MTB 344 was waiting but, once again, the set of tide and current were misjudged and it was not before 0345 that all were safely aboard the mother ship.

The Little Pisser then made her way out to sea and raised St Catherine's Head at 0700 the following morning. They made their way back to Anderson Manor where Peter Kemp was amongst those waiting to greet them: 'before breakfast they returned, strained and exhausted but content with their night's work ... Although they had taken no prisoners, we all felt it was an encouraging start.'[7]

Writing up his after-action report on Operation *Barricade*, March-Phillipps estimated that three Germans had definitely been killed, with another three probably killed and a further three or four wounded 'as the range was almost point blank'. One of the raiding force had been badly bruised after falling on a metal stake. There were no other British casualties. He went on:

> Though the operation was only partly successful, because no prisoners were taken, it has proved beyond doubt that a handful of men and one M.T.B. can cause damage on the occupied coastline.
>
> The casualties inflicted on the enemy were not heavy, but they were sufficient to have a very demoralising effect. It is doubtful if the Germans ever realised who or what was attacking them, as the explosion of the plastic bombs used was far exceeding their size. The M.T.B. commander, one mile away, reports seeing distinctly bits of debris flying up in the flames and smoke, and states that the explosion resembled that of a much heavier bomb.

At the time of writing March-Phillipps was evidently still unaware that they had overshot their intended target by almost a mile:

> The navigation, with no more than a compass, was exceedingly accurate, and the actual target was only missed in the final approach. But this fact serves to show that a small party of determined men can find some target or other by moving along the coast ... Small parties are better than large parties. It is not easy to keep touch in the dark and a large party of men cannot move quickly for this reason ... The ideal size for such a party is ten or a dozen men and such a party can produce an effect out of all proportion to its size ...

He concluded his first raid report with a plea for further expansion of a concept both he and Appleyard had come to believe in passionately:

> The effect of such raids, though small in itself, [sic] can be cumulative if they are continuous. If carried out frequently and over a wide area they would have a demoralising effect on the enemy and corresponding heartening effect

on our own troops. They present the best form of training both for comman-dos and home forces.[8]

Operation *Barricade* took place on the night of 14–15 August 1942. Operation *Jubilee*, the raid on Dieppe, took place four days later. At least one source suggests that six members of SSRF took part in this raid as part of X Troop, a mixed party including, in addition to SOE, members of both MEW and SIS.[9] Their task was to move ashore to the town hall and German headquarters behind the assaulting formations and remove docu-ments and interesting pieces of German equipment. The failure of the main assault, however, also led to the failure of their mission. Yet one on-line unverifiable source[10] suggests SSRF were there for a darker reason alto-gether, and that amongst those tasked to land at Dieppe was Freya radar expert, Flight Lieutenant Jack Nissenthall. His task – had the assault been a success – would have been to inspect and remove secret German Freya radar equipment from a nearby radar station on cliffs between Dieppe and Pourville. It was, it is claimed, vital that Nissenthall should not be captured – not, one may presume, because he might have told his captors why he was there but because, under interrogation, he might have dis-closed to the Germans what Britain knew about the Wurgburg and Freya radars and the counter-measures, post-Operation *Biting*, that had been put in place. Nissenthall, it is claimed, carried a green cyanide capsule he was prepared to take in the event of imminent capture. To make certainty doubly sure, the claim stands that the SOE men from SSRF were there to act as both bodyguard and executioners, with orders to kill him if his capture appeared inevitable. Perhaps unsurprisingly, there is no mention of this particular mission briefing in any of the SSRF papers seen by this author.[11] In the event, Jack Nissenthall lived to return safely to England with members of No 4 Commando.

Operation *Barricade*, though modest, had been an undoubted success. It established precedent, created a point of reference and gave credence, both within SOE and Combined Operations, to a new concept. Had it failed, cross-channel pin-prick raiding by SSRF might have been put back several months, perhaps even cancelled altogether. As it was, Operation *Barricade* served as a prelude, an appetiser, for what was to come.

†††

What was to come, a fortnight later, after a series of frustrating delays and cancellations due to what became known as '*Dryad* weather', was Operation *Dryad*, a raid whose skilful execution, untarnished success, lack of British casualties, audacity and amusing, operational postscript perhaps temporarily blinded those who did not have to brave dark nights in small boats to the intense danger inherent in night raiding. As Peter Kemp put it years later:

> There was a tremendous tension before any raid. It was frightening because either you pulled it off without any loss to yourselves or you were inclined to lose the whole party, because if the enemy spotted you coming in you were a sitting duck. And so the actual paddle, the paddling in was very, very tense indeed. And it was essential, of course, to do it without making any sound at all. And that was very frightening.[12]

Operation *Dryad* took place on the night of 2–3 September 1942.

Casquets is a group of tide-scoured rocks 6 miles west of Alderney in the Channel Islands and forms part of a sandstone ridge that has proved to be the graveyard of many merchant ships over the centuries. The largest island among these outcrops is 280 yards long and 150 yards wide. From 1724, Casquets had boasted a lighthouse 80 feet tall, with two further distinctive coal-fired stone towers built to prevent confusion with other lighthouses on the French mainland nearby. After the German occupation of the Channel Islands in June 1940, Casquets lighthouse had been turned into a naval signal station manned by a tiny garrison of German troops. Isolated, cut off from the mainland and the possibility of rapid reinforcement, Casquets' best defence lay in the swirling strength of the 6–7 knot spring tides that tore and swirled around its barren rocks. That same isolation, however, meant that in the summer of 1942, it might have been tailor-made for the attentions of the SSRF. They thought so, too.

The objective of Operation *Dryad* was very simple: to take prisoners. A secondary objective was to remove whatever code books, documents and naval papers they might find lying around. The raid was to be commanded by March-Phillipps with Appleyard second in command. Also on the raid were Hayes, Lassen and Winter.

Planning for the raid had begun, as usual, at Anderson Manor with all ranks spending hours in the conference room studying charts, aerial photographs and even a large-scale plasticine model of the rock, lighthouse and adjoining buildings. Appleyard carried most of the initial responsibility: it would be up to him to find their way through the heavy swell and fierce tide-race they could expect as they approached the rocks. Casquets guarded its lighthouse well with the Channel Pilot warning mariners: 'The great rates attained by the tidal stream in the neighbourhood of the Casquets renders approach to them in thick weather hazardous.'[13]

Having been turned back by fog within a few hundred yards of their objective, bad weather or mechanical breakdown aboard MTB 344 – yet again – repeatedly frustrated their attempts to land. At last, as Appleyard wrote to his parents shortly afterwards, referring to the Casquets raid as 'another successful little party', it went ahead: 'You remember I said that some time ago we went somewhere and were beaten by fog at the last moment and although we knew we were within a few hundred yards of our objective we couldn't find it? ... Well ... last Wednesday night, which was the ninth or tenth night on which we have tried this particular job, we got it in the bag.'[14]

As so often with these things, it was the waiting beforehand that the men found difficult: all were highly trained, highly motivated and intelligent. Which meant they also had imagination. Sometimes, that did not help. 'We spent the morning in the conference room and the afternoon resting', wrote Peter Kemp, now on the eve of his first raid:

> Although we had the greatest confidence in our commanders and in each other, it was difficult not to contemplate the numerous possibilities of disaster. Once we were in the MTB I should feel all right, but I found this period of waiting very hard to bear. We spent the time between tea and supper in drawing and preparing our equipment. There was plenty of it. I was carrying a tommy-gun with seven magazines, each with twenty rounds, a pair of wire-cutters, two Mills grenades, a fighting knife, a clasp knife, a torch, emergency rations and two half-pound explosive charges for the destruction of the wireless transmitter; on top I had to wear a naval lifebelt, an awkward and constricting garment that might save my life in the water but seemed very likely to lose it for me in action. We wore battle-dress, balaclava helmets and felt-soled boots.[15]

No mention of blackened faces smeared with soot or cocoa to tone down the gleam of white faces in the darkness: 'If I am to die on one of these parties', March-Phillipps had announced to the men aboard *Maid Honor* in Africa, 'I'll die looking like an Englishman and not like a damned n*****.'[16] In that England in September 1942, it would have taken a brave man indeed, one suspects, to black up in the face of such an attitude – accepted at the time – from a short-tempered commanding officer. Peter Kemp takes up the story:

> After a hurried supper we climbed into our lorry. The whole unit turned out in the stable yard to see us off; Tony Hall in an old suit and peaked cap, was ringing the mess dinner bell and shouting in the accents of an

American railroad conductor: 'All aboard! All aboard! Minneapolis, Saint Paul, Chicago and all points east!' We sang lustily, all tension now relaxed, as we drove through the green and golden countryside towards Portland. The lorry swung into the dockyard, drove onto the quay and halted close alongside the boat; we hurried aboard and dived out of sight below ... At nine o'clock we sailed.

With the forecastle hatch battened down to show no light, it was oppressively hot in our cramped quarters. The small craft bounced jarringly across the waves for the wind, which had been Force 3 when we started, was rising to Force 4 with occasional stronger gusts. My companions lay down to sleep on the two wooden seats and the floor; I sat up and tried to read a thriller.[17]

Others suffered agonies of sea-sickness in the hot, cramped, claustrophobic cabin as they crashed, pitched and rolled across the Channel.

Moving out into mid-Channel from the shelter of land, MTB 344 developed engine trouble and had to reduce speed. It was thus after 2230 before Appleyard knocked on the forecastle hatch and warned the raiders to be ready to come out on deck when called. When they did so it was to 'a beautiful clear night, bright with stars. The wind had dropped and the sea was moderating.'

Appleyard remembered: 'I navigated again for the whole job. It was pretty nerve-racking as it's a notoriously evil place and you get a tremendous tide-race round the rocks. However, all went well and we found the place all right, and pushed in our landing craft.'[18]

MTB 344 closed on Casquets at 2245. Manoeuvring to within 800 yards of the rocks, she put down an anchor on 50 fathoms of line and the raiders then transferred to the Goatley for that moment of helpless exposure, the final approach. They left the gunboat at five minutes after midnight. The original plan had proposed that two Goatleys would be launched by two separate motor launches, each carrying six raiders. On the day, only one gunboat was used and therefore only one Goatley was lowered carefully off the stern. The men dropped silently into their places. 'Right! Push Off!', March-Phillipps called softly: 'Paddle up!' They moved away silently into the darkness. It took twenty-five minutes of hard paddling to reach a small bay where waves were breaking white on dark rocks. 'Many and conflicting eddies of tide were experienced on the approach which took considerably longer than was anticipated, probably because the approach was later than had been calculated and the NE-going flood tide was by then running hard' reported March-Phillipps. The plan had assumed the Goatley would make for a recognised landing point but, instead, she let out a kedge anchor of her own as the boat was paddled in close to a face of shelving rock directly below what was marked on their charts as the engine house tower. Timing their leap to the surge of the swell in the darkness, all eleven raiders led by Appleyard with the bow line scrambled away after a moment's precarious imbalance up the slippery rocks, leaving Capt. Graham Hayes aboard to keep the boat from surging forward onto the rocks, with Lt Ian Warren now manning the bow line which Appleyard had tied off. Encumbered by our weapons we slithered about, trying to get a purchase on the rock, until March-Phillipps hissed angrily: 'Use the rope, you b-bloody f-fools, to haul yourself up!' They hauled themselves up, ten men against a lighthouse, the black brooding mass of the signal station towering over them in the darkness.[19]

They moved up the 80-foot cliff in single file, the rattle of any dislodged pebble and the chink of weapons and equipment masked by the rumble of surf and the heavy, echoing boom of the sea in the chasms and deeply cleft inlets below. Coiled dannert wire had been used to choke the gully ahead and they cut their way past this only to find their way into the courtyard blocked by a heavy knife-rest wire entanglement. Still no shots, no shout of detection. They scrambled over a wall and dropped into the courtyard, unchallenged and silent in their felt-soled boots. Here they broke off into small teams and headed for separate objectives. John Burton and Peter Kemp made for the wireless tower where, hurtling up a steep staircase, fingers on triggers, they found an empty transmitting room crammed with wireless sets, generators and electrical equipment. Nearby were an open notebook, code books and signal pads. The final haul included a code book for harbour defence vessels, signal books, records, a W/T diary of calls sent and received, procedure signals, personal letters and photographs, identity books, passes and ration cards, the station log, the ration log, the light log and even a German gas mask and cape. Rich pickings.

Appleyard and Winter's objective was the main light tower itself: 'The door was open and after a lightning ascent of eighty feet of spiral staircase we found the light-room empty!' The lighthouse and the engine room were both deserted: all seven men of the German garrison were in the main building, either in bed, in the living room or getting ready to turn in. Surprise was complete: 'The whole garrison were taken completely by surprise. I have never seen men look so amazed and terrified at the same time!'[20] There was a moment of humour too. 'Long John', Captain The Lord Howard, remembered:

I was leading a German down the corridor and in those days it was unusual for people to have long hair and he had very long hair tied up in a hair net and as I was walking him down I suddenly heard Gus's voice behind me saying: 'F-Francis, you can't take that! It's ... it's a woman!'[21]

March-Phillipps admitted later in his official report: 'A characteristic of those in bed was the wearing of hairnets which caused the Commander of the party to mistake one of them for a woman.'[22] Hairnets notwithstanding, not a shot had been fired, no violence had been used and the prisoners, to a man, were reported as being 'very docile'. SS these were not. Many still in their pyjamas, the prisoners were hustled away back down the cliffs to the waiting Goatley that was being skilfully held off the rocks by Graham Hayes and Ian Warren. Re-embarkation, however, brought its own problems: the prisoners had to be slid down a 45-degree slope and then man-handled one by one into the Goatley as she rode the heavy swell with the gap between rocks and boat varying between 5 and 20 feet. This was accomplished without mishap and the raiding party then began to climb aboard. They had been ashore just thirty-five minutes.

Meanwhile, up at the lighthouse, the radio had been smashed into pieces by John Burton wielding an axe – gunfire might have alerted Germans elsewhere, for Alderney was only a few miles due east. The retreating raiders brought back down the cliffs the garrison's old-fashioned, bolt-action Steyr-pattern rifles and an Orlikon small-calibre cannon. Two large boxes of stick grenades – one of which was open – were left behind. It had been intended to bring the weapons home as war booty but they were dumped in the sea to save weight as the overcrowded Goatley was paddled back in the darkness towards *The Little Pisser*. Luckily, she had already changed position. MTB 344 had dragged her anchor to the north and Lt Bourne had weighed anchor and was already closing down on Casquets when the Goatley began her return with nineteen on board. By this time, however, two of the raiders had been injured: Peter Kemp had been stabbed in the right thigh by a fighting knife held by one of the men as he lurched into the Goatley just as it dropped away on the swell. His wound was deep, stiff and painful. It would take a visit to the naval hospital in Portland, a shot of morphia and a minor operation to set him back on the road to full recovery. Appleyard's injury, however, was potentially more serious and longer-lasting. He wrote breezily to his parents:

I was left as the last man [ashore] and so, of course, had no one to hold the boat in for me and no rope to slide down into it. I had to swim about twenty feet out to the boat which, as soon as the tension came off the bowline, was swirled back from the rocks by the swell and I crocked my ankle whilst sliding down the rock into the water – my leg got doubled underneath somehow. However it is nothing really and should be strong again in a week or ten days. In fact, his ankle was more than just 'crocked': the bottom of his tibia – the shinbone – was fractured.

The men of SSRF boarded MTB 344 at 0135. They arrived back at Portland at 0400, where Sergeant Tom Winter stepped ashore wearing a captured German helmet: 'You look like a bloody Hun', was March-Phillipps' parting comment.

Winter's sense of release, of careless, post-raid euphoria was perhaps understandable. In the cold light of dawn, however, the discovery of such an armoury of weapons in the lighthouse gave pause for sober thought: 'If a good watch had been kept, or if any loud noises had been made on the approach or landing, the rock could have been rendered pretty well impregnable by seven determined men',[23] wrote March-Phillipps in his after-action report. Luckily for him and his men, *Obermaat* Mundt, *Funkgefreitern* Dembowy, Kraemer and Reineck, and *Gefreitern* Abel, Kepp and Klatwitter were not men of such calibre. Back in Britain, according to Appleyard, they were all soon 'talking quite well'.

Cross-Channel raiding would always depend upon skill, daring and a high level of training. But it would also depend upon luck, upon encountering a series of bored, slack, inattentive sentries in an army not noted for failing to learn from past mistakes or habitual inefficiencies. Perhaps sensing that it was asking a lot to expect every operation to run as smoothly as *Dryad*, Appleyard confided to his father:

> Don't tell the others about this, Dad. I tell you because if it should happen that one time I get left behind on one of these parties and so am out of action for the rest of the war, I should like you to feel that I'd had my share of the fun and that it wasn't entirely a wasted effort.[24]

This time, on Operation *Barricade*, the men of SSRF had been lucky. They would need that luck to continue.

But, in that summer of 1942, it looked like being a long war.

'A small and very unobtrusive party ...'

No medals this time, but plenty of praise for the unit: Bourne for his boat-handling and Appleyard for his navigation. There was a telegram too from Lord Louis Mountbatten, the Chief of Combined Operations. Appleyard recorded:

> The 'battle of Whitehall' is, of course, now going a lot better. Never was the old adage 'nothing succeeds like success' more apparent, and our few small successes have helped enormously in London. In fact, people now are only too willing to give us what we ask. Gus has had several interviews with Mountbatten, and he has written us a personal letter of congratulation and encouragement.[1]

The man with a sharp, aristocratic eye to his own advancement, and who had made sure newspapermen went in with the first wave at Dieppe, authorised the publication and general release of a snappy little booklet entitled *Combined Operations*. Its Chapter Three – 'The Steel Hand from the Sea' – lifted Appleyard's restrained account of the *Dryad* raid and turned it into the sort of breathless panegyric typical of the period:

> A slight noise – it may have been the click of the door as it closed softly – caused him [Obermaat Mundt] to turn in his chair. Leaning against the door were two men with black faces [sic] wearing crumpled uniforms, somewhat damp around the ankles. Two Colt automatics, negligently poised, were in their hands. He got slowly to his feet and passed a hand across his eyes but, when he dropped it, the figures by the doorway were still there. Chief Mate Munte [sic] began to sway and, as one of the special service men stepped forward, collapsed fainting with terror on the floor.[2]

There was more in a similar vein. There may have been reporters at Dieppe. There certainly wasn't one on *Dryad*. SOE in London was appalled, and not just because of *Dryad*, but because of wider-ranging concerns about Combined Operations' trumpet-blowing as it related to their mutual security. Not everything in the relationship between SOE and Combined Operations, it appears, was sweetness and light. Describing what he called 'The more important points of difficulty' between SOE and Combined Operations, SOE's 'CD', now Sir Charles Hambro, put on record a few months later:

> I have been much exercised in my mind lately over the lack of operational security shown by the CCO [Chief of Combined Operations] Organisation in connection with those operations in which our own people have taken part. I have spoken to General Haydon who is the Deputy of CCO and Brigadier Gubbins has also written him a letter. I hope as a result that things will improve, but the thirst for publicity amongst CCO's staff is, I fear, much removed from the SOE policy of keeping their light under a bushel. As an example, I was slightly horrified to hear that CCO were producing a booklet of their achievements in which the description of a raid on Norway included details of how the local Norwegians had helped them – the local Norwegians being in some cases our own SOE people.

Hambro went on to claim current plans for co-ordination:

> will avoid the two organisations making plans to attack the same objectives, but in their thirst for activity the CCO staff are inclined to make plans to attack objectives of a type that would definitely come within the SOE charter and in fact would be more successful and less expensively attacked by SOE methods.[3]

Hambro was writing to SOE's Chairman, Lord Selborne, in late December 1942. Earlier that same month Combined Operations mounted Operation *Frankton*, the intrepid canoe raid by ten Royal Marines on Axis shipping in Bordeaux docks that later entered legend as the Cockleshell Heroes. The attack by kayak was sanctioned because it was perceived as the only way such ships could be reached. But it wasn't. From late July that same year, SOE had their own team of agents with explosives on the same docks at the same time ready to attack the same ships. The incident became notorious and was cited as an example of just how bad co-operation could sometimes become between two essentially rival organisations.[4] That December Sir Charles Hambro warmed to his subject:

I think it is difficult for the CCO staff in planning their operations to real-ise in every case what political repercussions, especially on SOE, result from some of their operations. In fact, the damage done to SOE and SIS is very often out of all proportion to the results achieved by the raid ... CCO [Mountbatten] is always ready to consider any suggestions which we may have in this respect, but if you [Lord Selborne] get the occasion to impress on him the necessity for consulting us as early as possible in his planning it would be a good thing.[5]

Just four days after Operation *Dryad* SSRF mounted another raid – Operation *Branford*.

The Operation was to be commanded not by Major March-Phillipps but by Capt. Colin Ogden-Smith.[6] *Branford* was a reconnaissance, not a fighting patrol. Its objective was the tiny barren island of Burhou, half a mile long and 300 yards wide, that lay 3 miles north-west of Alderney and less than half way between that island and Casquets light. The intention of the reconnaissance was to establish if the island was occupied by the enemy and if light pack artillery could be landed there to provide fire sup-port for a possible invasion of Alderney. Amongst the ten men who went to Burhou with Ogden-Smith that night was James Edgar, former member of the Gordon Highlanders and Intelligence Corps and recent SOE courier. Edgar seemed to have spent most of the war so far either in Field Security or locked alone in a first class railway carriage on a crowded steam train puffing north, ferrying seven packages – always seven – of differing size of what he felt sure were explosives between London and Leuchars airfield in Scotland for onward transit to Lerwick, Shetland and the 'Shetland Bus' (the SOE/SIS operation that ran agents, radios and explosives into enemy-occupied Norway).[7] He was recruited into SOE because of his skill with languages: he spoke fluent French. From there he transferred into SSRF after announcing that he was 'fed up and said I would like to get into some action. And then I found myself being interviewed by March-Phillipps in London.' He remembers him chiefly because he had:

the most appalling stutter. Dare I say it? He made a rather poor impression. What was my opinion of him, March-Phillipps? Well, I didn't really get to know him. He separated from us down at our army establishment very much on his own. He, being a regular army officer [sic], still carried on as they did. He had a horse and a batman and at six o'clock in the morning he went for his usual ride. We never really saw March-Phillipps ... March-Phillipps was mainly upstairs where they created models of lighthouses and so on. Only the officers saw those before a raid, not the other ranks. The person we saw was Appleyard ... in my opinion, Appleyard ran the whole show really ... He was wonderful; an absolute gentleman.[8]

Appleyard, boat-bound now because of his injured leg, had elected himself Navigating Officer for Operation *Branford*.

They sailed from Portland aboard MTB 344 at 2100 on the night of Monday, 7 September 1942. The weather was fine with a light wind and a gentle swell from the south-west. Within the hour the port engine packed up and they turned for home: an MTB with one engine out would fall easy prey to marauding E-boats. The boat's mechanic persevered, however, and nursed the engine back to life. Fuel pressure restored, *The Little Pisser* swung back on course with a decision taken that, at the slightest further engine problem, the mission would be aborted. The engine ran smoothly and MTB 344 closed on the Ortac Rock, between Burhou and Casquets. The sea was by this time very confused and before Ortac was finally identified, breaking water was seen in every direction as if the sea was boiling over reefs. Course was altered on one or two occasions to avoid what appeared to be dangers, until Ortac stood out indisputably and the confused and breaking sea was identified as the Pointer Bank and the Danger and Dasher rocks, which have plenty of water over them. After that it was all plain sailing.[9]

They dropped anchor at 0015 and Capt. Ogden-Smith, Second Lt Lassen and six other ranks transferred to the Goatley for the 600-yard, eight-minute paddle to the rocky shore. The sea this close inshore was now absolutely calm with no appreciable tidal set and, with the Goatley held off by kedge anchor, the landing party of six men – cox and bowman were left aboard – scrambled ashore to make their way over 60 yards of broken rock that was wet and slippery with kelp and seaweed to the dry rockline above the reach of high water. From here they made their way uphill towards the crown of the island 400 yards away where once had stood a small stone-walled house long shattered by German artillery practice. Here the team separated to complete their search, Capt. Ogden-Smith taking two men and Corporal James Edgar taking the others and heading west:

> We came across this little hut which was empty ... All I was told to do by Ogden-Smith was go across the other side of the island and investigate it, see what's there ... I was thinking always, are we going to meet some Germans, are we going to get shot up or something?[10]

The island was deserted. There was no sign of any recent habitation nor of any new defence works. On reconnaissance missions such as this, the discovery of what was not there was as important as the discovery of what was. The raiding party withdrew back to the waiting Goatley and were home again, docked at Portland, at 0430 without further incident. Capt. Ogden-Smith was able to report: 'Pack artillery or mortars or loads requiring two or three men are practicable. Wheeled or tracked guns would present great difficulties, there are no sand beaches and all landings would have to be made over rock.' Second Lt Anders Lassen came in for praise, once again, for his 'excellent judgement and seamanship throughout the operation'. Major March-Phillipps added his own views on the end of his officer's report at the end of a third successful mission:

Navigation among the Channel Islands is difficult, but once that difficulty is mastered these islands would appear to present innumerable targets, with obvious advantages over mainland targets in that they are so much more easily recognised. An MTB once within that wilderness of rocks and tide is safe from hostile surface craft and indistinguishable from the rocks themselves, and the landing craft is in a similar position.[12]

It was to prove a prescient and astute observation.

The intelligence gleaned by Operation *Branford*, prized from the enemy foreshore and brought home at dawn to Combined Operations Headquarters by the courage of a few brave men, was interesting, but stayed locked away deep in some file, for Alderney was never invaded. Appleyard wrote home shortly afterwards:

We were out again the other night (Monday) but it was a small and very unobtrusive party whose mission was purely a reconnaissance with a very particular end in view. No one was met, and I am quite sure no one on the other side ever knew we had been. It was in the same district as the previous one in which we robbed the nest and removed the seven eggs! ... I was unable to go ashore, of course, because of my ankle, but I navigated the party and, from that point of view, it was by far the most interesting of anything we have yet done. It was great fun, as there was quite an element of cheek involved![13]

Operations *Barricade*, *Dryad* and *Branford*: three raids – and innumerable false starts – which all took place in just twenty-four days. And next week, almost certainly, there would be more; and the week after that. Perhaps that was why Appleyard's letters home now contain, behind the mandatory cheerfulness of a young officer writing home to anxious parents, a sense of sober reflection:

Thank you for your prayers, Dad. And Mummy's too. I know they are a great help, and many of us pray very earnestly for the success of these parties ... When you pray, don't just pray for our safety, but also pray for our success and our cause, and for one of the greatest things our little unit may help to achieve – the building up of morale in our own forces. When you pray for me, pray for courage and steadfastness and for my team spirit and loyalty to the other chaps on the job.[14]

It was a sentiment of thoughtful, responsible Christian morality that might have surprised Commodore, later Vice Admiral, John Hughes-Hallett RN, Mountbatten's naval adviser. After the war, in his address to the Royal United Services Institute in November 1950, Hughes-Hallett referred to both March-Phillipps and Appleyard as those 'most gallant and imaginative young army officers'.[15] It seems unlikely, however, in view of what had passed between them and what was still to come, that he spoke so highly of them when they served – as they were about to – under his own particular command.

14

Disaster

Major March-Phillipps had not taken part in Operation *Branford*, the raid on the deserted island of Burhou. But he had appended to the end of Capt. Ogden-Smith's after-action report his own astute appreciation of the advantages of silent, inshore raiding amongst the off-lying rocks and islands of places like Burhou. It was an appreciation that, by default, highlighted the disadvantages of using MTBs and Goatleys on less shielded, mainland targets where objectives would be harder to pick out against a continuous shoreline, where MTBs would be exposed to sudden attack by E-boats, and where both MTBs and Goatleys would have nowhere to hide. It was, perhaps, a counsel of perfection. And wars have little time for that.

Their next operation was scheduled for the night of 11–12 September 1942, just four days after the successful completion of *Branford*. This time – March-Phillipps' recommendations notwithstanding – Operation *Aquatint* would be back on the Normandy mainland, down the coast apiece from Barfleur and the site of Operation *Barricade*.

Their mission would be to destroy enemy installations, kill Germans and take prisoners to the west of Port-en-Bessin, a village on the coast north-west of Bayeux on the very eastern edge of what, two years later, would become D-Day's *Omaha* beach.

The shoreline offered a long, flat open beach with high bluffs, or cliffs, behind. In the briefing room upstairs in Anderson Manor, March-Phillipps and Appleyard studied the area intently. On 26 June 1942 a photo-reconnaissance Spitfire had taken high-resolution photographs of the French coastline. Under close scrutiny, these pictures from RAF Medmenham[1] showed there was a gap in the cliffs about half a mile east from the village of Sainte Honorine to the west of Port-en-Bassin where a cluster of houses were believed to be used to billet German troops. The plan was to go ashore, scale the cliffs, move inland along the clifftop, attack the first

German-occupied house they came to, capture a few prisoners and bundle them back down the cliffs to the waiting Goatley – and away. That, at any rate, was the plan.

Their operational orders from COHQ stated that the senior officer had full discretion to cancel the raid 'should he, for any reason whatsoever, consider that it is inadvisable to proceed'.[2] On the night of 11–12 September they duly set out for their target area. As they closed within a few miles of the enemy coast March-Phillipps found the night too foggy. He cancelled the raid. *The Little Pisser* swung her bows to the north and took them home with not a shot fired. Now, the next night, 12–13 September, they were going in again.

For everyone involved at Anderson Manor, it was a time of increasing tension. Head gardener Reg Mullins remembered: 'They used to go up on the farm there, Mr Stevenson's farm. They used to have a fine time up there. Hay-making, messing about, anything to occupy the mind until these nights came, you know.'[3] Others, Tony Hall for example, found their courage in solitude:

I always felt frightened, and if one was involving oneself in something that was definitely possibly fatal – being of my age – there was still some time when one thought that the church was the place one went to. And there was a chapel at Anderson, you see, and I remember I used to go and absolutely wet my knickers, you see, but the thing was on the old basis: don't let *me* be afraid. And the last, the final night when we sort of took off, I went there and, hidden away in a corner, was Gus as well. You know it … it helped me. And if he saw me it must have helped him.[4]

Tony Hall did not have a monopoly on fear: 'I think he [Gus] was a very brave person', recalled Marjorie March-Phillipps, 'because I think he was a very brave *nervous* person. I've told you [Henrietta March-Phillipps] often that he wrote to me and said "Please send me lots of Sanatogen [a nerve tonic] – it makes me feel very brave!"'[5] That afternoon, before they left Dorset, March-Phillipps tried to call Marjorie:

I had been in the office in Baker Street and had gone out to do something, or get something, and came back and I can remember very exactly the very nice girl who was supposed to be working for me telling me that he'd rung up and … it was most extraordinary … he'd rung up – to say goodbye. And it was a most astonishing physical sensation of my heart, or something, just absolutely dropping like a stone.[6]

As in Operation *Branford*, Appleyard was to go on *Aquatint* as navigator aboard MTB 344; his ankle injury still prevented him from going ashore. Peter Kemp's deep stab wound to the thigh on the earlier Operation *Dryad* to Casquets meant that he had only just left hospital and was convalescing at home with his wife in their rented cottage in the nearby village of Spettisbury, about 5 miles from Anderson Manor:

This was the second consecutive night that they had attempted the raid having run into fog the first time when they were within a mile or two of their objective; this part of the coast was heavily defended, and so it might have been wiser to allow a longer interval.

Reynolds and Torrance, who were not included in the raiding party, drove over to us for dinner. It was an uncomfortable meal; conversation was artificial and constrained, for all our thoughts were with our friends crossing the Channel on their desperate mission. As we stood in the garden afterwards silently looking down over the vale of the Stour and watching the shadows creep across the meadows beside the river, Torrance put my fears into words: 'Don't telephone, Peter. As soon as we have any news I'll come over myself and let you know.'

I slept little that night: Burton, my close companion for the last eighteen months, was with March-Phillipps and I hated not to be there beside him in the battle … All next day I loafed about, irritable and unhappy, with no word from Anderson. Long after dark I heard a truck draw up to the gate and rushed out to meet Torrance. His thin, dark face was puckered with anxiety and grief: 'We've lost the lot! Apple came back tonight with Freddie Bourne – I've just left them in the Mess.'[7]

MTB 344 had sailed from Portsmouth and passed the Needles at 2012 on the evening of 12 September 1942.

The night was unusually dark with patches of fog in coastal regions. It was dry and there was a light breeze out of the north east. Sea state was Slight, wind Force 2–3[8] as *The Little Pisser* picked up speed in open water and began banging her way due south. On board – in addition to Lt Freddie Bourne and his crew of seven – were Capt. Geoffrey Appleyard beside him on the bridge acting as navigator, Major Gus March-Phillipps and ten members of the Small Scale Raiding Force, many of whom were officers: Capt. Graham Hayes, Capt. John Burton, Captain The Lord Howard, Lt Tony Hall, Maitre André Desgrange, Company Sergeant Major Tom Winter, Serjeant Alan Williams and Privates Jan Hellings from the Netherlands, Adam Opocznski (cover name Orr) from Poland and Richard Lehniger (cover name Leonard) from Czechoslovakia. Lassen was not on the raid. He had been rewarded with a weekend pass for his work on Operation *Branford*.

The passage out was uneventful and Cap Barfleur was rounded on dead reckoning almost exactly two hours later at 2210 although the land, once again, was obscured by fog. Keeping close inshore to avoid German minefields, speed was reduced to 12 knots to lessen main engine noise as, keeping to the main inshore Le Havre–Cherbourg shipping route, MTB 344 laid off a course that would take her directly to a position off Sainte Honorine. Taking lead-line soundings every two miles during the last 6 miles of the approach, MTB 344, now on her auxiliary silent engine, approached the target area with those on the bridge straining to catch sight of land. There was now no fog but it was so dark that, despite the 100-foot cliffs that rimmed the coast, France remained unseen until half a mile off shore. They were searching, particularly, for that gap in the cliffs they had identified on the aerial reconnaissance photographs:

> As far as I remember we went the night before and we were meant to climb up a certain cliff and if one went along one could see a little kink in the cliff. And we couldn't find the ruddy kink in the cliff … so we went the following night and we *still* couldn't find it. Then Gus said: 'What do you think, chaps? Shall we have a bash?'[9]

The men's replies are not recorded. Almost certainly, there was no debate – nor, indeed, was March-Phillipps asking a genuine question. This was now the second time they had approached the enemy shore on the same mission. To March-Phillipps, a further cancellation must surely have appeared insupportable: they had come across the miles of empty sea to kill the enemy, not to evade him. Precisely *where* that enemy might be encountered may have mattered little. From this remove, March-Phillipps' remarks appear to have been a statement of intent qualified by the uncertainly of their precise location, rather than a genuine question to heavily armed men tensed, nervous and girt for battle. Appleyard reported afterwards:

> Owing to the extraordinary dark nature of the night it was not possible to locate the spot at which the cliff was climbable even from only 400 yards to seaward and, as the climb could only be made at one particular point, it was decided that the landing would have to be made on the beach at Ste Honorine itself. The MTB was therefore anchored in three fathoms of water NNE of the gap in the cliffs and between 300–400 yards offshore at 0017 hours.[10]

The canvas-sided Goatley was lowered carefully over the stern and the men embarked. The die was cast:

> I was supposed to be quite a dab hand with a tommy-gun, so I was the one who got in first, so if there was any trouble as we immediately landed I'd be the one who'd go 'brrrrrrrr' with my tommy-gun. As I was holding on to let the next person in, the boat was going up and down and I thought to myself: Oh, God – how the hell are we going to get back from this one? And I hadn't the slightest idea. But it didn't worry one at that time, you know. You see, you're young, you're strong and ... nothing can assail you. I'd got some spectacles, spare ones in my battledress, and I remember throwing one damp pair away and putting on a clean pair as we left, rather like putting on a top hat or something to go ashore.[11]

They cast off from MTB 344 at 0020 and made for the right-hand side of the gap in the cliffs seen 300–400 yards away in the darkness.

They were more than 3 miles off course. Although they did not know it, they were paddling now, not towards lightly defended Sainte Honorine with its high cliffs but towards the long, flat, open beach at heavily defended Saint-Laurent-sur-Mer away to the right, or west. Ahead, a small, steady white light could be seen at the foot of the cliffs and, as they drew closer, another white light flashed once from the top of the cliff. Committed now, they paddled on silently towards the shore.

The beach they approached and the defences they were about to encounter were a country mile apart from those they had faced on Operations *Branford* and *Barricade*. The Normandy coast and, particularly, the shores that rimmed Baie de La Seine from Barfleur to the north-west to Honfleur below Le Havre to the east – those long, flat, exposed sandy beaches – made the area one of the prime sites for a possible allied invasion. And, long before the arrival of Erwin Rommel, the Germans knew it. Now, with the failure of the major allied raid on Dieppe less than a month previously and Canadian troops bloodily repulsed, German defences were on high alert all along the coast whilst the slave-labour construction of Hitler's much-vaunted Atlantic Wall by the Todt Organisation had begun in earnest five months previously.

The coastline facing MTB 344 that dark night was defended in depth. The area to the centre and north-west of that whole area of Calvados was the responsibility of 7th Army's 716th Infantry Division headquartered in Caen. The Saint-Laurent-Sur-Mer sector of that static Division's area of responsibility was handed to 726th Infantry Regiment commanded by 47-year-old Colonel Munstermann whose headquarters lay a few miles inland at Bayeux. Under *his* command were the 2nd and 3rd

Battalions, Infantry Reserve, who were responsible for six *Stützpunktes* (strong points). Each of these consisted of several small bunkers equipped with anti-tank guns, searchlights and machine-guns. They were ringed with barbed wire and mines and supported in turn by three or four *Widerstandneste* (resistance nests). These were surveillance posts supported by machine-guns, concrete emplacements and firing bays linked by narrow trenches. As the men of SSRF paddled towards the sandy shore they were unaware that they were off course and approaching the killing grounds of *Stützpunkt* 29 and its three *Widerstandsnest*, WN 29A, WN 29B and WN 29C. This was not some overlooked, remote and isolated backwater like Casquets. This was a potential invasion beach. And the men from Anderson Manor were unlikely to encounter elderly reservists wearing hair nets.

WN 29A was located 220 yards from and about 100 feet above the beach. Between beach and position was a belt of marshy ground. WN 29A was manned by twenty-seven men including four NCOs equipped with rifles, two heavy machine-guns, two 9mm Schmeisser sub-machine-guns – considered by many to be the best personal weapon of the war on any side – a few Luger P.08 pistols and two grenade launchers.

WN 29B was below, on the beach, 275 yards away to the west. Protected by barbed wire, it was manned by two NCOs and nine men. Between them they had seven rifles, a light machine-gun, a sub-machine-gun, pistols and a flamethrower.

WN 29C was also on the beach, but further west again from WN 29B. It was manned by an NCO and thirteen men armed with rifles, light and heavy machine-guns, a flamethrower and a 75mm PAK anti-tank gun.

Each unit patrolled ceaselessly, maintaining visual contact between each *Widerstandsnest*. Sometimes they took with them a guard dog held on a short leash.

The Goatley, with eleven men aboard, approached the shore. They were on a falling tide two hours after high water:

> As soon as the Goatley touched down on the beach at about 0020 hours, we saw that we were too near the houses to be able to leave it there with safety. We pulled the boat 200 yards to the east away from the houses and then hauled it up above High Water mark to the base of the cliff. There we left Capt. The Lord Howard in charge of the boat and the rest of the party made their way inland just east of the houses … We went inland and made a good recce for the next fifty minutes … After this we made our way back to the beach again to commence operations from there.[12]

In *Geoffrey*, Ernest Appleyard, writing from post-war sources, claims March-Phillipps and his men then heard a German patrol approaching and decided to ambush the patrol and attempt to capture a prisoner:

> The German patrol walked straight into the trap but the fight that developed was so fierce that all seven of the enemy were killed. When Gus was searching the dead for maps and other useful documents, another and much larger German patrol was heard running towards them ... To attempt to stay and fight these superior forces was hopeless and so Gus's party ran for their boat.[13]

This account, written in good-faith by a man who was not there, does not accord with the recollections of one who was. Tom Winter's account of Operation *Aquatint* continued:

> We had just reached the back of the beach when we heard a patrol coming which consisted of about seven or eight men. They came along the track at the top of the cliff from the East. We were inland of the track on a small depression and well under cover and would not have been discovered had it not been for the dog which was with the patrol. We intended to try and get back to the MTB and get away, but the dog scented us.[14]

They had been bumped by Patrol No 1 from the 3rd Reserve Company of 726th Infantry Regiment, who had been ordered to maintain walk-round contact with all three *Widerstandsnest* that night. Presently they expected to meet another patrol moving west to east towards them. Patrol No 1 commanded by Corporal Wichert consisted of four men armed with rifles, hand grenades and a sub-machine-gun. One of the men, Private Kowalski, carried a light machine-gun and with *him* was a guard dog, held tightly on a leash. Private Kowalski's dog started to growl, then bark and stain at the leash. Challenged by both Wichert and Kowalski, their '*Halt! Wer da?*' was greeted by a single shot. Wichert loosed off a burst of automatic fire, which was answered by a shower of British hand grenades. These fell in the shelter trench behind the observation post and did no damage.[15] The Germans now noticed the Goatley on the beach and lobbed down stick grenades. Amid the chaos, the flashes of grenades, the lights, the crackle of small-arms fire and the confusion of shouted orders, Tony Hall moved forward to grab a prisoner:

> I remember grabbing hold of one chap, a Goon, and dragging him down to the beach, and he was saying the whole time '*Nicht Deutsch! Nicht Deutsch! Checkish! Checkish! Nicht Deutsch, Checkish!*' and I was sort of

saying 'Oh, we'll sort that out in the boat, you know' and then somebody came up and clobbered me from behind.[16]

Tony Hall had been hit on the back of the head by one of the German sentries using a metal-headed stick-grenade as a club. His would-be prisoner scrambled away to raise a wider alarm: by 0132 the entire German coastal zone would be on Level 2 Alert. Knocked unconscious, Tony Hall, the peacetime writer and radio producer who had prayed for courage in the quiet, peaceful chapel at Anderson Manor just a few hours earlier, was left for dead on the beach.

Captain The Lord Francis Howard had been in charge of the Goatley on the beach directly beneath the shower of grenades thrown down by the alerted German patrol: 'In the scrap, I got shot in the leg and could hear the patrol saying in German: "Look, there's a boat."' March-Phillipps and the rest of the men dragged the Goatley down to the receding water's edge, scrambled aboard and began paddling out into the darkness of the open sea towards MTB 244. It was a desperate business. They were paddling for their lives with no way of shooting back. Equipped only with wooden paddles, they were now at the mercy of a full-alerted enemy, their only ally, darkness. Howard remembered: 'We got a certain way out – and then everything went up. Flares and more shooting.'[17]

Tom Winter recorded:

We tried to fight our way out, but unfortunately the Headquarters of the German detachment was not very far [away] in one of the houses and the alarm was raised. We managed to disperse the patrol and succeeded in getting 100 yards out to sea in the Goatley. Verey lights went up and they soon located us and started firing but we were not in a position to return the fire. We had all got away except Lt Hall who we left on the beach, presumably dead, as he had a terrible wound in the back of his head ... Capt. The Lord Howard was wounded while assisting the party to re-embark, but we managed to get him away in the boat.[18]

'Coming out again the boat, I think, would have sunk anyhow,' recalled Howard:

Whether it was actually holed or a shell landed nearby, I don't know. But certainly, long before we got anywhere near the naval boat [MTB 344], the ship sank. Turned over, in fact ... It was a small boat with a canvas bottom. It was really very unsuitable ... And Gus and several of the others tried to swim out to the boat [MTB 344]. The only person I've met since who got anywhere near it told me that he actually got fairly close to the boat but it was, of course, dark. The boat didn't see him ... and though they didn't see him he saw it sailing away ... The only reason I survived was that I actually was swimming about in the dark, being tossed around, I hit something and it happened to be the over-turned boat.[19]

The man who got close but not close enough to MTB 344 was Tom Winter. 'It was, of course, very difficult swimming because the tide was still on the flow [*sic*] and we could not make much headway. The Germans were firing at us all the time.'[20] Winter somehow made it back to the beach. Weapons lost to the sea, exhausted, floundering ashore in sodden battle-dress, he was fired on again at very short range. The shots missed. He was then taken prisoner and dragged off to German headquarters.

Some 400 yards off-shore staring out from the bridge of MTB 344, Appleyard and Bourne could do nothing but wait and watch in an agony of uncertainty as the fate of their friends played out on the enemy shore. After the initial flurry of tommy-gun fire and grenade explosions seen at 0050, Appleyard reported – although perhaps unsurprisingly, timings between MTB and shore party survivors do not mesh precisely – that red and green Verey lights, grenade explosions and more machine-gun fire spread up and down the coast for the next half hour. To begin with, MTB 344 remained unseen. Then, at 0120, she was spotted in the light of flares as she lay out at the edge of darkness and came under accurate machine-gun fire from three machine-guns on the clifftop. One of these rounds put the starboard engine out of action and a larger gun on shore – perhaps a 3-pounder – started firing heavier shells at the gunboat, all of which exploded harmlessly further out to sea. Aboard MTB 344 they then heard English voices calling from somewhere ahead but the messages were confused and indecipherable: 'As the MTB was now fully illuminated by flares and under considerable fire at 400 yards range, the anchor cable was cut and the MTB steamed 2 miles directly away from the coast.'[21] Hidden once more by her cloak of darkness, *The Little Pisser*'s engine was declutched and the power throttled down slowly to give the audible impression that she was moving out to sea. The firing then ceased. Verey lights continued to illuminate the sea close inshore.

The men on MTB 344 were not about to abandon their friends. A pause – and then *The Little Pisser* began to creep back towards the danger zone at slow speed on silent engines and with her infrared contact light burning at the masthead. She came to within half a mile of the beach and stopped again. She stayed there, rocking to the swell as they watched and listened, straining for sight and sound, for forty-five minutes. There was no more firing but the Verey lights continued to be sent up while, on the clifftop, the Germans attempted without success to bring a searchlight into action. Appleyard, Bourne and the Vickers gunners on either side of the bridge scanned the darkness. Nothing. No signals, no sign of their friends. What might possibly have been the Goatley was spotted in the fizzling light of one of the flares. It was lying broadside on to the right of the beach above high water mark and almost up against the sea wall. No one was with it and the sighting could not be confirmed in the uncertain light.

At 0225 MTB 344 came under fire again but this time from the sea. She had been picked up in silhouette against the shore in the light of the flares. Now seven or eight shells exploded between her and the shore, fired apparently from at least two unseen German patrol craft closing in astern from the north and north-west to cut off her line of retreat. A dozen more shells screamed over from seaward, one of which landed 20 feet off the starboard beam, drenching the ship with a cascade of water: 'E-boats were well-armed, fast. We wouldn't have had a chance with them. We had two twin Vickers on each side of the bridge, .303 only. We wouldn't have stood an earthly against them.'[22] Now the machine-gunners on the cliffs spotted them and opened fire, too. It was time to leave. MTB 344 swung away to the east down the coast and slid once more into darkness. Lt Freddie Bourne recalled:

We had to cut and run ... No way we could have got the Commandos back. One of the chaps tried to swim out. We heard them in the water but they were too far off for us to do anything and by that time we'd got a searchlight on us and we couldn't rescue them.[23]

A mile eastwards and then they altered course north, deliberately cutting across the top of a German minefield to ensure they were back in the safety of home waters before dawn broke. What passed between Lt Bourne and Capt. Appleyard on the bridge as MTB 344 bashed home during that miserable return with dawn lightning the sky off the starboard beam is not recorded. Perhaps they shared little more than silence as each absorbed the impact of such sudden, catastrophic loss; perhaps they discussed the possibility of a swift return on another night, infrared contact light burning at the masthead, to pick up survivors who, even now, might be going to ground to await rescue in a day or two. There would have been time to spare for such thoughts, such discussion; under-powered and on only one engine, MTB 344 made only 12 knots as she limped back across the Channel in a lumpy sea and swell with the wind now rising F4. She docked at Portsmouth at 1035.

Hobbling ashore, Appleyard made his way to HMS *Hornet* to make that initial single page, raid notification report to C-in-C Portsmouth.

He then caught the late morning train to London to report directly to Brigadier Gubbins at SOE Headquarters in Baker Street. After that, he knew, there would be other people he would have to inform. For the sensitive young officer who had just lost all his closest friends, it was the end of what must surely have been the most harrowing twelve hours of his life.

By then it was mid-morning in Normandy, too. Company Sergeant Major Tom Winter had been dragged to the local command post. There he had found Captain The Lord Howard lying wounded on the floor. There too was André Desgrange who was unhurt. All three were told they were to be shot. There was no sign of the others.

Not all had struggled ashore to capture the previous night. Capt. Graham Hayes – always a strong swimmer – had worked out his own salvation and, jettisoning his weapons, had swum away from the lights westwards up the coast. He had then landed near Vierville-sur-Mer, crawled ashore, walked inland and presently found warmth and refuge with a brave French farmer. It would be the first stage of a lengthy and courageous escape attempt.

The Germans reported Lt Tony Hall dead. In truth, he was lying unconscious in a German hospital with a serious head wound that would lead to his eventual repatriation. Capt. Burton, Private Hellings and Private Orr initially evaded capture. John Burton's widow recalled:

The Germans had the beach very well defended and the raid was a disaster. John, a Dutchman [Hellings] and a Pole [Orr] managed to get off the beach and swim for the MTB but that was under such heavy gunfire that it had to leave before they could reach it. They swam down the coast for some way and then went ashore. In the daytime they hid and were given clothes and food by the French, and at night they walked. One night they walked right into a German patrol [Fallschirmjager on exercise], so that was the end of that. They had been trying to get to the Spanish border, but found out that they had been going round in circles. They were handed over to the SS who put them up against a wall and said they were going to shoot them but then, for some unknown reason, changed their minds. John was sent to a prisoner of war camp in Germany. He didn't know what happened to the other two.[24]

Jan Hellings and Adam Orr had been captured near Rennes. Adam Orr – alias Polish Jew Abraham Opoczynski – was sent to Dachau concentration camp and from there to the Bad Tolz Kommando, an SS work camp. He died on 12 April 1945, aged 23, and is buried in the military cemetery in Durnbach, 30 miles from Munich. Jan Hellings was sent to two different Stalags, one of which was in Fallingbostel, Lower Saxony. He appears to have survived the war.[25]

Major Gustavus March-Phillipps (34), Serjeant Alan Williams (22) and Private Richard Lehniger (42) were all dead, killed by gunshot wounds and/or drowning.

'The next morning I was taken out and had to drag up the beach the bodies of Major March-Phillipps, Sgt Williams and Pte Leonard', reported Tom Winter many months later:

> I had not seen or heard anything further of the fate of Lt. Hall, only that the Germans reported him as dead and brought in his shoulder titles. I was taken back to the headquarters again, where we waited for a lorry to take us to Caen. The bodies were taken away and buried at St. Laurent, according to an Intelligence officer. Lord Howard had been taken to hospital during the night and Lt. Desgrange and I were taken to Caen in the charge of a guard and the Intelligence Officer, where we underwent a very stiff interrogation.[26]

Winter was kept at Caen for eight days. When he was escorted up to the hospital to see Captain The Lord Howard recovering from his wound he found Lt Tony Hall, still unconscious. After the war, Winter, the man who had moved March-Phillipps' body, was asked about the manner in which the Major had met his end: 'It's been said that he drowned, but I don't think so. I am sure that he died of wounds.'[27]

Marjorie March-Phillipps heard the news of her husband's death at Dunham Massey where she had started her parachute course. She was also – although she did not know it at the time – two months pregnant with her daughter Henrietta: 'I *knew* something had gone wrong. Anyway, we did our training and then on Monday evening somebody had left the evening paper and I found this paper and I saw the paragraph which was a German communique ...'[28]

That communiqué, issued at 1250 on 14 September by the Official German News Agency stated:

> During the night of the 12–13 September, a British landing party, consisting of five officers, a Company Sergeant Major and a private, tried to make a footing on the French Channel coast, east of Cherbourg. Their approach was immediately detected by the defence. Fire was opened on them and the landing craft was sunk by direct hits. Three English officers and a de Gaullist Naval officer were taken prisoner. A Major, a Company Sergeant Major and a Private were brought to land dead.[29]

Appleyard returned to Anderson Manor. Among those who greeted his return, anxious for news, was James Edgar:

Appleyard told me that the whole outfit were to look at the horizon where they were landing to see if there was a break in the horizon, a dip in it, up which they were possibly able to make their way inland. And Appleyard told me that, if they didn't find that little dip, silhouetted, as it were, they were to put off the operation. Well, this is what Appleyard told me himself. And March-Phillipps didn't obey their original plan ... We were simply told by Appleyard that they had all been shot up. A Verey light was sent up by the Germans – that's what did for them ... Appleyard was quite devastated, there's no doubt about it.[30]

Peter Kemp remembered the mood amongst the men when the news broke at Anderson Manor:

We had been prepared for casualties, but not for such a catastrophe as this. The death of the gallant idealist and strange, quixotic genius who had been our commander and our inspiration, together with the loss of so many good friends, all in the space of a few hours, was a crippling calamity which nearly put an end to our activities. Indeed, it probably would have done so but for the energetic reaction of Appleyard who refused to let our grief for our comrades arrest his determination to avenge them.[31]

James Edgar was right. Some time later Appleyard wrote to Major Cholmondeley, the man whose manor house home they had appropriated with such high hopes back in March and admitted:

His death was a tremendous blow to me ... Gus meant a very great deal to me and he was my closest personal friend. We had been together for over two years and the occasion when he was killed was the one and only occasion in all that time that we were not actually alongside each other in every 'party'.[32]

Now, for Appleyard, there was a debt to settle, a dead friend to avenge. There would be another raid. Soon.

Loss and Condolence

When Appleyard reported back to COHQ in London on the disaster that was Operation *Aquatint*, there was an extensive debrief. That same day Combined Operations' Intelligence Officer GSO2 Major Ian Collins issued a memorandum entitled: 'Lessons Learnt and Notes for Future Consideration Ref: S.S.R.F.'[1]

Top of the list of twelve points was a statement of the painfully obvious that 'The risk of carrying out a frontal assault even on a supposedly lightly defended objective is considerable.' Having stated that the plan had to be changed once it was found impossible to identify the small beach and narrow gully that had been their primary landing objective, Collins went on to note the need for choosing a landing place where 'a safe and quick get away can be effected'. With hindsight, it should perhaps have been noted at the early planning stage that, on the exposed Normandy coast, there were likely to be precious few of those once the German defences had been alerted and started putting flares or starshell up over the flat and open sea. Yet alerting the German defences was the implicit and desired consequence of all such raids. In any event, noted Collins, the raiding force should in future be backed up by two Goatleys, not just one.

There should also be an agreed recovery plan in case raiding parties got left behind. Lt Bourne and Capt. Appleyard received a mild rap over the knuckles for hazarding their boat: 'MTB incurred too great a risk in lying so close off-shore and was lucky not to be sunk', but there was praise for their navigation throughout which he described as 'excellent'. At that early stage the morning after the raid, however, the true extent of the navigational error that put the Goatley so far west of their objective had yet to be realised.

News of the disaster that had befallen the men of Operation *Aquatint* – that the entire raiding party of six officers and five other ranks were now to be posted missing – was distributed four days later by Lord Louis Mountbatten, the Chief of Combined Operations. Stating that 'it is particularly requested, for operational reasons, that further circulation of this report may be severely restricted',[2] Mountbatten sent it to the C-in-Cs Portsmouth, Plymouth, Portland and Dover, to Gubbins at SOE, to their friend and mentor Brigadier Robert 'Lucky' Laycock at the newly formed SS Brigade and to the Air Officer Commanding Nos 11 and 12 Group, Royal Air Force. It was also circulated to a host of smaller commands and organisations.

Two days later Mountbatten made time to write another, more private letter in his own hand. It was to Marjorie, the newly widowed wife of Gus March-Phillipps. By then his death, at least, had been confirmed. Mountbatten wrote to her at the home she and Gus had just made in Alford Street:

> I write to you to express my deep sympathy in the loss of your husband.
>
> There is little I can say except to tell you of our impressions of him during the short time he operated under my command and it is because these impressions were so strong that I wish to write to you.
>
> He was convinced that the spirit that had led so many Englishmen into many dangerous ventures was still alive and his determination to attack the enemy and carry out the kind of raids he had in mind was so strong that he overcame every obstacle; and having done so carried out three brilliant and successful raids.
>
> This success was very largely due to his own skill and leadership and to the fine spirit he had infused into the special force he commanded. We can ill afford to lose someone of his character and ability.
>
> Both myself and my staff had grown personally very fond of him during the short time we came to know him. We shall miss him very much, and I would like to express our sympathy to yourself in your greater loss.
>
> Yours sincerely
> Louis Mountbatten[3]

There was also the standard war casualty letter of elegant condolence from King George VI:

> The Queen and I offer you our heartfelt sympathy in your great sorrow.
>
> We pray that your country's gratitude for a life so nobly given in its service may bring you some measure of consolation.
>
> George RI

Gustavus March-Phillipps had been a firebrand patriot seemingly from an earlier, Elizabethan age who had marched to the beat of Drake's drum.

Once he had nursed plans to raid Harfleur on St Crispin's Day, the anniversary of the battle of Agincourt. Now, the inspirational, short-tempered visionary who Peter Kemp said combined 'the idealism of a Crusader with the severity of a professional soldier', the former novelist who had knelt by his bed in prayer each night, was gone.

Peter Kemp wrote to Marjorie:

> [A]lthough I only knew him for so short a time, he made an impression on me that will last all my life. His sincerity, personality and power of leadership, his magnificent ideals and his personal charm and kindness made him one of the finest men I have ever had the privilege of knowing and I am proud to have served under him.[4]

According to one account, Lassen sensed his leader's death. He had been granted weekend leave and had spent the night at the home of a Mrs Knight in Bournemouth. Earlier that evening he had taken to pacing the room restlessly and gazing out at the weather. In the middle of the night he had woken up 'with a loud yell' convinced, in that moment, that Gus had been killed.[5]

Desmond Longue remembered March-Phillipps from the *Postmaster* days: 'He was a tremendous patriot. Almost to ... to the point that one looked at him and wondered whether he was really true.' Henrietta, the daughter he would now never see, agreed: 'Yes – sometimes I wondered if Gus and Apple were really true too – they were so very idealistic – above all, so very patriotic. Looking back from now it would be easy to laugh.'[6] The nervous ex-Indian Army officer who kept himself dosed with Sanatogen and whose papers included a 1938 certificate from the Pelman Institute for 'The Scientific Development of Mind and Memory', the Elizabethan buccaneer born into the wrong age, left a legacy that perhaps echoes some of that ambivalence expressed to Brigadier Gubbins by Julius Hanau in London before Operation *Postmaster*. What was it that made Gus March-Phillipps impressive, enabled him to elicit such fierce loyalty from some men and yet repel others in equal measure?

'I've spent ... I suppose I've spent thirty years it is now, jolly nearly, trying to work out the answer to that question and one knows that one invents all sorts of false reasons', reflected Jan Nasmyth in 1972:

> One thinks of him as being a great commander and a great leader of men and that sort of thing ... But in many ways he wasn't. In many ways he was an extremely bad one. I've met people who said they couldn't get on with him at all, and some people thought he was a snob, obviously, and other people

said he's so nervy that he had a terrible effect on people, and he certainly did that to me. I mean, in the end I quit the outfit because I was more or less nervously demoralised by Gus. He had this terrible temper, besides being very nervous. But – and I think, you see, it's very hard to describe – that Gus seemed to be able to live almost an inspired life at times. These were times when he had reached some sort of level of balance inside himself.[7]

Tony Hall, the man left on the beach in Normandy after being struck on the head by a German stick grenade as he tried to grab a prisoner during *Aquatint* had no such ambivalence, no such doubts, not even thirty years later:

He [Gus] somehow wrapped up for one all that one loved in this country and all that one loved when going to the aid of other people. He represented to me exactly what I wanted for one and a half years ... I wanted a hero to lead me. And he was a hero.[8]

In Africa, Gus March-Phillipps had sometimes whiled away the hours of boredom writing poems. Perhaps one of these might stand as his epitaph:

If I must die in this great war
When so much seems in vain
And man in huge unthinking hordes
Is slain as sheep are slain
But with less thought: then do I seek
One last good grace to gain
Let me die, Oh Lord, as I learned to live
When the world seemed young and gay
And 'Honour Bright' was a phrase they used
That they do not use today
And faith was something alive and warm
When we gathered round to pray
Let me be simple and sure once more
Oh Lord, if I must die
Let the mad unreason of reasoned doubt
Unreasoning, pass me by,
And the mass mind, and the mercenary,
And the everlasting 'why'.
Let me be brave and gay again
Oh Lord, when my time is near
Let the good in me rise up and break

The stranglehold of fear;
Say that I die for Thee and The King
And what I hold most dear.

Major Gustavus March-Phillipps, DSO, MBE, 1908–1942

†††

It was low water. At dawn on the same day that they had been killed, Tom Winter and André Desgrange were ordered to carry the bodies of their three comrades above the high water mark on the beach where they had been washed ashore. They were filmed doing so by a German propaganda unit. On 15 September, all three commandos were buried in the French village cemetery of Saint-Laurent-sur-Mer when, once again, the ceremony was filmed. Three carts, each carrying a coffin bedecked with flowers, were driven to the cemetery preceded by a section of 3rd Reserve Company stationed at Saint Laurent. German officers brought up the rear. Local civilians were forbidden to attend but two men, Jules Scelles and First World War veteran Henri Leroutier,[9] watched secretly from behind a wall. After the service a guard of honour fired a three-gun salute over the graves.

Major Gustavus March-Phillipps, Private Richard Lehniger and Serjeant Alan Williams had been laid to rest side by side. They lie there still.

†††

The Intelligence Officer at Combined Operations Headquarters made further recommendations in the light of *Aquatint*'s failure:

9. It is strongly recommended that as soon as possible another raid is carried out for the sake of morale; next suggested raid (island of Sark) is to be carried out approximately Sept 20. The fact must be faced that we are certain to have some mishaps.
10. Every encouragement should be given to SSRF to bring their numbers back to normal. Capt. Appleyard is seeing Brigadier Gubbins. A detachment from No 12 Commando could probably be made available immediately.
11. Captain Appleyard MC to be appointed SSRC [Small Scale Raiding Commander].
12. Question of awards to SSRF.[10]

Capt. Geoffrey Appleyard was now promoted Major, Commanding Officer, SSRF. He had a meeting with Gubbins on 21 September and it appears likely from the cryptic single word diary entry 'Anderson' that Gubbins visited Anderson Manor – possibly to quite literally rally the troops – on 26–27 September.[11]

The attack on Sark would, indeed, be the next raid by the men of the Small Scale Raiding Force. Operation *Basalt* would earn its place in history, however, not for yet more displays of courage in the pursuit of some shining Elizabethan ideal but for precisely the opposite: for the raiders' deliberate killing of prisoners who were both trussed and unarmed. According to testimony given by Colonel General Alfred Jodl, Hitler's Chief of Staff, at the International Military Tribunal at Nuremberg in 1946, the SSRF raid on Sark and the tying of prisoners was seen as one of *the* signal events of provocation that led to the issue of Hitler's infamous *Kommandobefehl* (commando order) later that same month. Signed by Jodl, this led to the execution of scores of captured commandos and members of the Special Air Service Regiment (SAS). It would also lead directly to the execution of one of March-Phillipps' men cast ashore on Operation *Aquatint*, who was even now making his way doggedly towards the illusion of safety and freedom.

The Tying of Hands

In the immediate aftermath of Operation *Aquatint*, two other raids were considered and then abandoned before *Basalt* became a reality. The first of these was Operation *Woodland*, a raid on Cap Levy near Cherbourg by twelve SSRF to capture enemy personnel and destroy a searchlight and machine-gun position. This had advanced some way down the planning pipeline before it was cancelled: the losses endured on Operation *Aquatint* had stripped SSRF of the experienced men it needed to mount the raid. Replacements would arrive shortly, certainly, but they would need to be trained and assimilated into the ways of night raiding. Until then a raid that involved up to twelve SSRF was simply too ambitious. Operation *Woodland* was scrubbed. *Blarneystone* was cancelled for different reasons: a straightforward recce along almost identical lines to that on Burhou, to see if the tiny Îles St Marcouf some way off shore almost opposite what would become D-Day's *Utah* beach in Normandy, was cancelled because of bad weather and lack of suitable raiding craft. The date of that proposed raid is not known but it is possible that it too had been planned before disaster overtook Operation *Aquatint*. And that the lack of MTB/ML availability for the two men of SSRF who might have carried out the recce – possibly by kayak – was linked to the bullet-damage to the engine that put MTB 344 out of action and back into the Camper Nicholson workshops for overhaul and repair.

Sark had long been on Appleyard's raid wish list. After the successful Casquets raid – Operation *Dryad* – he had written home to his father: 'By the way, Sark light was on! Showing a red flash every fifteen seconds. I should like to land on Sark again sometime.' Now his wish was to be granted. Sark, nestling between Jersey and Guernsey and lying 20 miles west of the Cherbourg peninsula, had been visited by the Appleyard family several times during peacetime and he knew his way around the island. When the raid was over – and ever mindful of security – he wrote to his younger brother Ian:

Last Saturday night really was fun. We spent over four hours there and had a really good browse round before we rang the bell and announced ourselves. It was so strange to see old familiar places again. Such as the tree under which you found half-a-crown. Remember? I recognised it immediately.

Fun? For Appleyard, just possibly. It would not be so for all.

Leaving Portland just after 1900 on the night of 3 October, this Operation *Basalt* represented their second attempt to reach the island. The first – on 19 September – had been thwarted by weather, time and the conflicting sea conditions and currents they encountered close to the island. The mission had been abandoned. Now, a fortnight later, conditions appeared ideal: the sea was smooth with a slight swell and the wind was light and variable from the south-east. The aim of *Basalt* – the first raid after Gus' death – was to take prisoners. To accomplish this Appleyard – he would lead the raid, ankle injury notwithstanding – took with him six officers and men from SSRF reinforced by Capt. Philip Pinckney and four men from No 12 Commando, making a raiding party of twelve in all.

Pinckney was a remarkable officer and, according to one of those who served with him for three years, 'one of the finest officers in the war'.[2]

On 23 June 1942, whilst still attached to No 12 Commando, Pinckney proposed to his commanding officer that he and Jeffrey Quill, the famous civilian test pilot, a personal friend and only the second man to fly the Spitfire, should be carried to the French coast by MTB. Paddling ashore by canoe, they would then make their way to the German aerodrome at Cherbourg-Maupertus and stake out one of the new Focke-Wulf 190s the British boffins were itching to get their hands on. Lying up overnight and observing the enemy aerodrome, they would then penetrate the airfield, wait until the aircraft had been warmed up and then shoot the pilot and whatever ground crew were standing around. Pitching the dead pilot out onto the runway, Quill would then fly the enemy aircraft to England leaving Pinckney alone in enemy territory to find his own way home. Operation *Airthief* was rendered unnecessary when a lost German airman, Oberleutnant Armin Faber, mistook Bristol Channel for the English Channel and landed an intact and wholly airworthy Focke-Wulf 190 at RAF Pembury in Wales by mistake. Quill recorded: 'I am afraid I have to confess to a certain easing of tension within my guts!'[3] After offering to snatch a Messerschmitt 109F instead, Pinckney was bitterly disappointed when the raid was abandoned. In September 1943, he was captured by the Germans on Operation *Speedwell* and shot.

One of those Pinckney brought with him for Operation *Basalt* was 21-year-old Horace 'H' or 'Stokey' Stokes,[4] a tough young Midlander from the Small Heath working-class area of Birmingham. He too had endured and survived the commando course at Achnacarry:

> In Scotland we were out for weeks on end, mostly at night, and it was here that I really learned to handle boats, how to fire a wide variety of weapons, how to use a 'fighting knife' and kill quickly and silently, and my stock-in-trade – explosives. Darkness was our daylight and we became completely proficient in operating at night completely in the dark.[5]

Meanwhile, in October 1942, there was a raid to be planned on Sark. Defences and garrison strength on Sark were largely unknown. In fact, they were to prove considerably more substantial than was anticipated. On Sark in October 1942 were a heavy machine-gun section, a light mortar group and anti-tank Platoon all from 6 *Kompanie, Infanterieregiment* 583 of 319th Division. A five-man engineer detachment was also on the island carrying out work on the harbour installations at Creux.[6]

MTB 344 approached Casquets on dead reckoning, passed these abeam without incident at 2053 and then altered course to the east and reduced speed. Sark was identified and closed on silent engine at 5 knots. A ridged spine of rock known as the Hog's Back curves down steeply to the sea just above the pinched mid-point of Sark dividing the land into two wide bays – Dixcart Bay and Derrible Bay – both of which offered obvious landing possibilities. Fearing these beaches might be mined, Appleyard opted instead to land on rocks directly beneath Pointe Chateau, the southern tip of the Hog's Back. It was a shrewd move. Both beaches had, indeed, been recently mined.

Nimble-footed Second Lt Anders Lassen was sent ahead to recce the steep climb up the rocks to the clifftop where it was reported a machine-gun post might have been recently installed. He slid ashore and disappeared into the moonless dark. The rest of the party followed more slowly. Appleyard reported:

> The ascent was very steep and difficult for the first 150 feet and made dangerous by shale and loose rock and the darkness, but the gradient then eased and the route ended up steep gullies of seathrift and rock to the top of the Hog's Back. The whole party was collected on top at 2400 hrs.[7]

One on the climb was Bombardier Redborn. He remembered: 'The navigation was excellent. We landed exactly at the right spot. We rowed in and the landing boat was made fast and left with a guard [Second Lt Young] while the rest of us clambered up the steep path which led to the top of the cliff.'[8] Presently, Lassen returned. There were no defence posts on the Hog's Back ridge, just barbed wire entanglements. However, as Appleyard's father told it:

As Geoff reached the top of the cliff after a stiff climb, and cautiously peered over the edge, he was horrified to see the vague silhouettes of a number of German soldiers about fifty yards away. He waited for some minutes in the hope that they would move on and then decided that here was an ideal opportunity to eliminate a complete German patrol and probably get a few prisoners as well. He therefore crawled stealthily towards the enemy and when he had so shortened the range that it was impossible for his men to miss, he prepared to give the order to fire. Then a doubt crossed his mind … He decided to investigate and crawled nearer and nearer. Then to their amazement his men heard him chuckle, stand up and call them forward. They found him examining a row of perfectly dressed dummies used by the island garrison for target practice![9]

They moved on, 'the stillness of the night was only broken by the cry of a seagull or when the wire was snapped with cutters. We fumbled around the whole time in the dark …'[10] Presently they heard a German foot patrol approaching and melted off the path into the undergrowth. The patrol passed by, oblivious.

Looking for trouble, weapons cocked, crouching low and leaning forward with ears straining for the slightest sound of danger above the cry of the seagulls and the distant murmur of the sea on rocks far below, the raiders moved off inland along the spine of the Hog's Back. En route they 'attacked' what they thought was a Nissen hut and wireless mast but which turned out to be the flagpole, butts and targets of a firing range. Luckily, no shots were fired. They pressed on, drifting westwards, pushing their way downhill through thick gorse and bracken towards a group of small cottages known as Petit Dixcart. These cottages – identified as the raiders' primary target – were reached at 0015. All were deserted.

Now they moved on to the secondary target, the isolated house of La Jaspellerie twenty minutes' march away to the west overlooking Dixcart Bay. To reach this they had to cross a shallow stream and then climb up through close, broad-leaf woodland and across an open field. The house was reported to contain a number of Germans. While the rest of the party stayed back three men – Appleyard, Corporal Flint and one other – carried out a swift recce. The square-faced, four-chimneyed house and outbuildings were in darkness. La Jaspellerie appeared locked and deserted. Calling up the rest of the party, Appleyard forced entry via a set of French windows on the south-east side of the house. 'We tried every door and window but all were locked, so we smashed a window in the French doors, undid the latch and tumbled into the room', Redborn recalled:

Downstairs was all empty but Major Appleyard and Corporal Flint who went upstairs were luckier. There they found an elderly lady. I did not see her myself because I and some of the others had to stay on watch downstairs. We had made a lot of noise breaking the window and, as there was always the possibility of an enemy patrol, we had to be prepared to shoot if surprised.[11]

The 'elderly lady' was 41-year-old Mrs Frances Pittard, daughter of an RNVR Captain and widow of the island's retired medical officer who had died four months earlier. Described by Appleyard as 'well-educated and intelligent' she proved a mine of valuable information:

The bulk of the party was then sent out of the house to form a cordon whilst two remained behind [Appleyard and Corporal Flint] and during the next hour interrogated the woman in detail. With the help of a large scale map of the island she produced, they obtained a great deal of information regarding the defences of the island, the billets and numbers of troops, living conditions, morale, etc.[12]

Mrs Pittard was offered the chance to return to England with the raiding party. Spurning the possibility of reprisals, she declined: 'This is my home', she said. 'I've lived here for fifteen years and I don't want to leave it. Besides, if I go the Germans will punish the Sarkees. I think it's best to stay and brave it out.'[13]

Critically, she told them the whereabouts of the nearest Germans: there were twenty soldiers garrisoned nearby, not in the Hotel Dixcart, as they had thought, but in the adjoining annexe. With time pressing, they moved on. They had already been ashore an hour longer than planned. Now Appleyard gave Corporal James Edgar new instructions:

I was ordered by Appleyard to hurry back to the cliff-top and to flash 'wait' as we had over-run our specified time and the boat might depart without us. In the moonlight I got lost in the whins [sic] and had to force my way, losing my belt with .45 colt in the process.[14]

Ten men set off towards the Germans in the annexe of the hotel where the Appleyard family had spent carefree holidays ten years earlier. Now they were searching for more than half crowns. Redborn remembered that:

when we neared what we believed to be the German quarters, Anders and I were chosen to deal with the sentry ... We went ahead to see the lie of the land. A little later we came back to tell what we had found out ... We returned to the spot where the sentry was on patrol. As there was only one man, Anders said he could manage on his own.[15]

It was the moment of contact, of silent, close-quarter killing, that Lassen had longed for. After the war David Smee, a fellow commando officer, recalled sharing a room with Lassen before a raid. It was an experience difficult to forget:

> He kept me awake most of the night, cleaning his pistol and sharpening his fighting knife while talking to himself about 'Killing the fuckers!' Nobody else could have put such venom into knife and pistol cleaning. It was in keeping with his enormously forceful nature. I was glad not to be his enemy.[16]

Now, at last, that enemy was near. He was 36-year-old *Obergefreiter* Peter Oswald.

> We lay down and watched him and calculated how long it took him to go back and forth. We could hear his footsteps when he came near, otherwise everything was still. By now the others had crept up so that all caught a glimpse of the German before Anders crept forward alone.
>
> The silence was broken by a muffled scream. We looked at each other and guessed what had happened. Then Anders came back and we could see that everything was all right. The Major believed that the way was clear for us to approach the annexe.[17]

Appleyard makes no recorded mention of Anders' killing of the sentry in either his letter to his father or in his formal after-action report to Lord Louis Mountbatten, Chief of Combined Operations.[18]

The annexe was connected to the main Dixcart hotel by a covered passageway. Appleyard's men entered this and then, poised for battle and with fingers on triggers, pushed open the door at the far end and rushed inside. There was no one there. They found themselves in a long corridor with doors running down either side:

> The Major gave orders that each man should take a room and all go in at the same time. I rushed into the room allotted to me and heard snoring. I switched on the light and saw a bed with a German asleep. The first thing I did was draw the curtains and tear the bedclothes off him. Half-asleep, he pulled them back again. I got the blankets off a second time and when he saw my blackened face he got a shock … I hit him under the chin with a knuckleduster and tied him up. Then I looked round the room for papers or cameras.

I got him to his feet still half-senseless and out into the corridor where Captain Pinckney, Andy and the others already stood; there were five prisoners all told. I covered them while the others searched the rooms once more and when this was done we took the prisoners outside.

When we were all outside, it happened. Until then, everything had gone fine but as soon as we were out in the moonlight they began to scream and shout, probably because they saw how few we were. All five of them had their hands tied behind their backs but they were not gagged. As soon as they started hollering we set about them with cuts and blows. Major Appleyard shouted: 'Shut the prisoners up!' and this began a regular fight.

I was not exactly sure what happened next as I had so much trouble with my prisoner – he had got his hands free and we were fighting. He was just on the point of getting away so I gave him a rugger tackle and we both fell to the ground. He got free again as he was much bigger than me but I grabbed at him and we rolled about in a cabbage patch. One of the officers shouted above the noise: 'If they try to get away, shoot them.'

Captain Pinckney's prisoner got free and started towards the hotel shouting at the top of his voice. The Captain went after him and a shot rang out. I had just about had enough of my German: I couldn't manage him so I had to shoot him and found that the others were doing the same with their prisoners. All, that is, except Anders who still stood and held two Germans tightly.[19]

Operation *Basalt* was a raid that was to linger in the memory: 'Years after the war I have had time to reflect on those moments, and situations like this are rarely understood by anyone who has never been in such a position', remembered 'Stokey' Stokes who was on the *Basalt* raid:

We were by now a small team of ten men, a long way from home on an enemy island miles away from our own transport facing a far superior force.

Anyone who has handled prisoners under combat conditions a long way from home on the enemy's doorstep will know how hard this is. Especially when your prisoners know that you are outnumbered and outgunned, and that their lives are about to change forever one way or another. People can react to this in many different ways: some are subdued, which is what you hope for, others you know will fight. Once all Hell breaks loose there is only one way to deal with this and it is to be aggressive and controlling right from the start. It's known as the shock of capture. You can't fuck about.

Our job wasn't to fight the whole island, our mission was to get prisoners home alive. By now everyone was being alerted to our position and we had only seconds in which to decide what to do. In the chaos two more German soldiers were killed leaving two ... both of these men had been properly restrained with their hands tied. One of them was completely subdued, the other struggled wildly in response to the loud and approaching sounds of his fellow comrades who were now heading in our direction.

We were told to bugger off and make haste back to the boat. I moved towards the front of the party with two of us forcibly taking control of the first POW. What seemed like a few seconds later we heard an almighty ruckus behind us and another shot was fired.[20]

Fighting his way through the thick gorse on the way back to the elusive Hog's Back, Corporal James Edgar heard the shots:

I discovered there was very, very thick gorse in front of me – shockingly sharp gorse and so I just dived into it and forced myself right through it. Whilst I'm going through it I hear: bang-bang, bang-bang, bang-bang, bang-bang and I said to myself: Oh, the boys have met up with them.[21]

Bombardier Redborn recalled:

More shots rang out with shouting and screaming. It was a hell of a rumpus and lights were coming on in the hotel. Anders, who had now freed himself of his prisoners, wanted to throw some grenades through the hotel windows but Major Appleyard said no, keep them, we may need them later. By now Germans were pouring out of the hotel and, when we saw how many of them there were, we decided to get away. We still had one prisoner who had seen what we had done to the others and he was stiff with fright and did everything we told him.

The most important thing now was to get back to the boat as quickly as possible. The island was waking up and the German headquarters was like a wasps' nest. How we ran.[22]

Inexplicably, there were no shots, no sounds of pursuit. Racing back to the clifftop in the moonlight, Lassen brought up the rear and helped Private Smith who had been wounded. The exhausted, terrified and bespectacled German prisoner, *Obergefreiter* Weinrich, floundered along surrounded by the ten fit, black-faced raiders and was dragged down the cliffs and bundled into the Dory. The rest of the party scrambled in without incident and paddled away from the shore. Once aboard MTB 344, her silent engine started, *The Little Pisser* slipped away unscathed into the darkness. In their haste to get away the raiders left behind two commando knives, a Sten magazine, a pistol, a pair of wire cutters, torches, a woollen cap, a scarf and several toggle ropes. All these items were recovered by the Germans now busy working their way along the Hog's Back to Pointe Chateau.

Operation *Basalt* was over. Not a man of the raiding party had been lost. But the controversy surrounding its execution was about to begin.

By binding the hands of prisoners who were then shot, Major Appleyard and his men presented the Germans with a propaganda opportunity they would not be slow to exploit: the Third Geneva Convention of 1929 – today's expanded protocols only came into force in 1949 – states that non-combatants, combatants who have laid down their arms and combatants who are *hors de combat* due to wounds, *detention* or any other cause shall, in all circumstances, be treated humanely. It also states, quite specifically, that they shall not be subjected to outrages upon personal dignity, nor to humiliating and degrading treatment. Geneva protocols might be light years removed from the horrors of death at dagger-point and the close-quarter mayhem of a night raid on Sark, but those were precisely the Rights the Convention sought to enshrine. Now, those Rights had been abused. And the incontrovertible evidence lay there, tied and crumpled, in the chill light of dawn.

One sentry, *Obergefreiter* Peter Oswald, had been stabbed to death by Lassen; Bombardier Redborn had shot his prisoner and Capt. Patrick Dudgeon, it appeared, had been responsible for the death of a third. According to Ian Warren, an SSRF Officer who was not on the raid to Sark but who discussed it the next day with Capt. Dudgeon back at Anderson Manor: 'He hit his prisoner with the barrel of his pistol, not the butt – and, forgetting his finger was on the trigger, blew the top of the German's head off.'[23]

The German cemetery at Fort George on Guernsey reveals the plain headstones of the three German Engineers who died that night: *Unteroffizier* August Bleyer, aged 28, *Gefreiter* Heinrich Esslinger, aged 30, and *Obergefreiter* Peter Oswald, aged 36. German records also show that a *Gefreiter* Just was found, slightly wounded and that a fifth man, *Gefreiter* Klotz, was discovered, naked but unharmed, in a garden. The sixth man was the prisoner, Engineer *Obergefreiter* Weinrich, soon safely back in England.[24]

Lassen's biographer, Mike Langley, writing in 1987, claimed that the tying of prisoners was standard practice with SSRF and that they were issued with strong grey cord specifically for that purpose. James Edgar claims they used fishing line. It was also claimed by the Germans that the prisoners were gagged but Lassen allegedly countered: 'It's not true we stuffed their mouths with mud. We used grass.'[25] Appleyard, the commanding officer who gave the order for the prisoners to be tied, makes no mention of this in any of his reports whilst stating that, after attempting to escape, *four* prisoners were shot and killed.

The Germans made much of their discoveries, linking the dead prisoners on Sark with the tying of prisoners on the Dieppe raid six weeks earlier and the capture of an unarmed combat leaflet showing exactly how a prisoner could be restrained without the use of ropes in such a way that the cramp which ensued would bring about his own death. At the Nuremberg War Crimes Trials in 1946, *Generaloberst* Alfred Jodl referred to all three incidents – Dieppe, Sark and Fairbairn's 'Grapevine' technique – in an attempt to justify Hitler's top secret *Kommandobefehl* (commando order), which demanded that all captured commandos should be executed immediately on capture. It availed him little.[26]

The German press ran with the story; the British press published their sanitised version of events and made much of Germany's plans – discovered on the raid – to deport men from Guernsey, Jersey and Sark to Germany as forced labour: 'Afterwards, we never thought any more about the significance of what we had done until the Press took it up', admitted Bruce Ogden-Smith, one of those who took part in the raid.[27]

Lord Louis Mountbatten, Chief of Combined Operations, was quick to distance himself from Appleyard's actions once the German account of the raid became known, writing:

> I specifically told Major Appleyard (if my memory serves me right) before he undertook the raid on Sark that he was not to tie the hands of any of his prisoners. Unfortunately this order was disregarded ... One of the prisoners gave out a great cry for help and ran away in the dark. The Commandos shot him as he ran. The others were brought back to safety with their hands bound. Their hands were immediately untied when they got into the boat.[28]

Yet, according to Appleyard's report, *Obergefreiter* Weinrich embarked alone. The Germans, it appears, were not the only artful dissemblers of misinformation.

MTB 344 returned without incident and docked at 0630 at Portland, where lorries were waiting to take them back to Anderson Manor. 'I hadn't been on the raid and was still asleep when they got back', recalled Ian Warren. 'Andy woke me. He held his unwiped knife under my nose and said: 'Look – blood.'[29]

Anders Lassen would not survive the war. Promoted Major and the recipient, by then, of the Military Cross with *two* bars, he would be killed with the Special Boat Squadron in Comacchio, northern Italy, on 9 April 1945, aged just 24. He would die, at night, on an ill-considered, unrecced mission storming a chain of successive German machine-gun emplacements on a narrow causeway. For this – and perhaps, for much else – the blonde Dane who had once killed a deer with a knife and who had stalked *Obergefreiter* Peter Oswold with such swift and savage efficiency, would be awarded a posthumous Victoria Cross.

German forces in Italy surrendered on 29 April 1945: the peace Anders Lassen would never know had been less than a month away. A legend in his own short life-span, Lassen was thus spared the challenges and confusions of peacetime adjustment, when nations sometimes turn their back on the killers that become heroes and the conduct that wins wars.

Capt. Patrick Dudgeon, the officer whose pistol went off by accident when he struck his prisoner outside the Sark Annexe, would also not live to see the end of the war. He would die as part of Operation *Speedwell*, a mission by 2 SAS, in September 1943.

Dropped hundreds of miles behind the German lines in Spezia, Italy, and tasked with disrupting rail links south, he and SAS Trooper Bernard Brunt, 21, were captured near Parma on 2 October 1943. According to the German officer interpreter, Capt. Dudgeon was 'the bravest of English Officers I met in all my life'. Questioned about his mission, Dudgeon countered: 'If you were my prisoner, would you betray your country talking about your mission?' Both victims of Hitler's post-*Basalt* commando order, they were then told that – with regret – they were likely to be shot. 'All right', responded 23-year-old Dudgeon, 'I'll die for my country.'

In a letter written after the war to Patrick Dudgeon's parents by interpreter Leutnant Victor Schmit to honour a pledge made to the condemned man, he wrote: 'When my Captain had withdrawn I sat beside your son on the straw and we were speaking together all night long.' They chatted about their childhood and youth, about military traditions and about English literature and history. When they parted they shook hands and Lt Schmit saluted both soldiers, clicking his heels. Once more Dudgeon was interrogated, this time by Divisional Commander General Von Zielberg. Again, nothing was divulged:

Your son saluted militarily and left the General. He asked me to stay with him until it would be over. He gave me your address and asked me to inform you. He asked for a Protestant priest. Before he died he asked to die with free hands and open eyes. He knelt down for a short while praying with his hands in front of his face. Then he got up and died like a hero ... At the end, after praying and looking at the shooting squad with a defiant expression in his face, several seconds before the execution order was given, Patrick Dudgeon began to sing 'God Save The King' in a loud voice, the private following him in doing so, which was touching for all the German officers, even the one who gave the final order.[30]

17

Friends and Enemies in High Places

Anderson Manor remained, for them all that late summer, their place of quintessential refuge. It was their haven of calm and recovery after the fear and maelstrom of dark-night Channel crossings and incessant raiding. By early autumn 1942 – and in less than two months – they had planned or carried out eleven raids,[1] killed at least seven of the enemy, wounded half a dozen more and brought home eight most useful and communicative prisoners. They had returned from the enemy shore with code books and ciphers, pass books and maps, signal codes, weapons and equipment and, perhaps most important of all, they had planted fear and glance-over-the-shoulder unease in the heart of the enemy they had left behind. None of this had been accomplished, however, without cost: eleven of their own men, including their inspirational leader, were now posted as either killed, captured or missing. Appleyard was amongst those who found Anderson Manor balm for the pain of loss, sorrow and conflict, writing to Major Cholmondeley, the man whose home they had requisitioned:

> I have been wanting to tell you how much we appreciate the Manor – it has proved an ideal house in every way and to this unit a real home of which we have grown very fond. There is such a quiet and peaceful atmosphere about the house and gardens and often, after a night raid, coming back in the first light next morning, tired and often rather strung-up and on edge, it has been a real relief and relaxation to get back to such a lovely place. I know that Gus felt this very strongly – he often remarked on it to me – and I think the atmosphere of this house has, in an appreciable way, contributed to the making of what has been regarded in the high places, up to date, as a very successful little show. We have a grand crowd of men here and they have universally respected the privilege of living in this house. I don't think you would be disappointed if you could see the house now – it is kept beautifully clean and, although sparsely furnished, is very comfortable.[2]

Those 'high places' mentioned by Appleyard in that letter were, indeed, the highest in the land. Whatever the long-term implications and even embarrassments of Operation *Basalt* might yet turn out to be – word of the hand-tying had yet to be made public by the Germans – in local and tactical terms, the raid had been an outstanding success. The very next day after returning from Sark, Appleyard found himself ordered to London to meet both the Prime Minister and the Chiefs of Staff in Churchill's private rooms at the House of Commons:

> Yesterday was a very thrilling day ... partly spent at the House – in the Prime Minister's private room. He unexpectedly congratulated me. The CIGS [Chief of the Imperial General Staff] shook hands and said 'It was a very good show!' That was General Sir Alan Brooke, of course. General Sir Ronald Adam [Churchill's Adjutant General and close confidant of Sir Alan Brooke] was also present (as were Pound [Admiral Sir Dudley Pound, First Sea Lord],[3] Anthony Eden [Foreign Secretary], and quite a few other well-known people) and he said almost exactly the same thing. The Chief of Staff has directed the Chief of Combined Operations to make Small Scale Raiding a major part of his policy and has said that we are going to be given every assistance and facility! Wouldn't Gus have been thrilled! That is the type of recognition for which he was always working.[4]

The unit conceived by March-Phillipps was giving the Prime Minister exactly what he wanted. Undeterred by stories of trussed prisoners – some reports suggest he was actually delighted – Churchill's growl rang out from Edinburgh a week later on the day he was made a Freeman of that city:

> The British Commando raids at different points along this enormous coast, although so far only the forerunner of what is to come, inspire the author of so many crimes and miseries with a lively anxiety. His soldiers dwell among populations who would kill them with their hands if they got the chance, and will kill them one at a time when they *do* get the chance. In addition, there comes out from the sea from time to time a hand of steel which plucks the German sentries from their posts with growing efficiency, amid the joy of the whole countryside.[5]

The Chief of Staff minutes of the following day, 13 October, reflected Churchill's mood for Action This Day and declared, under 'Future Operations':

Raiding Operations

THE PRIME MINISTER stated that he wished the Chief of Combined Operations to intensify his small scale raids, as he was certain that the Germans were being worried by them.[6]

That intensification took immediate effect. By the middle of October 1942 Mountbatten had announced that, with SOE agreement, the Small Scale Raiding Force would be increased dramatically in size. Anderson Manor would remain the headquarters of No 62 Commando, SSRF's cover name, but there would now be an additional four troops based in four more requisitioned manor houses scattered along the south coast. These would be at Scorries House in Redruth, Cornwall; Lupton House in Dartmouth, Devon; Wraxhall Manor in Dorchester, Dorset; and Inchmery in Exbury, Hampshire. The new troops would be staffed by a core of experienced SSRF soldiers augmented by trained commandos joining SSRF on temporary attachment, bringing the unit strength now to 18 officers and about 100 other ranks. Evidently, the newly expanded force would now need a more substantial chain of command and Major Bill Stirling – brother of David, founder of the SAS – was posted in as lieutenant colonel with Major Appleyard in charge of operations. More boats would be allocated to the unit, too.

On 18 October Hitler issued his Top Secret commando order. From now on, any subordinate commander who failed to execute *immediately* or pass to the Gestapo (which amounted to the same thing) any commandos, special forces or saboteurs who fell into their hands would be liable to face charges of negligence and punishment under military law.

Two days earlier Combined Operations Headquarters had indefinitely postponed a raid by SSRF which, had it taken place, would almost certainly have provided Hitler's *Kommandobefehl* with its first scapegoats. Operation *Facsimile* was finally abandoned because of prevailing weather conditions and the ending of summer. The onset of autumn gales and moonlit conditions notwithstanding, it is difficult to see, from this remove, why Operation *Facsimile* was permitted to progress from being one of a hundred hair-brained schemes destined for the waste-paper basket to a project that merited its own code-name and which, but for the weather, would definitely have been mounted.

Major Gwynne, the SSRF planner at Anderson Manor known as 'Killer' Gwynne because of his eagerness to take part in the raids from which his administrative role precluded him, was now to have his chance.

The plan – on paper – was simple: a party of two officers and two other ranks from SSRF was to be carried across to the Brittany shore by

MGB 312. There they were to paddle ashore by Goatley on the north coast of Brittany near Beg-an-Fry, land on rocks to avoid leaving footprints and move overland towards the German airfield at Gaël, north-east of Mauron. Gaël was approximately 30 miles inland. The team was then to spend up to a week lying up in enemy territory. During this time they would first recce and then attack Gaël aerodrome, destroying whatever aircraft they found there with special 2lb bombs of plastic explosive armed with six-hour fuses. Ludicrous steps were taken during planning to enable Gywnne and his men to carry out their reconnaissance deep inside enemy territory without detection. According to Peter Kemp – who erroneously places this raid *after* rather than before Operation *Fahrenheit* – Gwynne spent much of his time before the raid away from Anderson Manor:

> visiting various SOE experimental stations, in particular one concerned with camouflage. He reappeared at the end of his tour with two unusual pieces of equipment. One of them was a lifelike cow's head in papier mâché with holes pierced through the eyes; the other was a curious arrangement of fine-meshed camouflage netting … The mask was for road-watching … he would lie up in a field beside a main road and push his head, enveloped in the mask, through the hedge; thus disguised, he would be able to keep a watch on the road and observe the number and nature of enemy troops using it.

The purpose of the netting was even simpler: 'It enables a man to disguise himself at will as a rubbish heap or a pile of sticks', explained Gywnne.[7] Today's SBS would recognise the use of the netting, if not the cow's head of papier mâché whose composition presumably, would become interesting after heavy rain.

With recce and airfield attack successfully completed, Major Gywnne and his merry band were then to escape overland down the length of France into neutral Spain almost 400 miles away to the south. Not all of France was occupied by the Germans at that time (it would be, however, in less than a month's time), but the Zone Non-Occupée was still the best part of 100 miles away.

Lord Mountbatten designated Major Appleyard the overall force commander with Major J.M.W. Gwynne officer commanding the landing party. By that stage, one may presume, Appleyard had proved himself too valuable to risk on a mission which, from the outset, must have had little chance of success and from which the odds on a safe return were slender indeed. Briefing notes[8] disclose that the men would take sleeping bags, tommy cookers and four forty-eight-hour ration packs apiece. They were blithely expected to supplement these bulky rations with 'fruit, vegetables and nuts from the country'. A country, moreover, that was occupied by elements of 17 Infantry Division and 6 Panzer, while at Gaël itself 'the usual aerodrome garrison of 640 men may be expected, although it is considered possible that the garrison will be much under strength here owing to the relative inactivity of the aerodrome in the past'.[9]

By summer 1942, raids on enemy airfields in the vast empty spaces of the western desert, conceived by David Stirling, were becoming the stuff of legend. But Brittany was more than just western desert without sand and the thickly populated, heavily occupied hinterland of Brittany offered a more complex tactical challenge than Egypt's Qattara Depression. It is possible, of course, that there were other, more intelligent, secret orders that tied *Facsimile* in with SOE agents and saboteurs with strong local knowledge who were already on the Breton ground. If such orders exist, they remain untraced by this author; it is also possible that a direct paradrop of saboteurs into the area was also considered to obviate the dangers of a lengthy approach march by four heavily armed men weighed down with rucksacks containing rations, explosives, cookers and sleeping bags. Again, no trace of such a possibility has been discovered. It still remains difficult to understand, however, why Gaël aerodrome was not simply bombed to SOE markers; why SOE agents in place were not involved or, most particularly, why extraction home by sea was rejected in favour of that lengthy and extremely risky evasion south to Spain whilst living off nuts and fruit plucked from the sparse autumn hedgerows of wartime France.

There were several attempts to land *Facsimile* on the Brittany coast on the nights of 10–16 October. On 10, 11 and 12 October, MGB 314 was turned back because of weather and sea conditions. On 13 October the operation was cancelled by C-in-C Plymouth (Admiral Forbes) owing to what were termed 'other activities' in the Channel. On 14 and 15 October the weather was unsuitable. The briefing officer safely back in Combined Operations Headquarters suggested 'a slight or moderate wind is desirable for landing'. On 16 October – the last sailing opportunity of the autumn offering the right moonless conditions – they got rather more than that. After meeting wind Force 5–6 increasing on the outward leg with a heavy westerly swell, the frail, wooden-hulled gunboat that was MGB 314 wisely turned for home. After slamming through rough seas for three and a half hours Appleyard – who, as usual, had sailed as navigator – reported: 'Owing to the weather which may be expected in the next four months and the fact that from now on, owing to the falling of the leaf, cover ashore will be considerably reduced, it is no longer considered possible to carry out this operation before spring.'[10] Brigadier Godfrey

Wildman-Lushington,[11] Mountbatten's Chief of Staff, concurred. On 20 October Operation *Fascimile* was postponed indefinitely. It was a wise decision. It was also, quite possibly, a merciful deliverance.

For the men of Operation *Facsimile*, the attempted escape overland to Spain, however risky, would at least have been part of their post-operation evasion planning. It would thus have been something they would have had time to consider and prepare for. Capt. Graham Hayes, however, the evader from the disastrous Operation *Aquatint* a month earlier, had not enjoyed the same luxury of preparation. For him, heading south inland deep into enemy territory had been the one desperate option that might conceivably lead towards safety and survival.

Hayes had been brave – and lucky. After swimming more than a mile westwards up the coast in the dark towards Cherbourg – away from the gunfire, the shouting, the lights and the flares that engulfed his companions – the peacetime tall-ships' deep-sea mariner and aspirant wood-sculptor who had once kept a tame jackdaw named 'Grip' on his shoulder had stumbled ashore in the early hours of 13 September 1942. He then made his way inland to the village of Asnières en Bessin just to the east of Pointe du Hoc. Here, exhausted, soaked through and with dawn not far away, he had chanced all by knocking on the door of a farmhouse. His luck held, as he found himself befriended by French farmer Marcel Lemasson who, heedless of the dangers to himself and his family, ushered him in and closed the door.

While Hayes was being fed by his wife, Lemasson slipped out to confer with Paul de Brunville, the local Mayor who lived in the chateau across the lane. He too was a loyal Frenchman. After consulting his two children, Oliver (22) and Isabelle (20) – both of whom spoke English – Paul and Oliver de Brunville brought Hayes back to the chateau in the darkness that evening where he was hidden in the hayloft in the farm attached to the chateau's grounds. The next morning, at his father's instruction, Oliver de Brunville went to another trusted contact, Septime Humann in Jouay-Mondaye, who in turn promised to feed the stranded English captain further down the Resistance pipeline towards Spain and safety. A journey first by bicycle and then by train followed with Hayes at every stage watched, escorted and guided through check-points and barriers in a land thick with the grey-green uniforms of his country's enemies. From Asnières, Oliver de Brunville and Hayes cycled to Bayeux. From Bayeux Hayes caught the troop-crowded train to Caen and then on to Lisieux, further still to the east, a journey that, from its start point at Saint-Laurent-sur-Mer, carried him diagonally across what would, in two years' time, become the Normandy D-Day beachhead. Here, just to the east of

Liseaux north of Moyaux in the Le Manoir home in Le Pin of French *resistant* Suzanne Septavaux, Hayes was to be laid up by illness and a knee infection for the next six weeks. He did not know it, but by luck, good fortune and the selfless courage of others, he had hooked up with SOE's *Donkeyman* circuit.

Meanwhile, back in England, that same October, Second Lt Lassen was awarded the first of his three Military Crosses. Described as 'a very gallant and determined officer',[12] Lassen was awarded the MC for his inspiring leadership and outstanding contribution to Operations *Postmaster*, *Branford*, *Barricade* and *Basalt*. His face still battered and bruised from the fight on Sark and with front teeth missing after a collision with the rail of MTB 344 a few months earlier during some mistimed re-embarkation, he was then posted to the Commando Training Centre at Achnacarry. Here he conveyed a sense of realism, urgency and purpose to fellow Danes sweating their way towards course completion. Thanks to Lassen's powers of persuasion and recruitment, all sixteen Danes volunteered for onward deployment into SOE and SSRF.

The unit he had temporarily left behind in Dorset was now hugely expanded – it received a new and more formal charter of operations from Mountbatten on 22 October 1942.[13] It expanded not just with men, but with boats too, the essential means by which they would be carried to the enemy shore. Now *The Littler Pisser* – MTB 344, that veteran of previous raids – was joined by Coastal Motor Boats 103, 104, 312, 316, 317 and 326, all from the 14th Flotilla which, from the day of Churchill's 'hand of steel' speech in Edinburgh on 12 October, had became part of 'Force J' with its headquarters at HMS *Vectris* at Cowes on the Isle of Wight. 'Force J' consisted also of most of the surviving ships that had taken part in the raid on Dieppe – Operation *Jubilee* – and which had been kept together ever since. Perhaps unfortunately for Stirling, Appleyard and their men, 'Force J' was under the command of Captain, now Commodore, John Hughes-Hallett RN ('Hughes-Hitler'), the officer who had written so disparagingly about March-Phillipps' organisational skills in the early days of Anderson Manor. In future, although SSRF operations would be carried out under the 'unified command' of Lt Col Bill Stirling, who would submit plans for raids directly to Mountbatten, those plans would have to be copied to Hughes-Hallett and final operational control would rest with him. It was an arrangement and an appointment, evidently, which found no favour with the skipper of MTB 344, Lt Freddie Bourne, DSC, who, as a motor torpedo boat commander, came directly under Hughes-Hallett's command. He remembered bitterly:

He [Hughes-Hallett] made it absolutely clear to me, which I got very cross about, that he felt all these pin-prick raids over on the French coast which I had been partly responsible for were a total waste of the war effort. That was his personal view and he said it to me. I'll never forget that. I knew his Flag Lieutenant very well and Tim took me outside and said I wouldn't make too much of that, that's obviously just his own view. I said, well, that's not how we viewed it in the months I was working with the army and I'll never forget it.

I shot out of Cowes harbour in my MTB 344 back to Hornet [Coastal Forces Base HMS *Hornet* at Gosport, Hampshire] and created a bit of a furore because I went out far too fast and started rocking a few too many boats but I was in a fair old state at that stage ... We felt it was all worthwhile; it was keeping the enemy on his toes, he never knew where we were going to strike. Albeit it was very small stuff, but it was obviously a forerunner for something that could become much bigger.[14]

Once again, there was that apparently unavoidable clash between conventional naval thinking and those who had thrown away the rule book. Despite the high opinion of SSRF held by Brigadier Gubbins and Lord Mountbatten, by the Chiefs of Staff and even by Churchill himself, not everybody, it appears, thought the men of the Small Scale Raiding Force worth their rations.

Combined Operations moved fast to consolidate their authorised expansion in the minds of other agencies. On 31 October Colonel 'RN' – Robert Neville, one of Mountbatten's advisers and Chief Planning Co-Ordinator at COHQ – wrote to the Director of Military Intelligence reminding him of SSRF's existence and outlining their own plans to particularise and add to the strategic value of future missions:

The targets for these raids have been selected, hitherto, somewhat at random, the broad objective being that we should kill or capture Germans and obtain intelligence. In other words, there has been little relation of the objectives with definite requirements.

In accordance with the Prime Minister's and the Chiefs of Staff's Directive, it is now intended to increase the scope and activities of this Small Scale Raiding Force. It may thus be possible to select targets with the object, over and above that of killing Germans, of bringing back, for instance, some particular technical or other equipment, a specimen of which may be required by one or other of the services ... It would greatly assist us in this connection if you could inform us of any targets in which the War Office would be interested.[15]

Be careful what you wish for: Combined Operations presently received, from a wide variety of sources, a veritable shopping list of suggestions as to what they might capture and bring home for examination. This embraced everything from sea mines and the latest 25-hundredweight, multiple-barrel flak unit in its entirety (failing that, the latest anti-aircraft gun-sight would do nicely!); specimen rounds of ammunition, sniper rifles, grenade discharger cups for rifles, machine-gun mountings, details of beam transmission stations, gun dials, range tables, pay books and office records. In fact, 'Practically any documents which can be seized will be worth carrying home'.

From the Director of Naval Intelligence, however, SSRF received a word of timely caution:

> The progressive strengthening of the defences of the coastline of Europe makes it increasingly difficult to find targets which offer a reasonable chance of success ... The garrisons guarding small objectives such as lighthouses, isolated batteries and searchlights, previously satisfactory targets, are being strengthened as a result of CCO's operations on that coast ... In the past very many promising targets have been pointed out to CCO and every effort will continue to be made to do so in the future.[16]

Although Combined Operations may have hurried to consolidate their new authority to raid the German-occupied coastline with a new co-ordinated procurement objective, others, like Hughes-Hallett, remained unpersuaded. As late as 13 November 1942 Combined Operations' Director of Plans felt obliged to review both the arguments for the existing raiding policy[17] and those arguments still paraded against it by the Commander-in-Chief, Plymouth, Admiral Sir Charles Forbes, who took common cause with Commodore Hughes-Hallett RN in his dislike of 'pin-prick' raids.

In *favour* of the raids, the Combined Operations' Director of Plans echoed Appleyard's thinking, stating that they gave participants valuable experience 'which can be gained in no other way'. He emphasised that they provided an opportunity to gain intelligence whilst locking up large numbers of German soldiers and equipment in a passive, static role. He added:

> With the enemy's increasing manpower shortage, this aspect is highly important ... Some idea of the effect of our raids on the enemy can be obtained by considering how vexatious it would be to us if the enemy were to adopt a similar policy and force us to take the same sort of precautions that they themselves have had to adopt.[18]

In an earlier paragraph he had emphasised: 'There is evidence (graded A1) that, consequent upon a recent small raid, [Operation *Basalt*] Hitler personally has ordered the increase of garrisons of all outlying occupied islands, from Finland to Greece, since in general he considers them at present to be quite inadequate.' Over time the new vigilance of the coast defences would be worn down 'and a state of fatigue and strain induced all along the coastline'.

Conceding that raiding *must* have an adverse effect upon the work of Naval Intelligence, Director of Plans Minutes noted for the record that: 'Commander-in-Chief, Plymouth, doubts whether the advantages accruing from the raids are sufficient to outweigh the disadvantages that result.' He enumerated these as a tightening of security measures generally and a more frequent change of Nazi codes making the interception of German convoys in the Channel more difficult. There would be a general tightening up of 'weak spots' in German coastal defences and this would impact upon destroyer and RN operations generally.

None of these arguments prevailed. Besides which, observed the Director of Plans: 'The conflict between NID ('C')'s interests and other operations has always existed. D of P knows of no new factor to justify the alteration of the raiding policy at the present time. It is understood that close liaison is maintained between CCO and 'C' [SIS].' He concluded:

> While there is undoubtedly something in Commander-in-Chief, Plymouth's, contentions, D of P's opinion is that the most potent of the above arguments is that by these small raids the enemy is forced to lock up his dwindling manpower in an unproductive occupation. Furthermore, since there is nothing in the Commander-in-Chief's arguments that has not already been taken into consideration, D of P. considers that the present policy should be adhered to.[19]

And so it would be – for the moment, at least.

Even as the arguments flowed to and fro between Richmond Terrace and the offices of the Chiefs of Staff in sandbagged Whitehall, a further two raids had already been planned. Operation *Fahrenheit*, in fact, had been mounted just the day before. But Operation *Gimcrack* – a raid by twelve SSRF to take prisoners and wipe out the German garrison on the tiny Île Saint-Rion close inshore off the north coast of Brittany, had been cancelled: MTB 344 had been required by 'Force J' 'for other operations.'[20] Operation *Inhabit* – a raid on the Cherbourg Peninsula south-east of Omonville to recce coastal defences, take a prisoner and 'investigate a sinister German area of activity'[21] – also fell by the wayside.

Admiral Forbes' reasons for opposing small scale raids on the Channel coast appear, on the face of it, to be petty and insubstantial; thin gruel. They suggest that something of greater moment lay behind his opposition to the proposed activities of Stirling, Appleyard and the men of the Small Scale Raiding Force. Perhaps it did.

The writ of C-in-C Plymouth extended from Exmouth in east Devon to Penzance in Cornwall, lying as it did at the south eastern edge of the Western Approaches, that vast block of water extending far out into the Atlantic and as far north and east as the Orkneys. Admiral Forbes' command thus encompassed Dartmouth, Falmouth and the secret SOE base at Helford, whose Commanding Officer was the firebrand Gerry Holdsworth, the former 'Section D' SIS agent in Norway who had crossed cutlasses with Commander Slocum over the sanctioning of clandestine fishing boat missions to France for SOE rather than for SIS, and whose work Slocum had so thoroughly thwarted throughout 1942 (see Chapter 4). Although Commander Slocum as NID (C) reported, at this time, to Claude Dansey, SIS's *de facto* second-in-command to Sir Stewart Menzies, his work necessarily fell within the ambit of Admiral Forbes' influence. DoPs' minutes suggest that Forbes may indeed have invoked, if only in general terms, the secrecy and importance of Slocum's work for SIS as another reason to curtail the activities of SSRF. If Admiral Forbes took an overarching interest in Slocum's activities, then he would also have been aware of, and been concerned to protect, the clandestine interests of SIS operations out of Devon, Cornwall and the Isles of Scilly. He would have done so, moreover, with good reason.

Immediately after the fall of France in 1940 Sir Stewart Menzies,[22] the head of SIS, set up two new staff sections to gather information from within France, together with an 'O' (Operations) Section to open up physical communication with occupied Europe. This, as already noted, was headed by Commander Frank Slocum. To begin with, these staff sections, led by Commanders Kenneth Cohen and Wilfred Dunderdale, did well. Soon, SIS agents working for Dunderdale's '*Johnny*' network had been infiltrated into France through Spain and by mid-1941 had established a useful network of agents along the French Atlantic coast and set up clandestine courier lines into neutral Spain. By the end of that year, Commander Cohen had established particularly good agent coverage on the French Atlantic ports – new home of the U-boat fleets that threatened Britain's Atlantic lifeline. Better yet, agents in Brest had sent to one of Cohen's most effective operatives, Colonel Gilbert Renault (alias Remy), complete plans of the harbour defences and the latest reported movements of German capital ships put in to Brest for repair. Gilbert Renault set up his own agent network, Confrérie de Notre-Dame (CND), which rapidly expanded and eventually covered most of France. One of its early notable coups was the provision of precise intelligence that became the backbone for the successful Operation *Biting* raid on the German radar station at Bruneval in February 1942. Thus '*Johnny*' and CND provided two vital strings to SIS's intelligence-gathering bow in France. Later, intelligence would come back to England by a variety of means including wireless, aircraft pick-up and courier. But, in the early days, one of the most important and reliable routes back to England for letters, reports, packets of documents and stolen German papers was across the Channel – by sea.

And then, in February 1942, one of those strings broke. A series of ship arrests and agent losses led to the falling apart of the '*Johnny*' network. Gilbert Renault's expanding Confrérie de Notre-Dame now assumed critical importance: CND was to go on to become 'the largest and most productive of all the Free French intelligence networks in France'.[23] In June 1942 CND had already pulled off a coup of major strategic significance that was to save thousands of allied lives. In that month, Gilbert Renault had sailed to England with more than just his family aboard the disguised fishing boat *N51- Le Dinan* at the successful conclusion of SIS's Operation *Marie-Louise II*. He had brought back with him a blueprint of the coastal defences along the Normandy coast just as the Todt organisation was beginning to construct them:

> The map spread out on the carpet [of his flat in Square Henri Pate] was more than three metres long and 75 centimetres in width. It covered the whole of the Normandy coastline from Cherbourg to Honfleur: marked on it were a great number of concrete blockhouses, machine-gun nests, barbed wire entanglements and minefields. The calibre of the guns to be mounted was indicated.[24]

It was a detailed blueprint for the D-Day beach defences, handed to the allies two years before the invasion of Normandy.

It rapidly became evident that, given the increasing volume and quality of CND's intelligence harvest, a regular monthly 'mail-run' between the English West Country and the south-west coast of Brittany would be essential. One of those closely involved in clandestine sea operations at that time was Sir Brooks Richards, DSC:

> By September 1942 Remy's *Confrérie de Notre Dame* was on a vast scale. It had for more than a year extended along the Atlantic coast and up into Brittany, with particularly good coverage of Bordeaux and Brest: now it covered the whole of France ... This sea link became of such overriding

importance to SIS that Slocum ruled that NID(C)'s fishing vessels must be reserved exclusively for this purpose and must not undertake operations for other organisations in the Bay of Biscay for fear of compromising the system.[25]

It was this clandestine sea link, this conduit for priceless intelligence anywhere across the Channel and not just into the Bay of Biscay, that those in the Royal Navy and SIS now sought to shield and protect. To those who were informed, the argument against the pin-prick, nuisance raids of SSRF spoke for itself: measured against a blueprint of Hitler's Atlantic Wall or some yet-to-be-realised strategic prize, what price the alerting of the enemy coastline for the mere snatching of a sentry's pay book or the cutting of a German throat on some remote, rocky out-station?[26]

Operation *Gimcrack* might have been abandoned because MTB 344 was required by 'Force J' for 'other operations'. Operation *Fahrenheit* was not.

Operation *Fahrenheit*

Additional reinforcements for the expanded SSRF at Anderson Manor arrived towards the end of October: another two officers from No 12 Commando plus a further twelve NCOs. Earlier arrivals on loan from 12 Commando, Capt. Philip Pinckney and six of his men, had already taken part in Operation *Basalt*. Now Capt. Peter Kemp, one of the SOE old hands from *Knife* days, was ordered to train up Capt. Oswald 'Mickey' Rooney and six men to take part in an unspecified raid scheduled for the near future which he, Kemp, would lead. Operation *Fahrenheit* was just a fortnight away. The men from No 12 Commando made an impressive addition to the decimated unit at Anderson Manor. 'Rooney, a powerfully built, self-confident officer, who knew his men intimately and commanded their implicit obedience, had little to learn from me', recounted Peter Kemp:

> In fact, apart from pistol shooting and movement at night, he and his men knew more about the business than I … we spent the next two weeks together in unremitting training by day and night. In particular, we exercised ourselves in night schemes on land and water, in soundless movement and the use of our eyes in the dark. For such intensive practice we were soon to be thankful.[1]

At midday on Wednesday, 11 November 1942, the ten men of Operation *Fahrenheit* left Anderson Manor for Lupton House near Paignton, Devon, one of the new bases recently requisitioned for SSRF. Here they ate a hurried meal, changed into their operational clothing and sorted out their weapons and ammunition. All wore leather jerkins with a toggle rope secured around their waist. They wore standard army boots and their faces were unblackened.[2] This time, in addition to the usual side-arms and tommy guns, Kemp's raiders were carrying a silenced Sten, two of the new plastic explosive No 6 grenades trialled on Operation *Barricade* back in August and a Bren light machine-gun to cover their withdrawal. Their target was a semaphore station on top of cliffs on Pointe de Plouézec about 15 miles north-west of Saint Brieuc on the north Brittany coast. They were to carry out the usual reconnaissance, attack the semaphore station and, if possible, take prisoners. The semaphore station was believed to be guarded by barbed wire, a sentry, a small concrete guard-house and a dozen soldiers. There were, they were told, no mines or booby-traps to worry about and the way up from the shore towards the semaphore station was by a narrow, clearly defined track that should be easy to find in the darkness. All appeared straightforward, the geography rather like *Basalt*, but on a smaller scale.

The SSRF, still recovering from its devastating losses on Operation *Aquatint*, badly needed another successful, loss-free operation on the heels of *Basalt* to restore collective confidence. Bill Stirling, their new commanding officer, took Peter Kemp aside before they left. 'Rooney and his chaps are very keen and will obviously seize any opportunity for a fight', warned Stirling:

Naturally we want to inflict casualties and take prisoners; but *not*, I repeat, at the cost of losing men ourselves. It isn't worth it at this stage. If, when you get there, you don't think you can fight without losing men, I promise I shall be quite satisfied with a recce. Remember, Peter, I don't want any Foreign Legion stuff on this party![3]

Peter Kemp understood. He and Capt. 'Mickey' Rooney had already decided that, circumstances permitting, they would close with the sentry themselves and kill him silently with their fighting knives.

Leaving Paignton, the party made its way by covered lorry to Dartmouth where MTB 344 was waiting by the quay, engines running. On the quayside were Bill Stirling, Freddie Bourne, the captain of MTB 344 and Ian Darby, the unit's newly appointed Intelligence Officer. Clumsy with weapons, the raiders filed aboard and squeezed below decks:

Eight of us had to travel in a very small hatch on the starboard bow of the craft. It was pitch black in what could well have been a paint locker. Before the door was closed on us, a sailor handed in a bucket and in answer to a question from one of us said: 'to use as a toilet or if you are sea-sick.'[4]

Appleyard – his slow-healing foot now in plaster – limped up to the bridge where he assumed his customary place as navigator. *The Little Pisser* slipped her moorings and, engines burbling, gathered way slowly downstream in the gathering dusk, the fourteenth-century Dartmouth Castle standing out as dark, silent sentinel against the fading western sky.

The evening was fine with a clear sky, south-east wind Force 2–3, and visibility moderate with a moderate south-easterly swell that was soon breaking green over the boat. Captains Kemp and Rooney were sheltering against the upturned hull of the Dory lashed astern. Soon they were drenched through with freezing spray and chilled to the bone. The crossing took six hours, during which tidal drift and cross-swell pushed *The Little Pisser* off her dead reckoning course. It took an hour and three sides of a box search after a 3-mile over-run to establish their position with certainly before they finally picked up the light tower on Roches Douvres. Presently they made out the off-lying islands leading in to Pointe de Plouézec. The men were ordered on deck:

> The sight which met our eyes as we emerged from the dark confines of our accommodation was really beautiful. On our port beam there was a high cliff rising from a beach about 500 yards away and we were heading into a large bay with a peninsula of land about ten o'clock from us. After the darkness of our position in the bow of the MTB it almost looked like daylight.[5] No one had been sea-sick. As MTB 344 edged close to shore they sensed rather than saw something black rising out of the water behind them. In their heightened nervous state several on board *The Little Pisser* imagined it might be the first showing of the casing of a submarine closing in astern. In fact, it turned out to be the humped backs of several grey seals.[6] They could breathe again. At ten minutes past midnight MTB 344, running now on silent engines, dropped anchor half a mile off-shore in 7 fathoms. 'The target, the semaphore station, could be dimly seen against the sky', Appleyard reported later.[7]

Kemp and his men launched the 18-foot Dory over the side without a sound and paddled the fifteen minutes to their agreed landing place at the foot of the cliffs at Pointe de Plouézec. Here they had expected to find shingle. Instead, they found boulders. While the men went into all-round defensive positions, Capt. Rooney went off in search of a better landing place. Ten minutes later he returned: there wasn't one. With the tide now on the run they decided to leave one man with the Dory to ensure it did not become rock-bound and turned inland to find the track up the cliffs. Like the shingle they thought they had identified on the photo-reconnaissance photographs, the path too turned out not to exist. Instead they were faced with a steep and difficult 100-foot climb up through sharp gorse and loose shale with slippery grass underfoot. The Bren-gunner, Sergeant Nicholson, turned his toggle-rope into a sling, slung the Bren over his back and climbed hands free. Weapons at the ready, they forced their way up, the sharp-barbed gorse tearing at uniform, hands and faces. In the fear of exposure and discovery, the tiny rattle of shale slipping down the cliff behind them sounded, thought Kemp, like an avalanche.

It took twenty minutes to scramble hand-over-hand to the top. Crawling low over the crest of the cliff to avoid being skylined, they paused to catch their breath. About 100 yards ahead Kemp could see a line of telegraph poles indicating the track that led inland from the semaphore station. They moved swiftly across open ground to the track and estimated they were now no more than 150 yards from the barbed wire and the guard-house. Peter Kemp was just congratulating himself upon the absence of mines or booby-traps when he saw Capt. Rooney examining two small notice-boards, both of which faced inland. Each warned simply: '*Achtung! Minen.*' Peter Kemp did not speak German. But then, he didn't need to. Nothing had gone off on the way up to the track so Kemp and Rooney reasoned it was probably just bluff. After a further recce of the defences Capt. Rooney returned to confirm there was a double belt of barbed wire which blocked the path and the entrance to both semaphore station and guard-house and that the area was patrolled by two wide-awake sentries. The best plan, thought Peter Kemp, was to skirt off to the left and approach the target away from the sentries' patrol line. A hurried, whispered consultation and Peter Kemp led the way off the track into the darkness:

> We did not get very far. I had only gone a few yards, crouching low and straining my eyes to watch the ground at every step, when I all but trod on a mine. It was laid, with very little attempt at concealment, under a small mound of turf. Abandoning our hopes that the notices might be a bluff, we returned to the path. A frontal attack was the only solution.[8]

They decided to stalk the sentries, get as close as possible, shoot them with the silent Sten and then rush the wire. Killing the sentries with knives as originally intended was now out of the question: both were on the far side of the wire. Splitting into three groups, Kemp's raiders inched forward on their bellies to within ten paces of the two sentries: 'The night was uncannily still, the very slightest sound being audible ... the sentries were very much on the alert, pausing frequently in their talk to listen. Almost every word they said could be heard distinctly.'[9] One was young, the other appeared more elderly. Both were wearing army greatcoats and carried rifles with bayonets and each had a stick grenade tucked into their leather waist belts. The men from SSRF lay stock-still, pale, uncamouflaged faces averted, hoping the two sentries would move away. They didn't. The minutes must have dragged like hours:

> For a full fifteen minutes we lay there, listening to the lazy drawl of their conversation, punctuated all too frequently by periods of silence when they would peer towards us and listen. The nervous strain inside me grew almost intolerable, sometimes bordering on panic when I thought of the peril of our situation; we must carry on now, for I could never turn my party back under the noses of this watchful pair … I remember thinking how good the earth and grass smelt as I pressed my face close to the ground. Overhead a lone aircraft beat a leisurely way up the coast; from the direction of Paimpol came the distant sound of a dog barking.
>
> Out of the corner of my eye I saw Rooney make a slight movement. Then I heard a distinct metallic click as he unscrewed the top of his No 6 grenade. The sentries heard it, too. They stopped their conversation and one gave a sharp exclamation. I sensed rather than saw Rooney's arm go up, and braced myself for what I knew was coming. There was a clatter as one of the sentries drew back the bolt of his rifle, then everything was obliterated in a vivid flash as a tremendous explosion shattered the silence of the night. The blast hit me like a blow on the head. From the sentries came the most terrible sounds I can ever remember. From one of them came a low, pitiful moaning; from the other, bewildered screams of agony and terror, an incoherent jumble of sobs and prayers, in which I could distinguish only the words '*Nicht gut! Nicht gut!*' endlessly repeated. Even in those seconds as I leapt to action I felt a shock of horror that those soft, lazy, drawling voices which had floated to us across the quiet night air could have been turned, literally in a flash, to such inhuman screams of pain and fear.[10]

They stormed forward across the mangled wire. A small, yelping dog erupted from the guard-house and scampered away into the darkness. The guard-house itself was empty. The two sentries lay sprawled on the ground, their uniforms terribly burnt by the grenade. One was silent with his hands over his face. The other kept calling out to his mother and his God. Both were swiftly dispatched by a burst of close-range tommy-gun fire.

Kemp and his men raced forward towards the semaphore station. As Kemp joined Rooney a German loomed up suddenly out of the darkness firing rapidly with a small automatic pistol. His shots missed. Rooney and Kemp replied with their heavy .45s and the man dropped to his knees, still firing valiantly before he too was finished off with another burst of tommy-gun fire from Sergeant Barry. Up ahead in the semaphore station a door was suddenly thrown open. Silhouetted clearly against the light inside stood a German at the top of a flight of stairs, sub-machine-gun in hand. He presented a perfect target and paid for that folly with his life. He dropped to two bursts from the silenced Sten and fell forward onto his face. Trying to rise, he too was finished off with a burst of tommy-gun fire from Corporal Howells.

All surprise gone, the Germans inside the semaphore station now began to return fire in earnest from windows and the – now unlit – open doorway. Peter Kemp remembered afterwards:

> The garrison was clearly stronger than we had expected. If we stormed the building we should have to cross the open courtyard under heavy fire with a grave risk of casualties ... We had killed four Germans for certain without loss to ourselves. I decided to disengage now, before I had the added difficulty of carrying wounded through the minefield and down the cliffs.[11]

Like Appleyard and his men on Sark before him at the conclusion of Operation *Basalt*, Capt. Kemp and his men now raced back along the path to the top of the cliffs where Sergeant Nicholson was waiting stoically behind the Bren to cover their withdrawal:

> As we hurried through the minefield I was in a sweat of terror lest we should have a casualty here at the last moment: I do not know how we could have carried a wounded man down those cliffs to the boat. In fact, we were lucky, but the descent was dangerous enough as we slid and fell blindly in the gorse-covered gullies leading down to the beach. I was greatly relieved that there were no signs of pursuit from above, although the semaphore station was in an uproar and we could still hear the sound of small-arms fire when we arrived on the beach.[12]

There, miraculously, the Dory was afloat, held off the rocks on a falling tide by Sergeant Brian Reynolds who had spent two hours waist-deep in icy water. Now they discovered two men were missing as the Germans on the cliff-top put up a Verey light which bathed the bay, the cliffs and the raiders themselves in the vivid glow of a magnesium flare. As the last of the flare faded the two men scrambled aboard the Dory. It was time to go. Paddling hard out to sea, the Dory began making its way out towards MTB 344 and safety; 200, 300 yards off-shore and Operation *Aquatint* began to repeat itself. 'Another Verey light went up from the signal station, lighting up the tense, sweating faces of my companions as though in the glare of footlights. This time, I thought, they're bound to see us and I waited, almost resigned now, for the hiss and splash of bullets.'[13] Miraculously, none came. Darkness returned. They made the RV with the torpedo boat, clambered aboard and settled down as best they could for the long, wet and uncomfortable voyage home:

> Rooney and I sat huddled miserably in a pool of water on the bottom of the Dory, under the flimsy protection of a tarpaulin. I was feeling the reaction from the excitement of the last few hours. Although relieved that I had brought our party back intact I could feel no elation at our small success. Instead, I could not rid my ears of the terrible screams that had come from the mangled, wounded sentries.[14]

It was a memory – and a sound – that would haunt Peter Kemp for years.

At 0820 next day, an hour after dawn on a wet, grey, raw morning, *The Little Pisser* came alongside the quay at Dartmouth. Waiting for them were the SSRF Commanding Officer, Lt Col Bill Stirling, together with Darby, the unit's Intelligence Officer and a squad of field security police ready to escort away for interrogation the prisoners that had not been captured.

Operation *Fahrenheit* had been a qualified success. It had killed a few Germans and suffered no casualties to its own force. But its minor success, devoid of any strategic significance, would do nothing, unsurprisingly, to persuade SSRF's small army – and navy – of critics that shocking the enemy, as Bill Stirling put it, would ever be sufficient justification for an expanded policy of small scale raiding when weighed against the disruption such raids might cause to those monthly 'mail run' operations organised by Commander Frank Slocum and SIS in support of Gilbert Renault's Confrérie de Notre Dame (CND). That argument would persist and gather strength even as March-Phillipps' brain-child took on new commandos and expanded into those four newly requisitioned manor-houses that were to be the new troop bases scattered along the coast of the West Country.

Limping ashore from MTB 344 after Operation *Farhenheit*, Appleyard was soon heading home, north to Yorkshire, for a little well-deserved leave.

He had left Linton-on-Wharfe at the outbreak of war determined to do his very best, haunted above all by the fear of letting down the men under his command. He returned home now as something of a local hero. One evening after his return to a joyous family reunion there was a meeting in Wetherby Town Hall at which Herbert Hayes, Graham's father, made a presentation to him on behalf of the Wetherby and Linton Services Welfare Committee. The presentation was to mark the award to Geoffrey, the local lad made good, of two Military Crosses. The

Committee had raised a subscription and purchased a silver salver. It was given to him by the father of his childhood friend, now posted Missing.[15] On it was inscribed:

> Presented to Major J G Appleyard, MC, by the people of Weatherby and Linton in grateful recognition of bravery and services in the World War in defence of those good and lovely things that go to make life worth living.

Appleyard was profoundly moved. In reply he told his audience that he would value the gift for the rest of his life. A number of others should be standing there on the platform instead of himself, he said, among whom was Graham Hayes, one of his greatest friends and a man he had known for the past fifteen years. They had served together in the same unit, under the same commanding officer, a man whom both would follow into any situation with the utmost confidence. Killed recently in action, he too was an officer who stood for all the things the Nation was fighting for.

†††

Far to the south in Dorset, that fight was still going on. On 15 November 1942 a party of two officers from SSRF and an officer and seven other ranks from No 12 Commando under Capt. Ogden-Smith set out on Operation *Batman* in MTB 344. Sailing from Portland at 2145, on a smooth sea with very slight swell, light winds and with a sky completely overcast, their mission was to recce La Sabine, near Omonville, on the north-west corner of the Cherbourg peninsula and take prisoners. Poor visibility close inshore – it was less than half a mile in coastal fog on the other side – made it difficult to identify the correct beach for landing and, after moonset at 0050 made it darker still, time was wasted establishing their exact position. When they did, it was to discover they were on the wrong side of the north-western tip of the Cherbourg Peninsula. They estimated it would take too long now to work their way round the coast to the correct landing point. This, coupled with a rising northerly wind which would have placed them on a dead lee shore in a sea that was getting choppier by the minute, resulted in Operation *Batman* being abandoned. *The Little Pisser* swung round and headed for home. She arrived without incident at Portland at 0520.[16]

Cancellation, postponement, even the abandoning of a carefully planned mission, often took more cool, considered courage than a headstrong decision to bash on regardless. It was a view endorsed ten days later by Colonel A. Head in a Most Secret memorandum sent to

No 62 Commando on behalf of the Chief of Combined Operations, who evidently felt the need to remind Stirling's raiders of their mission brief. Reading that memo today one is struck by the possibility that, since it stated what by then must have been patently obvious, the real purpose of S.R. 865/42 lay masked in asserting Item 3:

> The following points about operations carried out by No 62 Commando should be borne in mind:
>
> 1. *Object of Raids.*
>   The chief object of these raids is to kill or capture Germans without suffering casualties and, if possible, without the enemy knowing the means by which their losses were sustained. Therefore, if the approach to the landing place goes wrong, or the alarm is likely to have been given in any way, the Force Commander should not proceed with an operation which is likely to result in considerable loses to his own Force, or which will involve an attack against an enemy who is prepared.
>   If initial surprise is lost it will usually be wrong to proceed with the landing.
> 2. *Identification*
>   The value of identification must be borne in mind and stressed to all ranks taking part in such raids. Shoulder straps, buttons, tunics, documents, equipment, etc., removed from dead Germans should be brought back whenever possible. One prisoner is worth about ten dead Germans.
> 3. *Binding Of Prisoners*
>   Until orders to the contrary are received, prisoners will, on no account, be bound.[17]

In the wake of Operation *Basalt* and the killing by SSRF of bound prisoners, Hitler had retaliated, not only by issuing his infamous *Kommandobefehl*, but by ordering the shackling of the 1,300 prisoners – mainly Canadian – captured at Dieppe. Canada responded by ordering the shackling of German prisoners in Canadian POW camps. This tit-for-tat squabble was only resolved by the intervention of the International Red Cross.

One of those who suffered no ill-effects from Operation *Basalt* was the raid commander, Geoffery Appleyard. In fact, quite the reverse. On 15 December he received an early Christmas present when the *London Gazette* announced that Lieutenant (temporary Captain, acting Major) John Geoffrey Appleyard, MC, had been awarded the Distinguished Service Order (DSO). The award recognised his outstanding personal contribution to the five SSRF raids carried out between August and October 1942 – Operations *Barricade, Dryad, Branford, Aquatint* and *Basalt* – and stated: 'The success of these operations has been largely dependent on his courage, determination and great skill in navigation.'[18] Lord Louis Mountbatten added his personal congratulations:

Dear Appleyard,
I was so very pleased to see that you had been awarded the DSO and send you my heartiest congratulations. It was a very well deserved award and you have played a most important part in the execution of all the small raids which have been carried out by the Small Scale Raiding Force.

I hope that opportunity and good luck will give you every chance of achieving still further successes in carrying out this type of operation and I feel sure that the skill and initiative which you have shown in the past will continue to contribute towards the future successes of the Small Scale Raiding Force.

Again my heartiest congratulations.
Yours sincerely
Louis Mountbatten[19]

In his reply to the Chief of Combined Operations, Appleyard did not waste the opportunity to hammer home the creed he and March-Phillipps had shared and evolved:

Thank you for your good wishes for the future of our small force. I speak for everyone in SSRF when I say that we are all determined to do everything possible to increase the effectiveness and the scope of these raids, and to make them an increasing source of worry and annoyance to the enemy.[20]

Appleyard may have answered to Louis Mountbatten for operations, but he was still seconded to SOE and Brigadier Colin Gubbins. He too sent his congratulations, addressing him familiarly:

My Dear Apple
Many congratulations indeed on your very well-deserved DSO of which I have only very recently heard. I am delighted for your sake, and that of your unit.

My best wishes for your success in 1943
Yours sincerely
Colin Gubbins[21]

When Appleyard attended the Palace for the investiture of his DSO it was his third appearance before his King in eleven months. 'King George paused during the proceedings to have conversation with Geoffrey and opened by saying: 'What, you here again? So soon?'[22]

Appleyard, most certainly, had stepped into a pool of limelight enjoyed by a very few. That autumn he received two prestigious invitations. The first was from the King and Queen to attend a Thanksgiving party at the Palace along with fifty other young British and American officers. The second was to spend a weekend at Chequers with the Prime Minister, his family and two young recipients of the Victoria Cross, Britain's highest award for valour. Operational commitments meant that he missed both.

As 1942 drew to a close, however, not everything was champagne, medals and garden parties. Behind the scenes in Whitehall, a row was brewing – and it wasn't a new one. The old argument about the conflicting merits of SSRF and the priority that should be accorded small scale raid-ing was gathering in intensity, sharpening in focus. Despite Mountbatten's early protestations as espoused by his Chief of Plans back in November, there was *still* a significant, ongoing and intractable conflict of interest between SIS and Combined Operations/SOE that, despite Churchill's romantic vision of that 'hand of steel' reaching out across the Channel, simply could not be permitted to continue.

As has been shown, the welcome expansion of SSRF in early October after Operation *Aquatint* had come with strings attached: plans had to be submitted to Hughes-Hallett and pre-raid clearance had now to be given by the naval commander-in-chief – Plymouth or Portsmouth – in whose sea area SSRF intended to operate. Thus, in December 1942, Operations *Weathervane* and *Promise* were both 'cancelled by C-in-C Plymouth owing to interference with SIS'.[23] *Weathervane* had been planned as a twelve-man recce, attack and prisoner snatch on a German OP at Pte de Minard, south of Paimpol in northern Brittany; Operation *Promise* was a similar mission on Pointe de Sahir, south of Trebeurden in the Baie de Lannion.[24] Both were vetoed. That monocled Admiral, Sir Charles Morton Forbes, GCB, DSO, commander-in-chief, Plymouth, was keeping German sentries alive in Brittany.

Eclipse

November 1942 closed with yet another review of the arguments for and against the stepping up of small scale raiding with the new Director of Naval Intelligence, Rear Admiral Edmund Rushbrooke, observing: 'The value of naval intelligence obtained from raids has been negligible compared with that which is obtained by other methods ... As far as operations of NID(C) [Slocum's section] and NID(Q) [SOE's naval section] are concerned, any increase in the enemy's vigilance is, of course, also most undesirable.' He concluded more constructively: 'From every point of view it would seem desirable that each raid should be considered on its merits, in the early planning stages, by an impartial authority with knowledge of the above considerations.'[1] But those 'above considerations' had more to do with SIS's view of their side of the hill than that of Combined Operations.

Admiral Rushbrooke's points were robustly rebutted by Mountbatten's Chief of Staff, Brigadier Godfrey Wildman-Lushington who pointed out on Christmas Eve 1942:

CCO [Mountbatten] has received clear and definite instructions from the Prime Minister and Chiefs of Staff to intensify small scale raids and his letters, to which C-in-C Plymouth refers, are in accordance with those instructions ... the arguments in favour of the raids are clearly formulated. There is no doubt that the most valuable result is that they tend to make the Germans employ more men on work of a purely defensive nature ... in so far as German Divisions in France are resting from the Eastern Front, the raids disturb their rest, and generally help to make the individual German long to go home ... Recent information indicates that the enemy dislikes these raids intensely.[2]

Such repeated purely tactical arguments, however, cut little ice. The Director of Naval Intelligence's suggestion of pre-raid review by 'an impartial authority' on 29 November 1942 was more than just a random straw in the wind; it was a portent of what was to come.

Mountbatten recognised the clash of priorities for what they were – a direct threat to his raiding policy – and resolved to address the issue head-on, writing to the Chiefs of Staff on 22 December 1942:

> At a meeting held on 13th October 1942, the Chiefs of Staff took note with approval that, in accordance with the Prime Minister's instructions, the Chief of Combined Operations would intensify his small scale raiding operations.
>
> Since then I have taken steps both to increase the small military force available for carrying out such raids, and the number of operations; but recent experience has brought to light two points with regard to the agreed small scale raiding policy which I feel should be brought to the notice of the Chiefs of Staff.[3]

Mountbatten went on to point out that the northern coast of France – with the exception of the Brittany peninsula – was strongly guarded, making it unsuitable for small scale raids. The Dutch and Belgian coasts presented similar difficulties. Which meant that the only bit of the French coastline suitable for raiding was that which lay west of the Cherbourg Peninsula – precisely the same area favoured for the same reasons by SOE and 'C' – SIS. Mountbatten did not mince his words:

> Intensified small scale raiding is likely to stir up these coasts, to increase enemy vigilance, and to make the task [of SOE and SIS] considerably harder, and there is no doubt that small scale raiding runs directly counter to their activities ... west of the Cherbourg Peninsula strong representations have been made that such raiding activities should cease owing to 'C's increasing difficulties caused by the occupation of unoccupied France ...
>
> In view of the intensification of these raids I think that the Chiefs of Staff should be aware of their implication on the activities of [SOE and SIS] and should give their general agreement for the continuation of numerous small scale raids in the areas which I have mentioned ...
>
> No guidance has yet been given to the various Commanders-in-Chief regarding the importance which should be attached to the despatch of these small scale raids; nor has the policy, stated by the Prime Minister and approved by the Chiefs of Staff concerning these small operations, been communicated to them. It is suggested that the attached signal 'A' should be sent stating their agreed policy in order that the Commanders-in-Chief will have some guidance in assessing their importance.[4]

Signal 'A' availed Mountbatten little. Early in the New Year the Chiefs of Staff met on 4 January to discuss small scale raiding. Mountbatten, however, arrived late. In his absence the Vice Chief of the Naval Staff, Sir Henry Moore, stated that the Admiralty had already encountered difficulties adjudicating between the conflicting demands of SIS, SOE and Combined Operations. He then circulated his own note suggesting the way forward. With Mountbatten still not in the room, the representative of the CIGS,[5] Lt General Archibald Nye, and the RAF's Air Vice Marshal Charles Medhurst, Vice Chief of the Air Staff, both stated that, as far as they were concerned 'the information provided by 'C' [SIS] was of such importance that his activities should have priority over both SOE and small raids'.[6] At which point, with battle-lines already drawn and the outcome virtually decided, Lord Louis Mountbatten, Chief of Combined Operations and the latest addition to the Chiefs of Staff Committee in his own right, entered the room.

Stating that in preparing to implement the Prime Minister's decision to intensify small scale raiding, he had come into competition with 'C', who claimed that his plans would 'interrupt and possibly destroy' the channels through which SIS obtained vital information, Mountbatten said – perhaps a little mildly in view of what was at stake – that he could not 'altogether' accept that view. But everybody else, it appears, could. Brushing aside his remarks by stating simply that it was the responsibility of the Chiefs of Staff to ensure that meeting the PM's raiding demands did not adversely affect the interests of SIS, General Nye then explained – presumably for the benefit of Mountbatten who had missed the crucial discussion – why the Chiefs of Staff had decided on the course of action they had. The crucial first two paragraphs of the new policy stated:

The Committee
(a) Agreed ... Where the proposed activities of SOE and SIS and minor raids clashed in any area ... SIS would ordinarily be given priority;
(b) Agreed that it was for the Admiralty to decide whether the Chief of Combined Operations' sea-borne raiding operations and the activities of SOE did in fact prejudice the security of SIS operations.

Paragraph four stated that the planning of *all* clandestine seaborne operations, whether originated by Combined Operations, SOE or SIS, would be co-ordinated by the Admiralty or the Flag Officer delegated by them with the conduct of each operation – from planning through to operational deployment – directed by the commander-in-chief concerned. For SSRF, this meant C-in-Cs Plymouth and Portsmouth. An exception would be made only in those instances when the Chief of Combined Operations was authorised to be the operating authority. Lord Mountbatten asked if the new policy would come into immediate effect: he had prepared a comprehensive programme of raids which he was anxious to start during the present dark period. Yes, replied the naval Vice Chief promptly, the Admiralty was prepared to take up its new responsibilities immediately. And that, really, was that. The Admiralty – and thus SIS – was firmly back in control.

But what had *not* been directly addressed – for the moment, at least – was Mountbatten's question regarding raiding west of the Cherbourg peninsula and, during that brief hiatus, the first raid of the SSRF in the New Year attempted to slip under the wire. Members of the SBS had now joined No 62 Commando. Operations *Criticism* and *Witticism* on the night of 8–9 January 1943 were one and the same thing: attempts, on separate nights by four members of No 2 SBS attached to SSRF, to paddle into St Peter Port, Guernsey, by canoe and destroy enemy shipping with limpet mines. All attempts were frustrated by bad weather.[7]

Operation *Frankton*[8] – the iconic Royal Marines' raid on Bordeaux docks in December 1942 by canoe-borne raiders who later gained immortality as the Cockleshell Heroes – had by then become 'notorious'[9] because of the lack of mission co-ordination between Combined Operations and SOE. As a result of this needless duplication on a mission which cost eight brave men their lives, the Admiralty set up a 'Clearing House' to ensure such wasteful duplication could never be repeated. Run by ACNS(H) – Assistant Chief of Naval Staff (Home), Rear Admiral Eric Brind – it was he who now bound the Small Scale Raiding Force's operational restraint still tighter, writing the same day SSRF/SBS abandoned Operation *Witticism*:

> The Operations now being undertaken by 'C' are of such importance as to make it necessary to refrain from small raids west of Cherbourg Peninsula for the present. Any particular operation required by CCO [Mountbatten] in the Bay will be considered according to the circumstances at the time.[10]

On the bottom of that handwritten memo from 'E.J.P.B.' – Admiral Brind – an unidentified hand has added a bitter note to the Vice Chief of Combined Operations the next day:

> I may have got it all wrong, but the situation implied in the last paragraph of ACNS(H)'s letter appears quite unacceptable. The suggestion, as I see it, is quite clearly that CCO [Mountbatten] can carry on planning and mounting raids for submission to ACNS(H) who has the right of last minute rejection.[11]

A pencil-corrected draft response for Mountbatten to send to the Admiralty from Combined Operations on 11 January 1943 states:

> I am assuming that this restriction does not apply to islands west of Cherbourg peninsula ... I will now be obliged to inform the Chiefs of Staff that, as a result of ACNS(H)'s decision, my small scale operations are being practically completely stopped ... I have no alternative but to submit that, for the reasons given in my memorandum attached, I am unable to implement the instructions of the Prime Minister COS (42) 146th meeting to intensify small scale raiding unless this decision is altered.[12]

A penned footnote in an unknown hand adds: 'Consider that the Norwegian situation (e.g. *Cartoon*) which is also being sabotaged [sic] by 'C' must also be mentioned.'[13]

Operations *Weathervane* and *Promise* had been cancelled by C-in-C Plymouth in December 1942. The New Year would see the cancellation of Operations *Underpaid* (a recce/prisoners raid on Cap Fréhel, Brittany), *Woodward* (Île Vierge), *Hillbilly* (Plouguerneau) and *Mantling* (Île Renouf).

The writing was on the wall, some of it put there by Major Ian Collins, Chairman of the Small Scale Raiding Syndicate. Briefing Mountbatten on 10 January 1943 about the implications of Channel restrictions that would leave the activities of SSRF 'very considerably curtailed',[14] he reviewed SSRF's bleak Channel options for February, recording on 14 January:

> I am submitting the programme for February, but the following facts must be faced.
> 1. It is unlikely that more than one or two operations at the most will take place as the Brittany coast is still closed to us ... MTB 344, after six months more or less continuous work, is going in for overhaul ... This would take from 3 to 4 weeks which more or less covers the non-moon period. MGBs (Class C) are not really suitable for operations in the Cherbourg Peninsula or the Channel Islands
> [...]
> 7. There is no doubt that with the few operations taking place the less risk we are inclined to take in attacking objectives, since as the effect of policy (series of small scale raids) is barred, one is less inclined to risk a force unless the object is very worthwhile, and the force itself cannot have the same confidence if only operating every two months.
> 8. As long as the present ban exists on any force operating every alternate night in the Channel west of the Isle of Wight, the number of days on which operations could take place is very limited.[15]

An undated draft letter for Mountbatten to send to the Chiefs of Staff at this time stated:

> A decision has been given by the Admiralty that I must refrain from any operations west of the Cherbourg Peninsula meantime ... I have no alternative but to submit that ... I am unable to implement the instructions of the Prime Minister to intensify small scale raiding unless this decision is altered ... I submit that the number of seaborne operations carried out by SIS in this area will be found to be so few that I still hold very strongly the opinion that this decision should be reconsidered.[16]

It was not.

Effectively forbidden from raiding west of the Cherbourg Peninsula, Mountbatten's Chief of Staff, Brigadier Godfrey Wildman-Lushington, fought a valiant rearguard action, pressing ACNS(H) on 21 January 1943 for confirmation that the *islands* west of the Cherbourg Peninsula were not included in his ban. He attached to his letter a summary of the planned raids which had been – or might yet be – affected by his decision. Operations *Woodward*, *Weathervane* and *Promise* – as already stated – were on the list; three unnamed raids against the Brittany coast were now ruled out and a further five raids against islands west of Cherbourg planned for the next non-moon period – i.e. between 30 January and 14 February – also now hung in the balance. Combined Operations Planning Staff waited anxiously for the Admiralty's reply. So too did Stirling's SSRF raiders in their five scattered out-stations along the south coast. The no-moon period passed with no decision. Most of February came and went in a shoal of bad weather – and still there was no reply. Nothing ventured, Combined Operations decided to press ahead with Operation *Huckaback* anyway.

In concept, *Huckaback* was originally planned as a recce-in-strength on three islets close to Guernsey: Brecqhou, Herm and Jethou. Bad weather scrubbed the original mission; when it was revised *Huckaback* – like Operation *Branford* on Burhou in September 1942 – was to discover if it would be feasible to land artillery to support a possible invasion, not of Alderney this time, but of Guernsey. Operation *Huckaback* was led by Capt. Pat Porteous of Lord Lovat's No 4 Commando, a man who had stepped into legend during the raid on Dieppe in August 1942. Shot through the hand during the initial assault on the Varengeville battery set back to the east of Orange 2 Beach on the western flank of the invasion area, he had first bayoneted his assailant, saved the life of his sergeant and then led his men in a desperate bayonet charge in the face of withering enemy fire before collapsing wounded on the objective. Two months later he had heard that he had been awarded the Victoria Cross.[17] Now he was leading ten commandos ashore on Herm, an island just 2,500 yards long and 800 yards wide. Scrambling up a steep cliff, they established that Herm was unoccupied and that Shell Beach on the north-east of Herm would support artillery. The party withdrew after three hours ashore without seeing anyone, German or civilian, and returned to Portland without incident.

And still no formal word from ACNS(H). Finally, prods from a Rear Admiral of equal rank in Combined Operations on 3 March 1943 elicited a grudging response eleven days later. But it was a response which failed to address directly the crucial question relating to those islands west of Cherbourg. Were they on or off limits? It did not say. But its bleak, concluding paragraph to Mountbatten left little room for doubt:

> In present circumstances I should feel bound to advise the First Sea Lord that the danger to SIS communications caused by very small raids would outweigh the value of those raids. I feel, therefore, that it is within the spirit of the Chiefs of Staff decision that these very small raids should give place to SIS communications for the present.[18]

Eighteen months earlier, when March-Phillipps' pygmy force had been thwarted by Commander Frank Slocum in their plans to use their spigot-armed 'Q' ship *Maid Honor* against unsuspecting German shipping outside Cherbourg, they had turned their gaze towards the distant shores of West Africa. Now SSRF found itself looking towards Africa once more. With the Channel effectively closed to them – again – might there not be a role for the SSRF harrying Rommel's Afrika Korps in North Africa?

In fact, even before Operation *Huckaback*, SSRF had taken matters into their own hands. A month earlier, on 23 January 1943, Lt Col Bill Stirling had sent Lt Anders Lassen and Capt. Philip Pinckney to Cairo to assist his brother with amphibious operations and sense out the raiding possibilities in what, for SSRF, would be a new theatre of operations. SSRF was to become part of 'a special raiding force [under General Eisenhower] in North Africa on the same lines as that now operating under General Alexander in the Middle East.'[19] The name of that unit was the SAS, formed by Bill Stirling's brother, David, in 1941. Already, it seems, the Stirling name was opening doors.

But, before one set of doors was finally closed, there was a final tribute to all that had been achieved by SSRF under March-Phillipps when it had been based at Anderson Manor. On 28 January 1943 the *London Gazette*[20] announced the recommendation that a Bar to the DSO be awarded to

Major Gustavus-Henry March-Phillipps, Service No 39184, for 'gallant and distinguished services in the field.'[21]

†††

And so to Africa.

For months, David Stirling's SAS had been harrying the German's extended supply lines along the coastal rim of North Africa as the fortunes of Rommel's Afrika Korps and Montgomery's Eighth Army swung back and forth between Tunisia, Libya and Egypt. First on foot – then carried deep into the desert behind enemy lines by the Long Range Desert Group (LRDG), whose peace-time experts had long mastered the arcane arts of desert survival, sand-dune driving, soft-sand extraction, and sun-compass and astro-navigation – Stirling's now jeep-borne, twin Vickers-firing raiders attacked airfields, blew up fuel dumps, shot up transport and destroyed hundreds of German aeroplanes on Axis airfields. In November, US and British First Army forces had landed far to the west in Operation *Torch* with Allied troops coming ashore in French Morocco and Algeria. Now both British armies – Anderson's First and Montgomery's Eighth – planned to squeeze Rommel's Afrika Korps in the jaws of an allied vice whose screws would be turned from both ends of the Mediterranean.

To David Stirling, that expanding and contracting Axis supply line stretching across Tunisia and Libya and eastwards to threaten Cairo had offered limitless scope for small scale, behind-the-lines, hit-and-run raiding operations. Sending his own SSRF into the same theatre, reasoned Bill Stirling – who had sat in his younger brother's flat in Cairo all those months ago, in July 1941, when David had first conceived the idea of the SAS – might perhaps offer his own men similar opportunities on the North African coast. Bill Stirling's early ideas found favour with Brigadier Charles Haydon, the Commanding Officer of the Special Service Commando Brigade. He wrote just before Christmas:

> I feel and always have felt that there is a genuine need for the formation of a unit to carry out irregular warfare in the true sense of the word by putting into practice a policy of long range sabotage ... The activities of such a unit should primarily be conducted in strategic support of a large scale operation such as the re-entry into France or the Invasion of Italy, though its employment should not necessarily be limited in this respect ... Thus, whilst the employment of the commandos proper should be tactical in aspect, that of No 62 Commando should be strategic ... No 62 Commando would undertake to paralyse communications 200 or 300 miles behind the enemy lines.

Establishing themselves by any conceivable methods in close proximity to their objectives considerably prior to D +1 of a major operation, their activities would be directed against airfields, industrial targets, etc., in enemy base areas ... In conclusion therefore, although I am very adverse to the formation of new specialised or semi-technical units whilst we have yet to find full-time employment for those already formed, I am nevertheless convinced that No 62 Commando could and would make a really valuable contribution to the war effort, provided that its terms of reference are widened and its war establishment increased as indicated in Lieutenant Colonel Stirling's report.[22]

Copied to Lord Louis Mountbatten, the Chief of Combined Operations and one of Stirling's two commanding officers, Brigadier Haydon's memo was a useful endorsement.

Mountbatten, it transpired, had already been to North Africa on a high-powered salesman's drive on behalf of SSRF and Special Forces. There he had met both General The Honourable Sir Harold Alexander, the British Commander-in-Chief, Middle East Command, and General Dwight Eisenhower, the supreme allied commander in North Africa. At a meeting at Camp Amfa on 16 January, Mountbatten opened by saying experience suggested Combined Operations could offer Eisenhower considerable assistance when it came to small scale raiding – particularly amphibious raiding once the Germans had been pushed out of Tunisia – and pressed the American general to decide whether or not he intended to create another SAS-style unit. If he did, then he, Mountbatten, would undertake to provide the men and equipment the American needed. Eisenhower stated that, yes indeed, he would welcome the addition of a force in his command along the lines of 1 SAS. General Alexander concurred. It was all Mountbatten needed to hear.

According to one account, Lt Lassen and Capt. Pinckney's initial overtures were well received in both HQ Cairo and Eisenhower's headquarters.[23] Thus encouraged, on 2 February 1943, Lt Col Bill Stirling handed over command of SSRF in England to Peter Kemp at Anderson Manor and set out for Africa.

††††

In summer 1941 West Africa had offered Maid Honor Force all the space and scope it could have wished for – General Giffard and Admiral Willis notwithstanding. But North Africa in early 1943 was a different place altogether. Rommel's Afrika Korps was retreating westwards towards Tunisia, its extended supply lines with that open southern flank to a vast and empty desert now a thing of the past: trapped between two great armies, in May 1943, 275,000 Afrika Korps troops would surrender and be shipped across the Atlantic to POW camps in Mississippi.[24] As German units retreated into Tunisia and supply lines shortened, the land became increasingly confined and unfavourable for jeep operations. SSRF came to North Africa in January 1943 hoping to find bountiful harvest. Instead, they discovered lean pickings. The suggestion, therefore, that Lassen and Pinckney found themselves welcomed and badly needed new arrivals knocking at an open door is contradicted by the SOE War Diary:

> B [Stirling] is sadly disillusioned partly through his own fault and partly owing to the CCO's [Chief of Combined Operations] excessive enthusiasm. There is at this moment no job for SSRF here. AFH [Allied Forces' Headquarters] felt that CCO sold them SSRF against their better judgement but as too late Recant [sic] they must do something with it ... 1st SAS had already informed the 1st Army [to the west] that the country and the largely hostile Arab population almost prohibited operations of the kind carried out by them already in the desert. There was no opening either for raids by sea.[25]

In England, SSRF had been thwarted by Slocum, the Admiralty and a set of initials – ACNS(H). In North Africa it seemed destined to be hostile Arabs, the Tunisian terrain and the speed of Montgomery's advance westwards that might frustrate their ambitions: 'Stirling's command would only be his own small party plus possibly a small detachment of the 1st SAS who were there and at present there was little future for him' records the SOE official history.[26] While there *was* a future for SSRF – albeit one that would emerge under a different set of initials – Stirling's attempts to locate his unit within the existing matrix of irregular units already operating in North Africa met with limited success and clashed with SOE's Brandon mission.[27] Stirling himself was described by one of his opposite numbers as 'a really bad piece of work'.[28] Like *Layforce* before it, SSRF as originally conceived was struggling to find a role. And, like *Layforce*, it too was destined to disappear, services no longer required.

Back in England, the days of Anderson Manor as a powerhouse of cross-Channel raiding were also waning. Between March and April 1943 one SSRF/SBS raid, Operation *Backchat*, would be compromised – possibly by enemy radar – and aborted before troops could be landed;[29] another, Operation *Pussyfoot* – a second attempt to recce parts of Herm unvisited on *Huckaback* – would be cancelled because of thick fog; an ambitiously planned Operation *Kleptomania* – a radar station and garrison assault/prisoner-snatch on Ushant, hardly a small scale raid, involving

four Hunt Class Destroyers, eight MGBs, No 1 Commando and up to *fifty*
SSRF, was eventually abandoned as impracticable; two further undated
raids – Operations *Hillbilly* and *Mantling* – were destined to be 'cancelled
... owing to interference with SIS'.[30] Now, with the French coastline closed
and with other units like COPP[31] weaned away from No 62 Commando to
take on the specialised business of stealthy beach reconnaissance on their
own, there was little left for SSRF to do in either England or North Africa.
On 19 April 1943 the Small Scale Raiding Force was quietly disbanded, its
former members dispersing back to the Commandos SAS and SOE.

By then Appleyard's childhood friend and the comrade posted Missing
since Operation *Aquatint*, Capt. Graham Hayes, had made his way first to
Paris and then, with the help of the Resistance, down an escape corridor to
Spain. But safety there was illusionary. Soon after crossing over into Spain
in November, Hayes had been betrayed and handed back to the Germans.
Post-war research revealed the Resistance circuit Hayes had turned to for
help in Paris had been hopelessly penetrated by the Gestapo. Thereafter,
his every step towards freedom had been tracked and observed, his unwise
letters of thanks to friends in Normandy intercepted, photographed and
turned into death-sentences for those who had risked their lives to help
him. Back on French territory, Hayes was taken back to Paris and impris-
oned at Fresnes.

†††

Out of the ashes of the Small Scale Raiding Force, Bill Stirling – his brother
David had been captured in January whilst he was asleep in a *wadi* by a
startled German dentist out on exercise – was given permission to form
another SAS Regiment, 2 SAS. The name and its connections – the brothers' cousin was Lord Lovat – evidently still counted for something. Before
his capture by first the Germans (escaped) and then by the jubilant Italians,
Lt Col David Stirling had laid plans to expand 1 SAS into a formation of
brigade strength: '*Now* I know what SAS stands for', confided one of Bill
Stirling's comrades as the light dawned – 'Stirling and Stirling.'[32]

Thanks to the January promise wrung out of Eisenhower by Lord Louis
Mountbatten, Major Appleyard and a few other SSRF old hands had
followed their Colonel to Africa by sea, sailing from the Clyde in mid-Feb-
ruary. Appleyard, meanwhile, considered himself still part of SSRF – for
the moment, at least. Arriving there in March 1943 – 2 SAS would not
be formed until May, the month the Germans surrendered in Africa – he
set about creating a new camp, just as he had in Freetown, for the men of
SSRF he anticipated would soon be joining him in Africa:

Our base is a most delightful place, right on the sea amongst the sand dunes and about ten miles from the nearest town. A really healthy spot (all in tents, of course) and in an excellent training area. We are making it our permanent base, rest camp, training, holding and stores depot. Wonderful surfing and great fun with the boats for training in surf work, etc., and the length and height of the surf is about Newquay standard ... The weather is very variable, some absolutely heavenly days, like the very best days of an English summer and of a perfect temperature, so that we are all already very brown about face and hands, and then there are other days like today, wet and dull with low, driving clouds.[33]

The camp was at Philippeville, 40 miles north of Constantine, in Algeria. Former SAS soldier and chronicler of the first fifty years of his regiment's history, desert veteran Michael Asher described it as 'a huddle of tents pitched in a grove of cork-oaks between the beach and dense *maquis* scrub that hid a malarial salt marsh. Beyond the scrub, forested hills rose to a height of a thousand feet, their knobbly peaks stretching across the skyline like knuckles.'[34] In that time and in that place, Appleyard found himself enchanted by the countryside:

This is a very fascinating country. It really is absolutely beautiful and infinitely varied – at times almost desert, and then a few miles later one could be in England on the Downs and then for miles it will be Mexico with dead flat plains stretching away to sudden scraggy bare rocky hills, and then suddenly one sees views of blue hills and valleys for all the world like Scotland ... As regards natural life, there are a lot of birds, some very English – swallows, martins, skylarks – and some very foreign – vultures, hawks, eagles, storks (all standing on their nests on one leg, etc). Flowers are not really out yet, but there are quite a lot of small spring wild flowers, mostly very small, but at times, looking across the ground, you get the most lovely 'patch' colour effects with the myriads of tiny little flowers – great yellow, brown, pink or purple patches cover the hillsides in places. But most lovely of all are masses of most gloriously scented wild narcissi ... Scorpions (yellow and black) abound in stony places and later there will be a lot of snakes ... At night the jackals come and howl round the camp (a weird and chilling sound).[35]

Once Stirling's new – and old – recruits for SSRF/2 SAS[36] began to arrive, there would be little time for them to admire spring flowers, narcissi or scorpions of either hue:

The training matched the course at Kabrit [1 SAS training base on the Great Bitter Lake in the Suez Canal Zone] – infantry skills, PT, demolitions, Axis weapons, route-marches and parachuting, which was run at a parachute school in Morocco. Final selection for 2 SAS depended on the ability to run to the top of a nearby six-hundred foot hill and back in sixty minutes. Failures were RTU'd [Returned To Unit].[37]

Plus ça change.

Yet, despite its pedigree, its intimate link with the founder of the Special Air Service Regiment, 2 SAS was slow to find its feet. According to Michael Asher '[2 SAS] was never to achieve the cachet of 1 SAS ... If 2 SAS had never quite lived up to its promise, it was mainly because many of the tasks it was handed were pointless or badly planned by outsiders.'[38] To begin with at least, that was not how it appeared to the men on the ground. Appleyard wrote:

As regards prospects, they are good, and things will be very busy soon. I think now that I shall not be coming home again quite so soon as I indicated at first. We can do such a really useful job here and there is so much co-operation and keenness ... after all, this is where the war is now and is going to be in the future.

The job Appleyard and his men trained for was small unit behind-the-lines reconnaissance, sabotage and disruption of enemy communications. Training for what, by June, would have become the new A Squadron, 2 SAS, translated into toiling up and down murderous countryside in broiling heat each carrying an explosives-laden rucksack whose webbing straps bit deep into aching shoulders:

I think you would be surprised to see me now! I am sitting, with a 5-days growth of beard on my face, stark-naked in the sun on a rock in the middle of a little stream with my feet in the water, cooling off some of the blisters! We are in a tiny little wadi in the midst of a cork forest and there are dense bushes of juniper, thorn, bamboo and broom all around, making this a perfect little hide-out for the day. We got in here about 5 this morning after being on the move since 7.30 last night and shall be off again as soon as darkness falls tonight ... I think this is quite the toughest thing physically I have ever done. We are each carrying 65 lbs (sixty-five) packs (rucksacks) and if you want to know just how heavy that is, Ian, [his younger brother] try it! This country is most incredibly difficult to move over and through, and the maps are abominable ... We started this scheme last Monday and now, with only fourteen more miles to go, should be back in camp just before dawn tomorrow. So far in our four night's travel we have covered about forty miles as the crow flies, but you cannot measure distance in this country in miles, as in that time we must have climbed between 6,000 and 8,000 feet.[39]

A little later in the same letter Appleyard's mood changes as a love of a home sorely missed bubbles to the surface:

I even heard a cuckoo the other day, and saw swallows and pied wagtails, going north presumably. I'll send my greetings with them! Linton must be looking very lovely now and when you get this the daffies will be out and April will be with you. The first nests – and the dippers. Tea at Malham, and perhaps ham and eggs. I suppose I'll miss all that this year. Still, there's a job to do here first and then, perhaps, a year hence it will all be over.[40]

Training soon gave way to live operations in early April with a raid on the island of La Galite off the coast of Tunisia. On the way to embark, Appleyard was shot – by an American. He was in a jeep which was passed by a large US truck going the other way, in the back of which sat a bored American plinking at passing road signs with a .45. The shot went through the jeep's dashboard and then entered and exited his shoulder without breaking bone. Shrugging off the suggestion of a stay in hospital, Appleyard got the wound strapped up and carried on with the night's raid: 'a very amusing night's entertainment with a few I-ties!', as he later described it.

The plan had been to attack La Galite in strength with forty men, capture a prisoner and send him back to the Italian CO with an ultimatum that, unless he surrendered, the town would be shelled by both the landing party and naval guns waiting off-shore. In fact, there were no guns at all. It was all bluff. Heavy seas badly damaged one of the landing craft on the way in and only a small party was able to slip ashore on a recce that did not carry sufficient authority to bluff anyone. The party withdrew without loss or detection.

They were lucky not to lose a man on another raid, too – an aborted attack on the Tunisian coast. The intention had been to land in two Dorys behind the enemy lines in Tunisia, make their way inland some 60 miles to Mateur, destroy a radar station and then break back through the enemy lines and return to base. Each man was carrying a 65-pound rucksack laden with explosives. '[W]hile still a long way from the shore the boat grounded', remembered 'Stokey' Stokes:

Major Appleyard climbed out of the boat and started prodding in front of him with the boathook to find the depth whilst we scanned the shoreline. Suddenly, he bloody vanished under the water and into the gloom. One of the skills you had to have was to be a very strong swimmer, which was just as well as a few moments later he appeared again soaking wet and told us we had hit a sandbar. We all knew the drill and got out of the boat and shouldered our rucksacks. The Dory now rode high with us and the rucksacks no longer in it. Suddenly the sand bar disappeared and we were now pushing the fucking boat up to our necks in water.

We continued and were now only a few metres from the shore with the water at ankle height. At that moment all Hell broke loose as 3 separate machine-gun positions simultaneously opened fire. These things could fire about 600 rounds a minute and the sound of incoming fire shattered what had been the peace and stillness of the night. We were too far away to assault any of the positions and our mission was already compromised so we had to bugger off pretty quickly.

We rushed the boat back into the water and jumped in completely forgetting that the damned thing wouldn't float and it grounded again. We needed to dump our rucksacks, push like mad, jump in and row for our lives back to the waiting MTBs. Quite how we survived is a mystery to me. And that was that, a complete fucking fiasco. We headed back to Tabarka, cold, soaking wet and minus our kit which was now at the bottom of the Mediterranean Sea. We arrived back in Tabarka and spent the rest of the night in the shell of what remained of the Hotel Mimosa, a shattered two-storey building. We waited for another three days at which point Major Appleyard cancelled the raid and we headed back to Philippville with our tails between our legs. I mention it just to show that sometimes things just went completely wrong, not just a bit wrong. And I remember thinking – not for the first time – that it would be a miracle if any of us were going to make it through the war.[41]

But on that raid, at least, not a man had been lost. What had been lost, however, apart from their weapons and all their equipment, was a precious, leather-bound anthology of favourite poetry given to Appleyard by his sister Jenny who had painstakingly hand-inscribed all her brother's favourite poems. It had been in Appleyard's rucksack. In a theatre of much killing and bereavement, it was a trivial and inconsequential loss. Nevertheless, Appleyard felt it keenly.

†††

As the allies' campaign drew to a successful conclusion in North Africa, their generals' eyes turned towards Italy, that 'soft underbelly' of Nazi Europe. Knocking Italy out of the war, reasoned Churchill to a Roosevelt reluctant to commit Allied troops to a southern invasion before the northern invasion of France, 'would cause a chill of loneliness over the German people and might be the beginning of their doom.'[42] Moreover, in Russian eyes, argued Churchill, their British and American allies would at last be seen to be doing *something*: 'Never forget there are 185 German divisions against the Russians ... we are not at present in contact with *any*.'

Standing in the way of a straightforward invasion of the toe of Italy was the German garrison on the stepping stone that was the island of Sicily. And standing in the way of a successful invasion of Sicily, reasoned allied commander General Dwight Eisenhower, were a cluster of small islands – and potential allied airfields – the most significant of which were Pantelleria, the Axis forces' Gibraltar, and Lampedusa. Pantelleria, 63 miles south-west of Sicily, had been sized up for invasion once before: in 1940 Admiral Roger Keyes,[43] hero of Zeebrugge in the First World War and – briefly – Director of Combined Operations in the Second World War, had planned to assault the island, storming ashore, at the age of 69, at the head of British commandos. The idea was vetoed by the Chiefs of Staff.

This time, Pantelleria, with its 12,000-strong Italian garrison, would attract its own bombing offensive. American B-26 Marauders of the 320th Bomb Group would fly more than 1,700 sorties to drop more than 4,000 tons of bombs on the guns, fortifications, radar station and airfield of an island 8½ miles long by 5½ miles wide. It was later estimated by Oxford Professor Sir Solly Zuckerman, Churchill's expert on the effectiveness of bombing from the air, that the precision daylight bombing of Pantelleria pulverised 53 per cent of effective opposition.[44] Unsurprisingly, perhaps, the battered Italian garrison surrendered even as Allied landing craft approached the island. The only British casualty, claimed Churchill afterwards, with a humour that may have been lost on Pantelleria's Italian casualties, was a soldier bitten by a mule.

A few weeks earlier, on 29 May 1943, and on the same island, Appleyard had been bitten by an Italian.

The aim of Operation *Snapdragon*, as ever, had been to capture a prisoner, recce a possible landing ground and gauge the strength of the Italian garrison through prisoner interrogation, all vital pieces of information that would be fed back to the British commander, General Harold Alexander, by Appleyard personally. A submarine, HMS *Unshaken*, was placed at the raiders' disposal.

'Stokey' Stokes remembered that, just before she surfaced, the 'silent service's' fabled hospitality came to the fore:

We worked a lot with the Navy and when operating on submarines it was the Captain's tradition, before blokes like us went ashore, to offer us a tot of rum … This seemed completely ridiculous to me, so when my turn came I just smiled and said 'no thanks' … it just struck me as bloody crackers to be sitting on a submarine swigging rum just before we tactically disembarked and made our way ashore. One of my best mates, whom I served with for a long time, had a laugh about this and pulled my leg. He said: 'Don't worry, Stokey. If you don't want it, I'll have yours.' His name was Ernie Herstell, and he was an ex-Hampshire Policeman; he was a great bloke.[45]

HMS *Unshaken* blew her tanks and surfaced half a mile off shore. Paddling towards land in two inflatable RAF rescue dinghies on a pitch-dark night with five men in each craft, Appleyard's dinghy crunched up onto the beach and he led the way to the base of steep cliffs. One of those on the raid was Lt John Cochrane of the Toronto Scottish serving now with 2 SAS:

We had one false start and then began the hardest climb any of us had ever experienced – we pulled ourselves up completely by instinct and every foothold was an insecure one, the rock being volcanic and very porous, crumbling away under our hands and feet. By what seemed to be a miracle, Geoff finally got us safely to the top – covered in scratches – for we had decided to wear shorts so that in an emergency swimming would be easier.

We were nearly discovered as we reached the top of the cliff which was about a hundred feet high at this point. Geoff and the others were crawling away from the edge towards a path that they could dimly see and I was just pulling myself up over the edge when we heard men approaching. We all froze where we were and then to my horror I felt the edge of the cliff on which I was lying begin to crumble.

Just as the patrol came level with Geoffrey, who was lying in the gorse not three feet from their feet, the worst happened. A large stone slipped from beneath me and I waited tensely for the crash as it hit the rocks a hundred feet below me.

The crash came and Apple and the others prepared to let the patrol have it at short range. But the Italians chattering to each other apparently didn't hear a sound and passed by, little knowing how near to death they had been. We breathed again and prepared to start the work we had been sent to do.[46]

That work involved grabbing a sentry. The unsubtle way they had decided to do this was to crack a guard over the head with a length of lead pipe and then lower him away over the cliff to the beach. Appleyard was to do the cracking. Upon reflection – and after scaling the 100-foot crumbling cliff – the plan was changed. Now they would merely stifle a guard, take him prisoner whilst he was still conscious and force him to make his own way down the cliff-face. Nearby, so we are told, they actually heard an Italian sentry singing *O Sole Mio*. So be it: he would be their man. Appleyard crept closer, leapt forward to get a stranglehold on the man's throat and botched it in the dark. The soloist let out a scream of fear. Four men jumped on him and Appleyard tried to stifle his cries by jamming his fist down his throat whilst whispering *Amico*! *Amico*! Whereupon the Italian bit deeply into his wrist. Hearing the scream, now another sentry came running. One of Appleyard's men, Ernie Herstell, ran forward to intercept him with a rubber truncheon and was shot in the stomach by a burst of fire. 'When the adrenalin is pumping and there is a split second to react between life and death you need razor-sharp senses', wrote 'Stokey' Stokes. 'I've had many years to wonder about that night and if I'd taken my tot of rum, instead of Ernie taking both, whether he would have survived.'[47]

More guards turned out and soon there was a running fight on the top of the cliffs in the darkness. 'Geoff accounted for at least three with his automatic and Sergeant Leigh got one and possibly two.' 'Stokey' Stokes remembers that fight on the cliff-top too:

> For what seemed like an eternity Major Appleyard and I were involved in one of the most violent fire-fights of my war with each one of us fighting a fierce battle, killing a significant number of the enemy. We knew that the operation was compromised and it was really a battle for survival. We had to conduct a fierce fighting withdrawal, leaving Ernie behind on the island.[48]

The SAS raiders were not there to fight pitched battles. Shouting 'Every man for himself!' Major Appleyard turned and disappeared down the cliff. The party scrambled, stumbled and slid back down the steep, crumbling cliff after him down to the shore, pursued by shots the whole way. The prisoner sentry, already knocked senseless, was dropped on the way down and broke his neck on the rocks below. They rifled his pockets for papers and then threw his body into the sea.[49] Back into the inflatables and another desperate paddle out towards safety, the Italians firing machine-guns and loosing off Verey lights in all directions. Presently they were out of Verey light range, the shooting slackened off and, once again, not a man had been hit. HMS *Unshaken* was lying out there somewhere, submerged and waiting. Appleyard had arranged with her captain, Lt Jack Whitton, RN, that, if they needed help in a hurry before the agreed time of rendezvous, he would drop two hand-grenades under water. Now he did so and the submarine rose obediently to the surface nearby. The men scrambled on board: 'We were all so grateful to the Captain of the *Unshaken* for remaining on station when he had every right to fuck off and leave us', observed 'Stokey' Stokes. 'He was a very brave man and against orders risked his crew to save us.'[50]

Their dinghies sliced to ribbons by two burly sailors, HMS *Unshaken* submerged and set course for Malta.[51] Only Ernie Herstell had been lost. It is tempting to surmise that, if the enemy had been German, it would have been a different matter entirely. Little had been achieved but, once again, Appleyard and his men had pushed their luck to the limit.

†††

Spring and early summer: the seasons for campaign and invasion. Pantelleria was invaded on 10 June. The invasion of Sicily began almost exactly a month later on the night of 9 July 1943. For Appleyard, however, the intervening weeks had represented a time of rest and recuperation. The strain of constant operations was beginning to tell – and had been noticed by brother officers. When the stand-down came it was not discretionary, but a direct order:

> By the way, I expect you will be relieved at the following news: I am to do no more operational work personally for at least six months. The reason is that I have been getting a bit 'operationally tired' lately, although I know it sounds rather unreasonable. I have been getting jumpy, which I am afraid is rather absurd but, under fire, it's a dangerous sign in the leader of a party, even though I am fully able to control myself.
>
> Although I feel a bit low about planning operations, etc., for other people when I am not going myself, I am quite convinced that some of those who have had less operational work in the past year than I have had, can, for the time being, command these small parties in a more vigorous and determined manner than myself at present … But don't worry – I am quite normal – not on the edge of a nervous breakdown or anything and am actually feeling better every day.

Once again, his thoughts turned towards family and home in Yorkshire, writing on 27 June 1943:

> How pleasant my room at home must look after its repainting, etc. Maybe I shall be seeing it again before long – lovely! Did I tell you there is every prospect (say 75 per cent chance) of my returning home about August? I won't be sorry to come back in a couple of months' time but I feel there are many more people who deserve a trip home more.
>
> Dearest love. God bless.
>
> Geoffrey[52]

Despite his compulsory rest from operations, Appleyard's next trip was not home to the safety of family in northern England but to the tracer-flecked skies of northern Sicily the night after the launch of Operation *Husky*, the allied invasion of Sicily. Operation *Chestnut* was 2 SAS's first airborne mission, mounted in support of that invasion, and, although he would not drop with his men, it was typical of Appleyard that he wanted to see them safely on their way, just as he had the men of SSRF from the bridge of *The Little Pisser* after injuring his ankle re-embarking during Operation *Dryad*.

Operation *Husky* consisted of a major amphibious assault on the east and south-eastern shores of the island supported by large airborne operations. Two task forces would land on the island – the Eastern Task Force under General Bernard Montgomery, made up of British 8th Army veterans from North Africa supported by Canadian troops, and the Western Task Force under General George Patton, consisting of the US 7th Army. Plagued by typical army on-the-bus, off-the-bus, on-the-bus, cancellations and uncertainties – eighty men were initially to be dropped off by two submarines – Operation *Chestnut* was planned to support that invasion.

'For whatever reason this plan was changed time and again, right up to the last minute', confirmed 'Stokey' Stokes:

> In the end a number of separate 'main' operations were undertaken and the main airborne drop was to be huge. Soldiers get used to people messing around with things and generally adapt to it but this felt different. It was as if it was being made up as we were going along.[53]

In its final configuration two teams of ten men from 2 SAS – HQ Teams PINK and BRIG – would be dropped on the north of the island on the night of 12–13 July. Their mission would be to disrupt communications in the German rear, attack convoys, shoot up Axis vehicles, blow up the Catania–Messina rail link, cut telephone wires and attack the German Headquarters near Enna. They were then to radio in for main force airborne reinforcements. Classic SAS raiding, in fact, but without the jeeps. Or, as it turned out, the luck.

Two Albermarle aircraft of 296 Squadron took off from Kairouan, Tunisia, at 2000 for the two and a half hour flight to the drop zones north of Randazzo, and Enna,[54] Sicily, with Major Appleyard flying as observer with HQ Party PINK. The green lights went on and both teams shuffled forward and dropped into the night through the hole in the floor. PINK was dropped low, 50 miles off course, at 300–400 feet onto steep hilltops of volcanic rock. Several of the men were injured. One went missing on the drop – Signaller Carter was later found unhurt, but it took the stick commander, the experienced Capt. Philip Pinckney, twenty-four hours to find out where he was. And only four of the six containers were recovered. BRIG fared worse. Given the green light 5 miles off target, the BRIG party was released far too high – one report suggested they exited the aircraft at 2,000 feet. They were scattered on the drop, recovered none of their containers and were spotted by the Italians during their descent. Capt. Roy Bridgeman-Evans and his team of four were captured shortly afterwards. It later transpired that an electrical fault on BRIG's aircraft had triggered the green light prematurely. As a result, 'S.S.M. Kershaw left the pilot's compartment to warn them to be ready to jump and found the plane empty'.[55] Once on the ground, the Eureka homing beacons that survived the drop failed to establish contact with Allied aircraft and the few radios that had dropped with them had been either lost or smashed on landing. The men of Operation *Chestnut* now had no way of calling in reinforcements.[56] Apart from shooting up a few lorries and blowing a few phone and telegraph poles, the raid was a washout. Concluded the official report: 'The value of damage and disorganisation inflicted on the enemy was not proportionate to the number of men, amount of equipment and planes used.'[57] Having achieved nothing of consequence, the survivors of Operation *Chestnut* worked their way back to the allied bridgehead.

The aircraft carrying Major Appleyard, however, did not return.

Armstrong Albermarle PMP 1446 vanished without trace. Geoffrey Appleyard, together with the pilot, Wing Commander Peter May, AFC, and four crew – F/Lt G. Hood, F/O J. Clarke, DFM, F/Lt T. de L'Neill and W/O F. H. H. Elliott – were posted Missing, Believed Killed.[58]

Despite an extensive search, no trace of their bodies or their twin-engined aircraft have been found.

Today Geoffrey Appleyard's name is inscribed on Panel 12 of the Commonwealth War Graves Memorial at Cassino, Italy.[59]

* * *

On the very same day that Appleyard disappeared, Capt. Graham Hayes, the childhood friend from the same Yorkshire village Appleyard had recruited into Maid Honor Force in 1941, was taken out of his cell at Fresnes Prison and executed by firing squad. Today, the body of Capt. Graham Hayes, aged 29, of the Border Regiment, Service No 129354, lies in Row B, Grave 1 of the Viroflay New Communal Cemetery, Versailles, outside Paris.

20

Endings

For many months, the families of Graham Hayes and Geoffrey Appleyard held tight to hope.

In 1946, after exhaustive inquiries, Graham Hayes' mother made contact with an RAF pilot, J.E.C. Evans, who had been shot down over France in June 1943. He too had been sent to Fresnes Prison, Paris. There, by tapping morse code on the pipes in his prison cell, he had managed to make contact with Graham Hayes in a cell nearby. Hayes told him he had been on a raid that had failed, that he had escaped to Spain and that the Spanish had then handed him back to the Germans. When they established contact, Graham had been in solitary for eight months but was in good spirits; he had been promised he would soon be sent to a POW camp in Germany.[1] Each morning and each night the two British officers sustained one another by shouting greetings in English. And then, one day, Evans shouted but there was no response. Graham Hayes had been taken from his cell and executed. Malcolm Hayes, his nephew, remembers:

> During the war when my uncle Graham had been missing for many months … my father, Denis Harmer Hayes [Graham Hayes's brother] was alone, driving to a meeting on the west coast connected with a torpedo testing range. For no apparent reason my father had the most terrible feeling of apprehension regarding his brother Graham. It was so strong that he felt sick, stopped the car and got out.
>
> Sometime after the end of the war when the German records had been looked at, it was seen that Graham had been executed by firing squad on the 13th July 1943 after nine months solitary confinement in Fresnes prison. When my father was told this, he asked his secretary to bring him the file re the torpedo range meeting to check the date: it was 13th July 1943.[2]

Major-General (as he then was) Colin Gubbins chose to break the news to Graham's father Herbert in his own hand, writing on 1 August 1945:

> I am deeply sorry to have to inform you that I have just received information that your son was shot by the Germans in France on the 13th July 1943 ...
>
> I would like to extend my deepest sympathy to you and your wife. Your son's fate is all the more tragic in that he had been at liberty for some time after the gallant raid in which he had taken part and which had left him stranded in enemy-occupied territory. I have not yet received details of his death but am still endeavouring to obtain them ...
>
> I knew your son very well personally; he was a grand soldier and a very gallant gentleman, and I am so sorry that he has gone. I lost my own son in Italy last year and know only too well how much it means.[3] But we can be proud that our sons never flinched from danger and saved our country and our people from the worst of fates. They will live in our hearts for ever.[4]

Before Graham Hayes left Linton to go to war, the promising young wood-carver had laid down a few choice pieces of oak to season for the duration. He planned to return and work these once the war had been won. Those pieces of oak were used by the village he came from to create his memorial, a memorial he shared with six others from the same village who had lost their lives – including his brother Malcolm, an RAFVR Halifax bomber pilot shot down over France in February 1943, when he was in Fresnes Prison, and the childhood friend who had died on that same day, Geoffrey Appleyard.

On 17 July 1942 Ernest Appleyard, Geoffrey's father, recorded: 'there arrived the saddest tidings that ever reached [our] family.' It was a letter from one of Appleyard's friends, Major Ian Collins, informing them that he was missing. After outlining what was known of that last mission his letter continued: 'You will see there is still real reason for hoping Geoffrey may be all right, and every effort will be made to find out.' Those efforts, however, proved fruitless. Unconfirmed reports that wreckage of the aircraft and aircrew had been found, recorded in the Operation *Chestnut* Casualty Returns, came to nothing. Other leads proved equally, cruelly, false: 'I am certain that my father [Ernest] would have followed any trail to the end in requesting information about the death', affirms John Appleyard, Geoffrey's half-brother.[5]

The Operations Record Book for 296 Squadron records the loss of Albemarle 1446, Appleyard's aircraft, and adds: 'The returning aircraft [from Operation *Chestnut I*] reported flak from our own naval forces from Malta to Catania [on the eastern flank of Sicily].' That aircraft was not shot down by what we have now learned to call 'friendly fire'. It is at least possible that Appleyard's aircraft was less fortunate.* In March 1944 his family received official War Office notification that their son was now presumed killed in action.

As the war drew to a close J.E.A. Appleyard began compiling *Geoffrey*, the slim volume of Geoffrey Appleyard's wartime letters home which, seventy years later, has provided the invaluable backbone to this story.[6] *Geoffrey* – which was privately published in 1946 and reprinted in 1947 – concludes with a section entitled 'As Others Knew Him'. The renowned English Christian theologian and member of the Oxford Group, The Revd Leslie Weatherhead wrote:

> I knew Geoffrey from his school-days onwards. At the time of his early manhood I said to a friend: 'If a visitor dropped down from Mars and visited each country to find out what earth's inhabitants were like, and if I had the chance to suggest whom such a visitor should meet in England, I should suggest Geoffrey Appleyard ... His body he may have given for England, but his soul lives on, part of the wealth of the universe, for it possessed qualities that do not die and over which war has no power.[7]

At war's end Graham's mother, Lillian Hayes, wrote to Marjorie March-Phillipps about the enduring, life-long friendship of Graham and Geoffrey: 'So those two who had played as boys together and faced life and death together, went on their way to start a new and free life, continuing, I feel sure, to wage war against the evil that is the cause of all this unhappiness and sorrow.'[8]

J.E.A. Appleyard wrote of his son:

---

* The same night Major Geoffrey Appleyard disappeared, 2,000 British paratroopers and glider-borne infantry mounted a disastrous airborne operation to seize Primosole Bridge 7 miles south of Catania on the east coast of Sicily. This was approximately 35 miles due south of Appleyard's intended DZ. Allied shipping opened fire on the British aircraft before they reached the coast and German guns joined in once they made landfall. Out of those 2,000 troops, only 200 were left to assault the bridge. This was seized and held for just twelve hours before they were forced to retreat. The night before, the men of Major General Matthew B. Ridgway's 504th Parachute Infantry Regiment, 82rd US Airborne, suffered catastrophic 'friendly fire' losses, with twenty-three aircraft shot down and at least 410 killed when nervous Allied shipboard gunners opened up on approaching Allied aircraft. Five days later, Ridgway could still only account for 3,900 of his 5,300 paratroopers. (*The Day of Battle*, Rick Atkinson, 110)

Although he may not come back, he never seems far away. Often indeed he seems very near; not least so when we are tramping over his beloved Yorkshire fells, the wind carrying the varied sounds of the moorland – the splash of a nearby stream, the whisper of the long grass, the bleating of lambs and suddenly, the lovely, bubbling cry of a curlew – the bird he loved above all others. Then we recall what Geoffrey said one day as the same call came faintly across the moor: 'That's how I'd like to return to earth when my time comes.'

Perhaps he has.

Ernest Appleyard – 'J.E.A.' – died in Torquay, Devon, in 1966, aged 83. The family business prospered, expanded and benefitted from a public flotation in the early 1960s. The Manor House at Linton was sold in 1950 and has since passed through several hands, its current owners apparently disinterested in its past. Although Kiln Hill still exists, the Hayes family has dispersed and left Linton. The Linton-on-Wharfe Memorial Hall, with its handsome oak tribute to the fallen of distant times, still thrives.

In May 1989 there was a summer fete and reunion at Anderson Manor for those who had served there as part of the Small Scale Raiding Force. A small brass plaque was dedicated in St Michael's chapel, where Tony Hall and Gus March-Phillipps had sought spiritual strength just before Operation *Aquatint*.

Etched into the oft-polished brass are the words:

IN MEMORY OF THE SMALL SCALE RAIDING FORCE (62 COMMANDO) AND ALL THOSE WHO SERVED WITH THE SPECIAL OPERATIONS EXECUTIVE AT ANDERSON MANOR DURING THE SECOND WORLD WAR.

That ceremony of dedication was attended by Henrietta March-Phillipps, the daughter Gus never knew, together with Peter Kemp, Tom Winter and a handful of other veterans.

Henrietta had been working in theatrical production and had gone into a Bristol antique shop looking for props. The shop was owned by Tony Hall. The fortuitous meeting that resulted led to the 1971 BBC radio documentary *If Any Question Why We Died: A Quest For March-Phillipps* produced by the daughter he never knew, who had grown up believing her father had been some sort of pirate. She was not entirely wrong.

Henrietta's brief marriage in 1978 ended in divorce. There were no children. She died of cancer in 1991 at the age of 48. Peter Kemp, the Spanish Civil War veteran haunted by the screams of those German sentries on

Pointe de Plouézec, became a writer and published author. His book about wartime service in SOE, *No Colours Or Crest*, was published in 1958. It became a classic of its genre and changes hands, today (2013) at anything up to £200. Peter Kemp died in 1993. Tom Winter, survivor of Operation *Aquatint*, died in 1996, aged 92, on the Isle of Wight after running a taxi business with former SSRF officer Ian Warren. In peace, as in war, the pair supported one another into the softening shadows of old age: both attended the Anderson Manor reunion in 1989. 'I interviewed both of them', recalled local historian Philip Ventham. 'They were at that stage both looking out for one another. It was very touching, really.'[9]

Post-war, Major Oswald 'Mickey' Rooney worked for Courages and then Charrington Breweries before returning to the family brush-making business and becoming a member of Lloyds. Married with five children, he later moved first to Little Laver, near Ongar, in Essex and then to Chipping Warden, near Banbury, claiming that all he ever wanted after the war was to 'live a normal life'. He died in 1995 aged 79, a few years after telling his son, Chris, 'I never expected to live this long.'[10]

†††

Anderson Manor itself still remains beautiful, weathered and unchanged. It appears, from the outside, exactly as Gus March-Phillipps and Geoffrey Appleyard must have viewed it that first fine spring morning in March 1942 when the gardens were alive with primroses, scented purple violets and crocuses. The Manor has, however, changed hands. Its current owners know its history and are reminded of its wartime past in gentle ways: digging up mole hills in the kitchen garden, they unearthed spent cartridge cases from Bren, tommy gun and .45 automatics – the kitchen garden had been a shooting range. There have been other reminders, too. One morning their young daughter came down for breakfast and announced 'that man' had been in her bedroom again. 'Man? What man?', asked her mother with a casualness she did not feel. 'The man', said the little girl, 'standing in the corner of her room'. He had been there three or four times before. She then described a man dressed in commando clothing. The girl was 3 years old. She had never seen or heard of a commando.

The Small Scale Raiding Force

Appleyard, Geoffrey, DSO, MC and Bar, MA	Killed	13 July 1943
Dudgeon, Patrick, MC	Executed	3 October 1943
Hayes, Graham, MC	Executed	13 July 1943
Herstell, Ernest	Killed	29 May 1943
Lassen, Anders, VC, MC and two Bars	Killed	9 April 1945
Lehniger, Leonard	Killed	13 September 1942
March-Phillipps, Gustavus, DSO, MBE	Killed	13 September 1942
Ogden-Smith, Colin	Killed	29 July 1944
Opoczynski, Abraham (serving as Adam Orr)	Murdered	12 April 1945
Pinckney, Philip	Executed	7 September 1943
Williams, Alan	Killed	13 September 1942

'Proper people', all

Notes

Prelude

1. The National D-Day Memorial in Bedford, Virginia, USA, has painstakingly confirmed 1,258 US deaths on Omaha Beach on D-Day. The research continues with many more names still awaiting confirmation. My thanks to April Cheek-Messier, Co-President, National D-Day Memorial, Virginia.

Chapter 1

1. *Dunkirk*, Hugh Sebag-Montefiore, 19.
2. *Geoffrey*, 45.
3. *Dunkirk*, 450.
4. Ibid., 453.
5. Ibid., 435.
6. Ibid., 457.
7. *Geoffrey*, 45.

Chapter 2

1. March-Phillipps' personal SOE file HS 9/1183/2.
2. Henrietta March-Phillipps made a BBC radio programme about her father in August 1970. This is the first of several excerpts. Others will be noted as 'BBC Henrietta'.
3. Interview with the author, 2013.
4. BBC Henrietta.
5. Brooks Richards Audio, IWM 9970.
6. *Anders Lassen*, Mike Langley, 21.
7. CAB 66/7/48.
8. Prime Minister Winston Churchill, speech to the House of Commons, 4 June 1940.

9. *Finest Years*, Max Hastings, 63.
10. *The Death of Jean Moulin*, Patrick Marnham, 90.
11. *British Commandos 1940–1946*, Tim Moreman, 9.
12. *Commando Country*, Stuart Allan, 84, and Cabinet Records CAB 120/414 at The National Archives, Kew.
13. *The Commandos*, 9.
14. Ibid., 27.
15. *The Commandos 1940–1946*, Messenger, 26–7.
16. *All Hell Let Loose*, Max Hastings, 48.
17. *Ian Fleming's Commandos*, Nicholas Rankin, 71.
18. *March Past*, Lord Lovat, 175.
19. Ibid., 177.
20. Ibid.
21. *Gubbins & SOE*, Peter Wilkinson & Joan Astley, 34.
22. *British Commandos 1940–1946*, 11.
23. Ibid., 12.

Chapter 3

1. *The Commandos 1940–1946*, 29–30.
2. '*If I Must Die …*', Gérard Fournier and André Heintz, 14–15.
3. *The Green Beret*, Hilary St. George Saunders, 21.
4. WO 106/1740.
5. *Green Beret*, 21.
6. *The Commandos*, 34, citing PREM 3/330/9.

7. *The War in the Channel Islands*, Winston G. Ramsey, 133.
8. Ibid., 136.
9. *The Watery Maze*, Bernard Fergusson, 49.
10. *March Past*, 187.
11. *The Second World War*, Vol. 2, Winston S. Churchill, 412.
12. *Geoffrey*, 51.
13. Ibid., 50.
14. *Anders Lassen*, 21–2.
15. BBC Henrietta.
16. *Geoffrey*, 54.
17. Ibid., 55.

Chapter 4
1. *Gubbins & SOE*, Peter Wilkinson and Joan Astley, 76.
2. *March Past*, 188.
3. BBC Henrietta.
4. *Anders Lassen*, 20.
5. BBC Henrietta, interview with Sir Colin Gubbins.
6. Gus March-Phillipps: SOE PF File HS 9/1183/2; Geoffrey Appleyard HS 9/48/1.
7. Colin Gubbins' personal diary for 1941 in the Gubbins Papers, 12618, Documents and Sound Section, Imperial War Museum.
8. Interview with the author.
9. *Hugh Dalton*, Ben Pimlott, 306–7.
10. *The Secret History of SOE*, William Mackenzie, 70.
11. *SOE in France*, Michael Foot (2004), 61.
12. *Secret Flotillas*, Brooks Richards, 91.
13. *SOE in France*, 64.
14. *Secret Flotillas*, 91.
15. PREM 3 185/1.
16. *SOE in France*, 64.
17. *Forgotten Voices of the Secret War*, Roderick Bailey, 77, quoting Sub Lt Robin Richards in audio interview.
18. *Secret Flotillas*, 307.
19. *Geoffrey*, 66.
20. HS 8/806.
21. *Geoffrey*, 67.
22. *Anders Lassen VC, MC*, Langley, 56.

23. *Geoffrey*, 105.
24. HS 9/ 1215.
25. *Anders Lassen*, 30.
26. Ibid., 24.
27. Ibid., 53.

Chapter 5
1. The Combined Services Detailed Interrogation Centre.
2. HS 6/345.
3. *SOE in France*, 153.
4. AIR 8/897.
5. AIR 8/897.
6. *SOE in France*, 154.
7. *Geoffrey*, 59.
8. *Anders Lassen*, 54.
9. War Office records WO 373/16 incorrectly records his MC as awarded for Gallantry at Dunkirk. This may have been an administrative error, although that is unlikely. Since SOE activities were unavowable, it is more likely that this was a deliberate concealment of the truth.
10. *Anders Lassen*, 60.
11. The author Nevil Shute served in the RNVR and worked in the Directorate of Miscellaneous Weapons Development. He wrote a novel, *Most Secret*, based precisely upon this scenario. It was first published by William Heinemann in 1945.
12. Excerpt from interview with Sir Brooks Richards. Sound Archive No 27462 at the Imperial War Museum, London.
13. *Secret Flotillas*, 94–5.

Chapter 6
1. *Anders Lassen*, 60.
2. HS 8/ 217.
3. *Anders Lassen*, 61.
4. BBC Henrietta.
5. *Anders Lassen*, 62.
6. *Geoffrey*, 80.
7. Ibid., 83.
8. *Maid Honor* Log Book held in the Perkins Papers, 14319, Documents and Sound Section, Imperial War Museum.

9. Letter held in the Perkins Papers, 14319, Documents and Sound Section, Imperial War Museum.
10. Entry in *Maid Honor* Log Book held in the Perkins Papers, 14319, Documents and Sound Section, Imperial War Museum.
11. *Ian Fleming and SOE's Operation Postmaster*, Brian Lett, 53.
12. HS 3/74.
13. *Ian Fleming and SOE's Operation Postmaster*, 52.
14. HS 3/86.
15. HS 7/219.
16. HS 3/86.
17. Memo from Rear Admiral Holbrook to the Director of Naval Intelligence, July 31 1941.
18. HS 7/221.
19. HS 3/86.
20. *Geoffrey*, 84.
21. HS 3/86.
22. HS 3/86.
23. Signal from Caesar to W, 6 October 1941. HS 3/86.
24. *Geoffrey*, 86.
25. *Anders Lassen*, 91.
26. Ibid., 78.
27. HS 7/223.
28. *Anders Lassen*, 81.
29. Ibid., 87.
30. *Maid Honor* Log.
31. HS 3/722.
32. HS 7/221, 21–2.
33. HS 7/222 (19–20 November 1941).
34. HS 3/86.

Chapter 7
1. *Geoffrey*, 99.
2. Ibid., 72.
3. HS 7/244.
4. *Ian Fleming and SOE's Operation Postmaster*, 109.
5. HS 3/86.
6. Ibid.
7. HS 3/91.
8. HS 3/86.
9. *Geoffrey*, 108.
10. HS 3/86.
11. Ibid.
12. Ibid.

13. Ibid.
14. Ibid.
15. Ibid.
16. HS 3/92.
17. *Secret War Heroes*, Marcus Binney, 132.
18. HS 3/91.
19. Ibid.
20. *Anders Lassen*, 82.
21. Ibid, 83.
22. ADM 199/395.
23. HS 3/87.

Chapter 8
1. *Geoffrey*, 72.
2. Guise report in HS 3/91.
3. *Geoffrey*, 73.
4. *Anders Lassen*, 84.
5. March-Phillipps report in HS 3/91.
6. Guise in HS 3/91.
7. HS 3/91.
8. *The Commandos 1940–1946*, 54.
9. Guise HS 3/91.
10. Ibid.
11. *Anders Lassen*, 85.
12. Hayes Report in HS 3/91.
13. Ibid.
14. Guise Report in HS 3/91.
15. Ibid.
16. *The Commandos 1940–1946*, 54.
17. March-Phillipps HS 3/91.
18. *Geoffrey*, 74.
19. Guise HS 3/91.
20. Hayes HS 3/91.
21. *Anders Lassen*, 86.
22. Leslie Prout in *Geoffrey*, 75.
23. Guise HS 3/91.
24. *Geoffrey*, 75.
25. March-Phillipps in his report in HS 3/91.
26. *The Commandos 1940–1946*, 55.
27. March-Phillipps in his report in HS 3/91.
28. Guise report HS 3/91.
29. According to Spanish sources, the Italian Governor of Fernando Po, Capt. Victor Sanchez-Diez, allegedly regarded the raid as an act of war by the British and, the next day, ordered a twin-engine De Havilland Rapide biplane

belonging to Air Iberia to search for the missing ships. The aircraft – armed with a single machine-gun and small bombs that would have been dropped by hand – returned without success. Source: Malcolm Hayes.

Chapter 9

1. Guise report in HS 3/91.
2. *Anders Lassen*, 85.
3. Guise HS 3/91.
4. March-Phillipps report in HS 3/91.
5. *Maid Honor* Log entry.
6. BBC Henrietta.
7. Detailed account by unknown author in the March-Phillipps Papers, 06/103, Documents and Sound Section, Imperial War Museum.
8. Guise HS 3/91.
9. BBC Henrietta.
10. HMS *Violet* survived the war. She was broken up in Bilbao, Spain, in October 1970.
11. HS 3/91.
12. Michie Report in HS 3/91.
13. *Anders Lassen*, 86–7.
14. Michie Report in HS 3/91.
15. *Anders Lassen*, 87.
16. Specht then allegedly spent three weeks in jail.
17. HS 3/87.
18. PREM 3/405/3.
19. Ibid.
20. Ibid.
21. HS 7/225.
22. Report of Tom Coker, Master S/T *Vulcan*. In ADM 116/5736.
23. Guise HS 3/91.
24. Longe in BBC Henrietta.
25. Guise HS 3/91.
26. HS 3/87.
27. Ibid.
28. As marked on original. Presumably refers to distorted grouping.
29. HS 3/87.
30. Ibid.
31. ADM 116/5736.

Chapter 10

1. *Duchessa d'Aosta* was sailed to Scotland and renamed as the allied transport *Empire Yukon*. She was scrapped at Spezia, Italy, in 1952. *Maid Honor*, however, sails on. It is the name of an Appleby family-owned Southerly 42RST sailing yacht commissioned by Geoffrey Appleyard's niece Penny and her husband, Adrian Heyworth, out of Herm in the Channel Islands.
2. HS 3/87.
3. *The Secret History of SOE*, William Mackenzie.
4. HS 3/87.
5. PREM 3/405/3.
6. These were promulgated in the *London Gazette* on 28 July 1942.
7. *Anders Lassen*, 89.
8. HS 7/235.
9. HS 3/89.
10. It would be found by autumn that 'One prisoner is worth about ten dead Germans.' (COHQ Most Secret Memo to OC No 62 Commando, 26 November 1942).
11. Commodore J. Hughes-Hallett, RN. Excerpt from Mountbatten Broadlands papers.
12. *The Commandos 1940–1946*, 152.
13. Ibid., 153.
14. Family tape loaned to this author.
15. *Undercover*, Patrick Howarth, 20.
16. Undated recording of interview conducted by Henrietta March-Phillipps with her mother, Marjorie Stewart. Recording passed to the author by her family.
17. Family audio tape loaned to the author.
17. *Geoffrey*, 111.

Chapter 11

1. *Geoffrey*, 112.
2. HS 8/806.
3. HS 8/818.
4. HS 7/ 229.
5. BBC Henrietta.

6. Recollections courtesy of Philip Ventham.
7. *No Colours Or Crest*, Peter Kemp, 43.
8. Ibid.
9. Ibid.
10. Ibid., 45–6.
11. Ibid.
12. HS 8/220.
13. *Anders Lassen*, 96.
14. Philip Ventham to author.
15. *Geoffrey*, 114.
16. Philip Ventham.
17. *Anders Lassen*, 98.
18. Ibid., 99.
19. Ibid., 101.
20. *Anders Lassen*, 94.
21. *No Colours or Crest*, 47.
22. HS 8/220.
23. Lt Freddie Bourne interview. IWM Audio No 11721.
24. *Anders Lassen*, 96–7.
25. Authorised, at Mountbatten's request, for all Commandos in May 1942. Today, it remains the symbol of the completion of a rite of passage and lifelong membership of an elite fighting force.
26. *Anders Lassen*, 102.
27. BBC Henrietta.
28. Ibid.
29. HS 8/220.
30. *No Colours Or Crest*, 49.
31. DEFE 2/694.
32. Paper: 'The Mounting of Raids', by Vice-Admiral J. Hughes-Hallett, *Journal of the United Services Institute*, November 1950. Broadlands Papers, University of Southampton. Paper in MB1/BS8.
33. *Geoffrey*, 113.
34. Ibid., 121–3.

Chapter 12

1. DEFE 2/109.
2. *No Colours or Crest*, 49.
3. DEFE 2/109.
4. Ibid.
5. The 'plastic bombs' which caused such devastation were evidently not ordinary metal-cased No 36 Mills fragmentation grenades. A possibility is that the men from SSRF were using an early variant of the No 80 WP (White Phosphorus) grenade which came into general issue early in 1943. The effect on unprotected troops of the phosphorus – self-igniting in the presence of air to a range of about 30 feet – could most certainly be described as 'devastating'. There is also the possibility that SSRF were being used as 'guinea-pigs' to carry out operational trails with a new sort of anti-personnel device developed by SOE scientists under Colonel G.T.T. Rheam at Special Training School 17 at Brickendonbury near Hereford. This would certainly justify the inclusion of a detailed description in March-Phillipps' after-action report of the plastic bombs' effect as witnessed from both land and sea. It would also go some way to explaining why the 'plastic bombs' as described are not given a recognisable name at this stage. This is the explanation favoured by this author. These 'plastic bombs' most probably evolved into the 'Grenades, P.E. No 6' used on Operation *Fahrenheit* (*see* Chapter 18).
6. DEFE 2/109.
7. *No Colours or Crest*, 49–50.
8. DEFE 2/109.
9. *The Commandos 1940–1946*, 149.
10. Commando Veterans Forum.
11. Still other sources suggest that, although there was indeed a protection team charged with Nissenthall's 'protection' and possible liquidation, it was not composed of members of SOE/SSRF but by ten Riflemen of A Company, South Saskatchewen Regiment (SSR).
12. BBC Henrietta.
13. Channel pilot.
14. *Geoffrey*, 115.
15. *No Colours or Crest*, 50.

16. *Anders Lassen*, 79.
17. *No Colours or Crest*, 51.
18. *Geoffrey*, 115–16.
19. DEFE 2/109.
20. *Geoffrey*, 116.
21. BBC Henrietta.
22. DEFE 2/109.
23. *Geoffrey*, 117–18.
24. DEFE 2/109.

Chapter 13

1. *Geoffrey*, 119.
2. *The Steel Hand from the Sea*, Combined Operations.
3. HS 7/286.
4. See *Cloak Of Enemies* by this author.
5. HS 7/286.
6. Killed in Brittany whilst fighting with the French Resistance on 29 July 1944.
7. James Edgar interview with the author, 2012.
8. Ibid.
9. DEFE 2/109.
10. James Edgar interview with the author, 2012.
11. Ibid.
12. DEFE 2/109.
13. *Geoffrey*, 118.
14. Ibid.
15. Vice Admiral Hughes-Hallett paper to RUSI, November 1950.

Chapter 14

1. PhotoRecon pic in DEFE 2/365.
2. DEFE 2/109.
3. BBC Henrietta.
4. Ibid.
5. Audio tape loaned to the author by the family.
6. BBC Henrietta.
7. *No Colours or Crest*, 57.
8. German wartime meteorological charts kindly made available by the Met. Office, Exeter.
9. Tony Hall. BBC Henrietta.
10. DEFE 2/365.
11. Ibid.
12. Tom Winter statement in DEFE 2/365.

13. *Geoffrey*, 124.
14. Tom Winter statement in DEFE 2/365.
15. '*If I Must Die …*', Fournier and Heintz.
16. Tony Hall. BBC Henrietta.
17. *Anders Lassen*, 108.
18. DEFE 2/365.
19. Lord Francis Howard. BBC Henrietta.
20. DEFE 2/365.
21. Appleyard after-action report written at HMS *Hornet* directly after he had returned from the failure of Operation *Aquatint*. In DEFE 2/365.
22. Lt Freddie Bourne interview. IWM 11721.
23. Ibid.
24. *Anders Lassen*, 111–12.
25. '*If I Must Die …*', 231.
26. Tom Winter statement post Operation *Aquatint*. In DEFE 2/365.
27. *Anders Lassen*, 110.
28. BBC Henrietta.
29. DEFE 2/365.
30. James Edgar interview with the author, 2012.
31. *No Colours or Crest*, 58.
32. *Geoffrey*, 133.

Chapter 15

1. ADM 179/227.
2. Ibid.
3. Amongst March-Phillipps' personal papers at The Imperial War Museum in file 06/103.
4. Letter from Peter Kemp to Marjorie March-Phillipps dated September 30 1942 in Gus March-Phillipps' papers, 06/103, Documents and Sound Section, Imperial War Museum.
5. *Supreme Courage*, Peter de la Billière.
6. BBC Radio documentary, *If Any Question Why We Died*, Henrietta March-Phillipps, August 1970.
7. BBC Henrietta.
8. Ibid.

9. 'If I Must Die ...', 123.
10. ADM 179/227.
11. Colin Gubbins' diary entry in the Gubbins Papers, 12618, Documents and Sound Section, Imperial War Museum.

Chapter 16

1. *Geoffrey*, 117.
2. *No Ordinary Life*, Peter Stokes, 45. This is a private unpublished manuscript, being the wartime memories of Horace "Stokey' Stokes, of 12 Commando, SSRF and 2 SAS.
3. DEFE 2/75.
4. In August 1939, 18-year-old Horace Stokes left home to attend a Territorial Army camp in Devon. He expected to be gone two weeks. The young Territorial soldier would not put on civilian clothes again for six years.
5. *No Ordinary Life*, 46–7.
6. I am greatly indebted to Winston G. Ramsey's *The War in the Channel Islands: Then and Now* for his detailed account of Operation *Basalt* and the composition of the German garrison on Sark during autumn 1942.
7. DEFE 2/109.
8. *The War in the Channel Islands*, 148.
9. *Geoffrey*, 130.
10. Ibid., 149.
11. *The War in the Channel Islands*, 149.
12. DEFE 2/109.
13. *Anders Lassen*, 120. In the aftermath of Operation *Basalt*, Frances Pittard would be deported to the French Mainland and an internment camp at Compiegne, near Paris (see *The War in the Channel Islands*).
14. Statement by James Edgar to author.
15. *The War in the Channel Islands*, 154.
16. *Anders Lassen*, 121.

17. Redborn, *The War in the Channel Islands*, 154.
18. DEFE 2/109.
19. *The War in the Channel Islands*, 154
20. *No Ordinary Life*, 70–72.
21. James Edgar interview with author.
22. *The War in the Channel Islands*, 154.
23. *Anders Lassen*, 123.
24. In their book 'If I Must Die ...' French authors Fournier and Heintz claim an SOE agent, Roman Zawadski, was also recovered from Sark during Operation *Basalt*. However, there is no record of this in the files and there is no record of an SOE agent by that name in the SOE Files at The National Archives, Kew.
25. *Anders Lassen*, 122.
26. Jodl was sentenced to death for crimes against humanity. His request to die before a firing squad was refused. He was hanged on 16 October 1946.
27. *The War in the Channel Islands*, 156.
28. Letter from Lord Louis Mountbatten at the Broadlands Archive, Hartland Library, University of Southampton, Ref MB1/b58.
29. *Anders Lassen*, 129.
30. Details recorded by Oundle School, Patrick Dudgeon's alma mater. He and Trooper Bernard Brunt are buried side by side in Florence War Cemetery, graves IX H.8 and IX H.9.

Chapter 17

1. Amongst the raids dreamed up by Gus March-Phillipps and Geoffrey Appleyard that never saw the light of day was an ambitious project to attack the mighty German battleship *Tirpitz* with limpet mines carried by members of SSRF sitting astride a two-man submarine propelled forward by pedal power. The project was abandoned –

perhaps wisely – when *Tirpitz* changed her mooring.

2. *Geoffrey*, 133.
3. He died in 1943 and was succeeded by Admiral Sir Andrew Cunningham.
4. *Geoffrey*, 128–9.
5. Speech by Prime Minister Winston Churchill, Edinburgh, 12 October 1942.
6. Minutes COS (42) 146th Mt (O) held on 13 October 1942. In ADM 116/5112.
7. *No Colours or Crest*, 69–70.
8. DEFE 2/109.
9. Ibid.
10. Ibid.
11. Promoted Major-General, June 1943. Died February 1970.
12. HS 9/888/2.
13. DEFE 2/622.
14. Interview with Lt Freddie Bourne. IWM Audio tape 11721, Reel 2. Recorded November 15 1990.
15. DEFE 2/ 1093.
16. Ibid.
17. First formalised on 9 May 1942 in CCO (CCS (42) 130 (O).
18. ADM 116/5112.
19. ADM 116/5112.
20. DEFE 2/694.
21. Ibid.
22. Sir Stewart Menzies, Chief of SIS from November 1939 to June 1952.
23. *Secret Flotillas*, 129.
24. Ibid., 143.
25. Ibid., 142.
26. Between January 1942 and March 1943 SIS mounted fifteen sea operations to the French shore. These were Operations *Valise, Turquoise, Pillar West, Mac, Marie-Louise 1, Marie-Louise II, Gilberte, Neptune, Grenville I, Grenville II, Grenville III, Hawkins, Tenderley, Tentative* and *Rodney*.

Chapter 18

1. *No Colours or Crest*, 59.
2. Rooney papers: information from private papers loaned to the author

by Chris Rooney, son of Major Oswald 'Mickey' Rooney.

3. *No Colours or Crest*, 62.
4. Rooney papers: information from private papers loaned to the author by Chris Rooney.
5. Ibid.
6. Personal anecdote recounted to the author by Chris Rooney.
7. DEFE 2/109.
8. *No Colours or Crest*, 64.
9. Ibid.
10. Ibid., 66.
11. Ibid.
12. Ibid.
13. Ibid.
14. Ibid.
15. In fact, on or about that same evening, Graham Hayes was laid up in Le Manoir, the home of resistant Suzanne Septavaux in Le Pin, outside Lisieux.
16. Although Appleyard 'signed off' the after-action report on Operation *Batman* on 19 November, it seems unlikely, given his leave commitments, that he was also navigator aboard MTB 344 on that particular mission.
17. ADM 116/5112.
18. Ibid.
19. ADM 116/5112.
20. Ibid.
21. Ibid.
22. *Geoffrey*, 138.
23. DEFE 2/694.
24. A third mission, Operation *Trelliswork*, had been planned at around this time as a canoe-mounted beach recce on Sept Isles, northern Brittany, by four SSRF. Pre-raid mechanical problems with the MGB carrier resulted in the mission's cancellation.

Chapter 19

1. ADM 116/5112.
2. Ibid.
3. Ibid.
4. Ibid.

5. Chief of the Imperial General Staff, General Sir Alan Brooke.
6. COS (43) 4th Meeting (Minutes 13 & 14) 4 January 1943.
7. DEFE 2/694.
8. See this author's *Cloak of Enemies* for a detailed account of this needless duplication.
9. *SOE in France*, 26.
10. ADM 116/5112, 'Most Secret' Memo from ACNS(H) to CNP 9 January 1943.
11. DEFE 2/957.
12. ADM 116/5112.
13. A raid on the island of Stord near Leirvik involving men of Nos 10 and 12 Commando.
14. Brief for CCO dated 10 January 1943. In DEFE 2/957.
15. DEFE 2/957.
16. Ibid.
17. Capt. Pat Porteous, VC, would survive the war. He died in October 2000, aged 82.
18. ADM 116/5112.
19. DEFE 2/957.
20. WO 373/93 (Microfilm).
21. That second DSO was never actually awarded. The wartime Awards Committee decided – in their wisdom – that the Bar to the DSO would only be awarded if it were discovered Gus March-Phillipps had in fact survived Operation *Aquatint*. If he were posted Killed in Action, then a Mention in Despatches would suffice. In another mission – Operation *Frankton* in December 1942 – the two Cockleshell Heroes who accompanied Major Hasler and Marine Sparks to attack German shipping in Bordeaux harbour were also simply awarded a Mention in Despatches. Had they survived and not been executed by German firing squad, both would have been awarded the Distinguished Service Medal. Both rulings appear perverse: the higher award, this author would argue, should better reflect the sacrifice of men who had nothing more to give.
22. HS 8/818.
23. *The Commandos 1940–1946*, 237.
24. Their commander, *Generalfeldmarschall* Erwin Rommel, would not be among them.
25. HS 3/61.
26. HS 3/61.
27. The BRANDON mission was a Special Detachment raised by SOE for sabotage behind enemy lines using saboteurs who spoke the language and who could pass as locals. HS 3/61; *Secret Flotillas*, 582.
28. HS 7/237.
29. The files hold conflicting evidence regarding Operation *Backchat*. DEFE 2/694 claims it was abandoned. HS 8/818 claims it was successfully completed.
30. DEFE 2/694.
31. Combined Operations Pilotage Parties.
32. *The Phantom Major*, Virginia Cowles, 255.
33. *Geoffrey*, 144–5.
34. *The Regiment*, Michael Asher, 222.
35. *Geoffrey*, 146.
36. The oblique stroke between SSRF and SAS [SSRF/SAS] is deliberate. As late as June 1943, Geoffrey Appleyard was suggesting to his family that letters addressed to SSRF would still find him. *Geoffrey*, 170.
37. *The Regiment*, 222.
38. *The Regiment*, 223.
39. *Geoffrey*, 149.
40. *Geoffrey*, 150.
41. *No Ordinary Life*, 'Stokey' Stokes, 84.
42. *The Day Of Battle*, Rick Atkinson, 7.
43. Admiral Roger Keyes, first Director of Combined Operations, July 1940–October 1941. He died in 1945. His son, Lt Col Geoffrey Keyes, MC, was awarded a posthumous Victoria Cross after leading the abortive Operation *Flipper* raid on Rommel's

Headquarters in Libya in November 1941 with the intention of killing the Panzer general. It later transpired that the target building was *not* Rommel's HQ, that he was away in Italy at the time and that Keyes may have been killed by a pistol round fired by a fellow British officer.

44. *Watery Maze*, Bernard Fergusson, 239.
45. *No Ordinary Life*, 91.
46. *Geoffrey*, 165–6.
47. *No Ordinary Life*, 93.
48. *No Ordinary Life*, 92. Herstell's body was never found. He is commemorated at the Medjez-el-Bab Commonwealth War Graves Commission Memorial in Tunisia.
49. *The SAS at War*, Anthony Kemp, 99.
50. *No Ordinary Life*.
51. HMS *Unshaken* survived the war. She was scrapped at Troon in 1946.
52. *Geoffrey*, 172.
53. *No Ordinary Life*, 97.
54. HS 7/238.
55. WO 218/98.
56. Both PINK and BRIG took carrier pigeons on the drop. Released on landing, one flew north and disappeared, the other was later found in southern Sicily, dead.
57. *The Regiment*, 224.
58. AIR 27/1645.
59. That of Wing Commander Peter Rodriguez May, Service No 28048, is inscribed on the Malta Memorial, Panel 6, Column 1.

Chapter 20

1. 'If I Must Die ...', 215.
2. Malcolm Hayes in letter to the author.
3. Capt. Michael Gubbins was killed in the Anzio bridgehead on February 6 1944. His body was never found.
4. Letter from Colin Gubbins loaned to the author by Annabel Grace Hayes, Graham's niece.
5. John Appleyard interview with the author.
6. Ernest Appleyard's wife Mary – Geoffrey's mother – died in Paris in October 1947 from early heart disease.
7. *Geoffrey*, 191.
8. Letter in the March-Phillipps papers, 06/103, Documents and Sound Section, Imperial War Museum.
9. Letter from Philip Ventham to the author.
10. Letter to the author from his son, Chris Rooney.

Bibliography

Allan, Stuart, *Commando Country*, Edinburgh: National Museums, Scotland, 2007

Appleyard, J.E.A., *Geoffrey: Major John Geoffrey Appleyard ... Being the Story of 'Apple' of the Commandos and Special Air Service Regiment*, London: Blandford Press, 1946

Asher, Michael, *The Regiment: The Real Story of the SAS*, London: Viking, 2007

Atkinson, Rick, *The Day Of Battle: The War in Sicily and Italy, 1943–1944*, Basingstoke: Picador, 2007

Bailey, Roderick, *Forgotten Voices of the Secret War: An Inside History of Special Operations in the Second World War*, London: Ebury Press, 2008

de la Billière, Sir Peter, *Supreme Courage: Heroic stories from 150 Years of the Victoria Cross*, London: Little, Brown, 2004

Churchill, Winston S., *The Second World War*, Vol. 2: *Their Finest Hour*, London: Cassell & Co., 1949

Cowles, Virginia, *The Phantom Major: The Story of David Stirling and the SAS Regiment*, Hove: Guild Publishing, 1985

Fergusson, Bernard, *The Watery Maze: The Story of Combined Operations*, London: Collins, 1961

Foot, M.R.D., *SOE In France: An Account of the Work of the British Special Operations Executive in France 1940–1944*, London: HMSO, 1966

Fournier, Gérard and Heintz, André, *'If I Must Die...': From 'Postmaster' to 'Aquatint': The Audacious Raids of a British commando, 1941–1943*, Bayeux: OREP, 2008

Hastings, Max, *Finest Years: Churchill as Warlord, 1940–45*, London: Harper Press, 2009

—, *All Hell Let Loose: The World at War 1939–45*, London: Harper Press, 2011

Howarth, Patrick, *Undercover: The Men and Women of the Special Operations Executive*, London: Routledge & Kegan Paul, 1980

Jeffery, Keith, *MI6: The History of the Secret Intelligence Service, 1909–1949*, London: Bloomsbury, 2012

Keene, Tom, *Cloak of Enemies: Churchill's SOE, Enemies at Home and the 'Cockleshell Heroes'*, Stroud: The History Press, 2012

Kemp, Anthony, *The SAS at War*, London: Penguin, 2000

Kemp, Peter, *No Colours or Crest: On the Author's Experiences as an Officer of the Special Operations Executive during the World War, 1939–1945*, London: Cassell, 1958

Langley, Mike, *Anders Lassen VC, MC of the SAS: The Story of Anders Lassen and the Men who Fought with Him*, London: Grafton Books, 1988

Lett, Brian, *Ian Fleming and SOE's Operation Postmaster: The Top Secret Story Behind 007*, Barnsley: Pen & Sword, 2012

Lovat, Lord Simon C.J.F., *March Past: A Memoir by Lord Lovat*, London: Weidenfeld & Nicholson, 1978

Mackenzie, William, *The Secret History of SOE: Special Operations Executive, 1940–1945*, London: St Ermin's Press, 2000

Marnham, Patrick, *The Death of Jean Moulin: Biography of a Ghost*, London: John Murray, 2000

Messenger, Charles, *The Commandos: 1940–1946*, London: Grafton Books, 1991

Moreman, Tim, *British Commandos 1940–46*, Oxford: Osprey, 2006

Neillands, Robin, *The Dieppe Raid: The Story of the Disastrous 1942 Expedition*, London: Aurum, 2006

Pimlott, Ben (ed.), *The Second World War Diary of Hugh Dalton 1940–45*, Basingstoke: Jonathan Cape, 1985

Ramsey, Winston G., *The War In The Channel Islands: Then and Now*, Old Harlow: After The Battle, 1981

Rankin, Nicholas, *Ian Fleming's Commandos: The Story of 30 Assault Unit in WWII*, London: Faber and Faber, 2011

Richards, Brooks, *Secret Flotillas: The Clandestine Sea Lines to France and French North Africa 1940–1944*, London: HMSO, 1996

Saunders, Hilary St George, *The Green Beret: The Story of the Commandos: 1940–1945*, London: New English Library, 1968

Schoenbrun, David, *Soldiers of the Night: The Story of the French Resistance*, London: Robert Hale, 1980

Sebag-Montefiore, Hugh, *Dunkirk: Fight to the Last Man*, London: Viking, 2006

Turner, Des, *Aston House: Station 12 – SOE's Secret Centre*, Stroud: The History Press, 2006

Wilkinson, Peter and Astley Joan Bright, *Gubbins & SOE*, Barnsley: Pen & Sword, 2010

Ziegler, Philip, *Mountbatten: The Official Biography*, London: Book Club Associates, 1985

Index

**Visit our website and discover thousands of
other History Press books.**

www.thehistorypress.co.uk

Maj J G APPLEYARD DSO MC*
RASC